Feminist Perspectives on Ethics

FEMINIST PERSPECTIVES SERIES

Series Editors:

Professor Pamela Abbott, University of Teesside
Professor Claire Wallace, Researcher at the Institute for Advanced
 Studies, Austria and Professor at the University of Derby

Forthcoming Titles:

Feminist perspectives on the body
Barbara Brook

Feminist perspectives on politics
Chris Corrin

Feminist perspectives on postcolonialism
Maryanne Dever and Denise Cuthbert

Feminist perspectives on disability
Barbara Fawcett

Feminist perspectives on language
Margaret Gibbon

Feminist perspectives on domestic violence
Laura Goldsack and Jill Radford

Feminist perspectives on environment and society
Beate Littig and Barbara Hegenbart

FEMINIST PERSPECTIVES SERIES

Feminist Perspectives on Ethics

Elisabeth Porter

LONGMAN
London and New York

Pearson Education Limited
Edinburgh Gate
Harlow
Essex CM20 2JE
England
and Associated Companies throughout the world

*Published in the United States of America
by Pearson Education Inc., New York*

*Visit us on the World Wide Web at:
http://www.awl-he.com*

© Pearson Education Limited 1999

First published 1999

ISBN 0 582 35635 0

British Library Cataloguing-in-Publication Data

A catalogue record for this book is available from the British Library

Library of Congress Cataloging-in-Publication Data

Porter, Elisabeth J.
    Feminist perspectives on ethics / Elisabeth Porter.
        p.   cm. — (Feminist perspectives series)
    Includes bibliographical references and index.
    ISBN 0–582–35635–0 (pbk.)
        1. Feminist ethics.   I. Title.   II. Series.
BJ1395.P67   1999
170'.82—dc21   99–12366
                                                           CIP

Typeset by 35 in 10/12pt New Baskerville
Printed in Malaysia, TCP

Contents

Series Editors' Preface

The aim of the Feminist Perspectives series is to provide a concise introduction to different topics from a feminist perspective. The topics were chosen as being of interest for students on a range of different degree courses and in a range of different disciplines. They reflect the current interest in feminist issues and in women's studies in a wide range of fields. The series aims to provide a guide through the burgeoning and sometimes rather arcane literatures which have grown around various feminist topics. The texts are written by experienced teachers and academics providing lively and interesting accounts of topics of current interest. They include examples and case studies or statistical information where relevant in order to make the material more accessible and stimulating. The texts contain chapter outlines and summaries for convenient, quick access. There are also suggestions for further reading.

In addressing the issue of ethics, Elisabeth Porter goes to the heart of some of the most heated debates in contemporary Western civilization. Issues such as abortion, reproductive technology, pornography, love and friendship are ones which have generated reams of prose. However, by looking at these issues from a distinctively women's point of view we can come to new understandings of these topics. Elisabeth Porter argues against the idea of any single moral system, but for an understanding of plurality and diversity. Nevertheless, she discusses particular principles such as justice, care, equality and rights which guide moral behaviour but upon which a feminist perspective throws a better light. In the first chapter, the author sets out this argument by counterposing the more male-stream view of ethics, based upon universal, rational moral principles, with a woman-centred one which brings in the idea of nurturance, caring and relationships with others. She looks at the way in which this can pose a variety of moral dilemmas for women which a masculinist perspective would ignore. Elisabeth Porter then explores these issues by looking at intimate relationships – love, friendship, passion and parenting. She then goes on to consider professional ethics in the public sphere, in particular those concerned with caring professions, but emphasizing the role of women as moral agents and the ways in which they can be empowered. In Chapter 4 she looks at how these issues resurface in public political life, focusing on how needs are translated into social and political rights and the role of women within this. In the last three chapters, Elisabeth Porter takes the examples of sexual politics (including lesbianism, heterosexuality, prostitution and pornography), abortion and reproductive rights to illustrate the complexities and ramifications of ethical issues. Thus, the book argues for a view of ethics which recognizes its social embeddedness.

Claire Wallace and Pamela Abbott

Acknowledgements

I am extremely appreciative to Norman, Shantala, Simon and Luke Porter for providing me with a loving, nurturant context in which to write. They have all taught me much about ethics, life and love. My sociology colleagues at the University of Ulster who kindly agreed to my semester teaching break. I am very grateful to my friend Fran Porter for her thorough proof-reading and offering of useful suggestions to make the text read more clearly. Special thanks also to my son Luke who made a helpful contribution in typing the index, and my daughter Shantala for typing corrections in haste and with great humour. This book is dedicated to the young women of her generation.

Introduction

Life is complex. We make difficult choices in our personal, social and political lives. Sometimes it is hard to know how to make good or right choices that satisfy ourselves and minimize hurt to others. Welcome to the world of ethics where we grapple with perplexing moral decisions. Ethics is the practical study of moral choices. It examines the situations, rationales and justifications in which choices are good or bad, right or wrong, decent or indecent, worthy or unworthy, desirable or undesirable, moral or immoral. Ethics explores the principles we draw on to deliberate on options; why some options seem right and others do not; the actual choice made; consequences; and personal accountability.

Traditional ethics highlights aspects of morality like the usefulness of a decision; the consequence of a choice; self-interest; maximizing happiness and minimizing pain; other-regarding acts; claiming rights; fulfilment of duties; and going beyond the call of duty. Feminists rarely recognize their experiences, thoughts, conflicts, judgements and choices in the abstract rules, rights and principles within traditional ethics. Feminist perspectives explain how the inclusion of women's diverse lives alters the understanding of ethical frameworks and formulates alternative ethics. Feminist ethics incorporate many types of feminisms with many different approaches to ethics.

Feminist ethics has three central features. First, its starting point is women's lives in all the myriad of variances. It includes women who are single, married (legal and de facto), separated, divorced, widowed; African, American (north and south), Asian, Australian, European, South American and every inter-racial variation; working-class, middle-class, employed, unemployed, uncategorized, professional, semi-skilled, highly educated, becoming skilled or illiterate; bisexual, celibate, heterosexual, lesbian; with children and without; marginalized or excluded, affluent or impoverished, privileged or powerless.

Second, feminist ethics interrogates the meanings, understandings and implications of traditional ethics for women. It notes the male privileging and exclusion of women's lives and the ways in which women's experiences often do not fit traditional frameworks. It asks questions, queries double standards, contradicts oppositional assumptions and stubbornly refuses to slot women in as if they are second-class citizens.

Third, feminist ethics proposes alternatives. It builds on the assumption that women's socialization, cultural expectations, gendering and life experiences typically are different to the experiences of men. The nature of this difference is debatable and the interpretation of differences influences the alternatives feminists propose.

Some feminists stress that differences depend primarily on sexuality or sexed bodies, others stress race, cultural differences, socialization or class. Increasing numbers suggest an interactive interplay between gender, ethnicity and class. Some feminists see difference as a problem that works against the acceptance of women as equals, others consider it a strength in highlighting diverse moral lives. A few imply a feminine superiority given the importance of nurture, co-operation and mothering.

Feminists are all shapes, ages and colours, and they adopt different ideologies or belief systems. They support values that are liberal, Marxist, socialist, nationalist, republican, religious, fundamentalist, environmentalist, transgressive, postmodern. Some support several value systems simultaneously, perhaps to different degrees. This book draws on the range of ideological viewpoints to demonstrate the rich diversity of feminism. Feminist ethics is interdisciplinary. Once, ethics was considered the exclusive realm of trained philosophers or theologians. Now, the relevance of ethics to all disciplines is conspicuous.

The uniqueness of this book lies in its attempt to break down dualistic, discordant or simplistic understandings of ethics. Frameworks that present simple options fail to grasp the complexities of life. Perspectives that assume either–or options provoke inclusionary–exclusionary responses. Dualism dictates hierarchically ranked options with traits traditionally associated with men valued more highly than those associated with women. For example, dualism views rationality, intellect, culture and the political to be superior influences on men's ethical judgements, and sensuality, emotions, nature and the personal to distort women's judgements. This book criticizes dualistic ethics and suggests that interrelationships, intersections, fluidity and syntheses are approaches that more adequately incorporate the fullness of being ethical humans.

Feminist ethics disrupts gendered dualism. It argues that:

- women and men need to work together
- the private sphere and the public domain are interrelated
- justice is not possible without care
- care without justice is oppressive
- rights and responsibilities are like a hand in a glove
- self-identity forms through relationships with others
- universal principles require particular application
- embodied practices assume actual bodies and reflective minds
- equality requires attention to difference
- knowledge informs opinion and bias influences beliefs
- one can be actively passive as well as passively active
- a rationality divorced from sensuality is incomplete.

The chapters can be read separately or in any order, but Chapter 1 provides important background to the following chapters. Each chapter offers a survey of feminist debates on key areas: the nature of feminist ethics; intimate relationships; professional ethics; politics; sexual politics; abortion; and reproductive choices. Case studies and comparative data are included. The book aims to summarize the major feminist debates; present a range of feminist literature; demonstrate the alternatives that disrupt, transcend or synthesize restrictive binary oppositions; and encourage the reader to read more, think critically and debate further.

Chapter 1 explores how *feminist ethics* differs from traditional ethics by being focused on women's experiences, cross-disciplinary and seeking alternatives. These alternatives emphasize personal experience, context, nurture and relationships. The particular details and contexts of moral dilemmas are central to feminist ethics. Knowing what is a right, good or decent choice presupposes that women are moral agents capable of making sound judgements, acting on their choices and being accountable for them. Feminist ethics apply to every moral choice.

Chapter 2 examines close and familiar *intimate relationships*. Changing family circumstances alter personal relationships with many people spending more time with friends and colleagues than with family. Feminist ethics pays attention to values like truth, reliability, trust, faithfulness, dialogue and mutuality. Expressing emotions responds to people's situations. All intimate relationships have duties, sometimes resulting in conflicts. Dialogue works through disagreements. Commitment to care may signal a strong relationship, but some women experience care as oppressive or taken-for-granted.

Sex and gender influence work ethics. Chapter 3 looks at *professions* and how workers are affected by sexism, discrimination, equal opportunities and disability. Professional care is a practice of attending to others' needs. Women generally are more skilled in these practices, accept responsibility for others and enter the caring professions of health care, social work, family law. Rather than clinical, dutiful care, these professions provide responsible attentive care in suffering, recovery, welfare needs or family crises. Feminist lawyers adapt justice and care to custody, rape, domestic violence and sexual discrimination. In business ethics, women are skilled in co-operative management and joint decision-making.

Chapter 4 demonstrates how *politics* is influenced by the ethics of politicians and citizens. Feminist theorists revise traditional concepts of equality, justice, rights, representation and political legitimacy. They work to overcome the dualisms between public and private. The representation of women's common needs by elected women politicians and the recognition by all representatives of differences of class, race, ethnicity, nationality, age, marital status, family, religion, culture, absence or presence of children, employment, health or disability are needed for full political participation. Diversity and plurality enable political negotiation across differences.

Sexual politics is the topic of Chapter 5. Unequal power relations use others as mere bodies, thereby undermining personhood. Feminist critiques of pornography are directed at objectification and the eroticization of dominance. Sadomasochism is problematic for feminist ethics. In prostitution any forced sex is wrong. A further ethical dilemma occurs when sex-workers claim their right to choose. Not all choices can be defended. For feminist ethics, the controversial issues are willingly being an object, total submission, dubious consent, sexual servicing, boundaries of sexual activity, commodification of sex, and censorship. Feminist sexuality is about bodily integrity and pleasure, not power or control.

Abortion, the focus of Chapter 6, is topical. Arguments supporting a woman's right to choose and a foetus' right to life lead to seemingly no-win debates. Working reasonable ways out of the rights impasse is crucial. Legal provision is important because legislation against abortion simply fosters unsafe backstreet solutions or transports it to other countries. Feminist ethics contextualizes abortion, taking into account women's situation. Feminist ethics advocates the need for legal provision of abortion while respecting the sacredness of life. Abortion addresses individual needs and social responsibilities.

Chapter 7 examines the technological progress and invasion into *reproductive choices*. Women who cannot conceive naturally are offered artificial forms of reproduction. The desperation to have a child in part reflects social pressures that make women feel incomplete until they are a mother. Feminists are alarmed at ways in which women are treated as disembodied creatures with wombs, eggs, cells, embryos. Contract motherhood raises ethical worries regarding the commercialization of the body. Bodily parts become commercial property, making poor women vulnerable to contractual arrangements with minimal regard to their full personhood.

The seven chapters are self-contained, in that readers with special interests in feminist ethics, intimacy, professions, politics, sexuality, abortion and reproduction can go straight to the relevant chapter. Hopefully interest will be stimulated to read further. Feminist ethics concerns every aspect of everyday moral choices. Feminist ethics is open to controversy. Readers should engage actively with these debates.

Chapter 1

Feminist Ethics

Chapter outline

This chapter begins with a brief description of traditional ethics before concentrating on the central features of feminist ethics, namely:

- personal experience
- context
- nurturant relationships.

It then examines different moral voices, or different ways of thinking through and deciding on ethical issues. Attention to others' particular life stories is important in ethics and stories are part of moral deliberation. Moral voices that emphasize care and responsibility differ from those emphasizing justice and rights, and feminist ethics examines the conflicting priorities between these different voices. Importantly, it strives to overcome the dualism of gendered ethical perspectives through integrating care and justice in attending to plural human needs. The chapter concludes by explaining that women's moral agency entails:

- moral capacities
- self-respect
- judgement and ethical practice.

Ethics

Ethics studies the morality of human conduct. Ethics asks questions with no easy answers. What should we do? How ought we to live? What sort of person should I be? Ethics is concerned with reasoned arguments on what is good and bad, right and wrong, worthy and unworthy, moral and immoral. It makes suggestions about decent individual and social action. Historical and cultural differences result in varying ethical responses. Ethics refers to moral deliberation, choice and accountability. Increasingly, ethics and morality are used synonymously. As moral agents we actively make choices we consider to be ethical. Given our ethical capacities, we strive to be moral.

Traditional ethics

All ethics are concerned with living decently, making right choices and being good people, but the starting points differ. Feminist ethics starts with the lived experiences of women in everyday moral deliberation. Traditional ethics starts with abstract rules, principles and maxims that guide individuals in making moral choices. The rationales behind traditional concepts vary, depending on whether the roots lie in Buddhist, Chinese, Christian, Indian, Islamic or Jewish traditions. The Western tradition of philosophical thinking about ethics exerts the strongest influence on contemporary **normative ethics**, the ethics that are concerned with guiding action (Singer 1993).

Greek ethics, starting with Socrates (469–399 BC), Plato (427–347 BC) and Aristotle (384–322 BC) leads through Roman and medieval thought to current ideas. It revolves around themes of contentment and happiness, and character virtues like wisdom, justice, courage and moderation needed to live a morally decent life. Subsequent theories centre on varying responses to the practical questions of what we ought to do and how we ought to live.

- Natural law theorists answer these questions in terms of living in accordance with human nature, particularly qualities such as rationality and objectivity.
- Kantian ethics claim that rational beings ought to obey a 'categorical imperative', a moral law which can be universally applicable to everyone. Duty, a respect for persons and autonomy feature strongly.
- In the social contract tradition, morality is conceived as an agreement made with fellow humans in order to benefit from co-operative social life. Self-interest, mutual advantage and impartial principles underlie contract theories.

- Egoist theories maintain that we live basically to further our own interests.
- In teleological ethics, the rightness or wrongness of our actions are determined by the consequences, goals and purposes.
- In deontological ethics, important aspects of how we ought to live are governed by rules that ought not to be broken. The right is not to be defined by the good.
- Utilitarianism argues that we should do whatever has the best consequences and increases our pleasure over pain.
- Rights-based ethics hold the injunction to respect the rights of others.
- Virtue theories focus on good character and the practice of wisdom.

These traditions hold a common view 'that there is one ethical structure that represents right for men: a composite of manly virtues, such as courage, endurance, physical stamina, wiliness and political judgement' and another set for women that includes 'timidity, tenderness, compliance, docility, softness, innocence and domestic competence' (Almond 1988: 42). This book explodes these gendered **dualisms** on which traditional ethics rest. Dualisms assume oppositional approaches, binary divisions, incompatible positions, antagonistic values. The divisions are hierarchically valued, with traits associated with maleness considered to be superior to those associated with femaleness. Both women and men reflect on moral options, weigh alternatives, make judgements and face the consequences. **Ethics** is the systematic and critical reflection on the goodness and rightness of human action. Any inference that there is one ethical framework for men and another for women is inconsistent with feminist goals of inclusivity, equality and justice for women and men.

Feminist ethics

Feminist ethics links moral theory and feminist thought (Tong 1993) and feminist theory with our 'moral prejudices' (Baier 1994). Feminist ethics is a moral reasoning about goodness and badness, rightness and wrongness, desirable and undesirable practices that is directed toward the personal, social and political changes that feminism requires to end women's subordination. It takes seriously 'the moral perceptions, self-images, and sense of moral value and responsibility of women' (Walker 1989: 15). Feminist ethics is cross-disciplinary and filters into business, education, law, management, medicine, nursing, philosophy, policy, politics, psychology, sociology and theology.

Feminist ethics criticizes the gender-blindness and biases in traditional ethics, and develops gender-sensitive alternatives. It conceptualizes issues of right action, social justice and the human good from 'the specifically gendered experience of diverse groups of women' (DiQuinzio and Young 1995: 1). It deals with questions like, 'What's the place in ethics of the moral traits traditionally associated with women like sympathy, nurturance, care, compassion?' or 'How can we resolve moral conflicts in feminist ways?' or 'What are the ethical ramifications of human relationships?' and 'How can feminist principles be lived in the workplace, /or classroom?' (Cole and Coultrap-McQuin 1992: 1) or 'How can women "dare to be good"?' (Bar and Ferguson 1998).

When feminist ethics poses the question, 'is it good for women?' (Shapiro and Smith-Rosenberg 1989: 199), what does it mean to say that feminism 'transforms ethics' (Frazer, Hornsby and Lovibond 1992: 3)? The answer is complicated because feminists debate alternatives. This is healthy, minimizing dogmatic, narrow views. At issue are two main claims. First, that women and men reason differently about moral matters. Whereas women, typically relying on a narrative mode of reflection, have an immediacy of moral response that is person and situation specific, men typically deliberate according to universal principles and abstract from concrete details about particular persons. Second, men and women typically develop different values 'in forming a sense of themselves as moral beings and in making decisions about the shape their interpersonal relations should take' (Tanner 1996: 171). Whereas women may worry about responding adequately to others' needs and sustaining relationships, men, being concerned to protect their autonomy and meet impartial standards, often worry about fulfilling requirements of equity and fairness. These two claims are debatable. However feminists vary, their similar themes are concerned with relationships, nurturance, experience, emotional responsiveness, attunement to particular persons and contexts and sensitivity to responsibilities (Baier 1985, 1986, 1987; Gilligan 1983, 1988; Noddings 1984, 1989; Rich 1979; Ruddick 1987, 1992, 1995; Walker 1989; Whitbeck 1984). Others (Card 1990, 1991; Code 1991, 1995; Grimshaw 1986; Houston 1987) ask whether maternal paradigms and nurturant responsiveness are part of women's oppression?

Every type of ethics is controversial, open to questions, uncertainties and doubts, and feminist ethics is no exception. Within different debates, there are three interrelated features of feminist ethics that are accepted as central to morality:

- personal experience
- context
- nurturant relationships.

While these features are important in other ethical perspectives, the distinctiveness of feminist ethics is being located in women's experiences, breaking gendered dualisms and building alternatives.

Personal experience

Ethics do not emerge in the abstract but in daily life dilemmas like sexual relations, parenting, friendships, work relationships. Systematic differences in gendered experiences 'can have ethical implications both in *generating* a different moral ideal', that is, in 'making women *think* differently about morality from the way men think about it' and additionally, 'in *justifying* a different moral ideal', that is, in influencing 'a genuinely alternative moral perspective' (Almond 1988: 43). Feminist ethics accuses orthodox ethics of being impersonal in building social contracts, personal maxims and moral guidelines on hypothetical dilemmas rather than in reality. What is important to feminist ethics is 'the experience of consciously choosing, of voluntarily accepting or rejecting, of willingly approving or disapproving, of living with these choices, of acting and of living with these actions and their outcomes' (Held 1993: 68). Feminists fend off any systematic depersonalizing of the moral or demoralizing of the personal, challenging assumptions about what we know and whom we are in a position to speak for (Walker 1989: 23; 1997). Personal experience is central to feminist ethics.

Context

Given that experience defines moral life, then 'the contexts in which experience is obtained may make a difference' (Held 1993: 69). For example, if you are surrounded by the demands of small children, the confusions of teenagers or the needs of ageing relatives, then the considerations needed to make moral choices differ from those who only need to consider themselves. Life experience alters the moral scope. Compare the situations of a single parent with two children who wants to take in her sick mother who adores her daughter but can't get on with her son, to a careerist single financier considering which nursing home to put his senile father in. Their different lives influence their outlooks. The idea that context informs morally appropriate choices is strong. The focal point of modern ethics is a hypothetical moral quandary where possibilities are presented, considered, costs weighed in relation to potential gains and losses, and where emotions are seen as potential disturbances and personal factors as mere distractions. The goal of such ethics is to formulate abstract rules and principles. Hypothetical dilemmas are distanced from the immediate realities and emotional intensities of complex lives.

Feminist ethics claims that not only is women's thinking frequently contextualized, but 'moral thinking in general *should be*' (Grimshaw 1986: 203) more concrete as well as general (Benhabib 1992). This claim criticizes sharp distinctions between facts and values, stressing instead the '*demands* of a situation, which are discovered through a process of *attention* to it and require an appropriate response' (Grimshaw 1986: 203). A baby cries, a toddler refuses to share, an adolescent is caught shop-lifting, a spouse is made redundant, a friend's father wants her to aid in his mercy killing – these are instances in which the specific contexts and persons involved influence the response. What is a good choice for one person may not be for another. This does not mean that abstract guidelines are irrelevant, but it means that abstract principles alone are insufficient. The response to a middle-class teenager stealing a lipstick may differ from the response to a homeless youth taking bread. Context matters.

Nurturant relationships

Care and nurture are intrinsic to a context-sensitive feminist ethics. Decent relationships of care belong 'to the centre and not at the margins of morality' (Benhabib 1992: 186). Indeed, we can talk of a 'feminist ethics of care' which argues 'for a recognition of connection and dependence as part of human life and moral subjectivity' (Sevenhuijsen 1998: 63). Humans are vulnerable; from conception through to birth, childhood, adolescence, young adulthood, adulthood and old age we all need care. Care takes many forms, from basic physical sustenance and domestic requirements, to socialization, emotional bolstering, spiritual counsel, comfort, encouragement, advice, companionship and nurturant touch. Traditionally, women have been socialized into caring roles which most women willingly adopt. Men can be caring. While some of us know harsh, cruel men, many of us delight in kind fathers, brothers, uncles, grandfathers, lovers, husbands, sons, son-in-laws and male friends. But families, friends, workplaces and social policies assume that women are primarily responsible for care. Given that women are the prime carers, whether through socialization, coercion, choice or some combination, they tend more commonly to display qualities conducive to empathetic nurturance than do most men.

Feminist ethics shows women's willingness to nurture and insists on the 'ready capacity for emotional involvement as essential to a humane moral stance' (Cole and Coultrap-McQuin 1992: 2). Global cultures that stress economic productivity, materialism and individualism, lack public values of care. Social and political priorities would alter significantly if our definition of a good society included those values traditionally associated with women and excluded from public consideration like 'attentiveness, responsibility, nurturance, compassion, meeting others' needs' (Tronto 1993: 2). Care is central to morality. Personal experience, context and care matter because relationships are fundamental to ethics. 'Most of us are wage-earners and political citizens, yet the moral issues which preoccupy us most and which touch us most deeply derive not from problems of justice in the economy and the polity, but precisely from the quality of our relations with others in the "spheres of kinship, love, friendship, and sex"' (Benhabib 1992: 184). Just as context informs moral choice, so too specific relationships require sensitivity and generate responsibilities. Indeed, 'many feminists emphasize morality as a way of being in relationship with others' (Cole and Coultrap-McQuin 1992: 8). Relationships are blessed and fraught with ethical implications.

Different moral voices

The catalyst to the escalation of writings on feminist ethics is the work of Carol Gilligan who analyses the sequence of stages in emerging moral judgements. Just as healthy children learn to walk before they run, so too, healthy young adults go through stages of moral growth toward moral maturity. Gilligan's influential 1983 work, *In a Different Voice*, responds to her colleague Lawrence Kohlberg's research which drew primarily on boys' responses to hypothetical dilemmas, the 'Heinz dilemma' being the most well known. Heinz' wife was dying, the chemist over-priced the essential drug, Heinz could not afford it, what should he do? Based on boys' responses, Kohlberg defined six stages of moral reasoning. In stage six, Kohlberg asserts the principles of justice and respect prevail so that to judge morally is to be impartial, ideal and universal. Gilligan was concerned that women were absent or scored poorly on Kohlberg's moral development scale. In his stage three conception, moral goodness is equated with helping and pleasing others. These attributes are assumed to be natural for women and necessary for decent family relationships. Kohlberg questions whether role-taking in this stage can assume the impartiality he sees as essential to mature justice reasoning.

After conducting her own research, Gilligan discovered that women typically mature through different stages primarily because their moral priorities differ (1983: 19). Gilligan's interest is not in hypotheticals but in actual moral deliberation. In listening to women tell stories about their thoughts and experiences, she claims to find a 'different voice'. The voice she hears speaks of the web of ongoing relationships women find themselves in, the conflicts women experience between their own desires and the needs of others, and the responsibilities they feel for those within their web of connections. She suggests there is something unique in the way that women typically cope with the conflict between meeting personal needs and desires and attending to others. She cites this conflict between self and other as the central moral dilemma for women.

Also influential is Nel Noddings who places responsibility and relationship at the centre of her ethic of care. For Noddings, care is not principles or universal maxims but an empathetic way of responding to others in particular situations. She defines caring as feminine in the deep classical sense of being 'rooted in receptivity, relatedness, and responsiveness' (Noddings 1984: 2), and considers care to be 'essentially feminine' (1984; 1989). Associating care with femininity provokes negative responses from other theorists who see this association as an entrenchment of traits and practices that historically have subordinated and repressed women. Gilligan's findings do not generalize about the sexes but refer to a tendency of women to use a different moral perspective. Her aim is not to disclose statistical gender difference in moral reasoning, but to interpret the different perspectives (1986: 326). From 1987 on, her work declares that care and justice 'frame the problem in different terms' (1987: 24).

Case study. Stages of moral development

Gilligan traces typical stages women seem to go through in dealing with conflicts between self and other. Gilligan's conclusion is that while men often formulate moral problems as a conflict of abstract rights and rules, women seem to construe morality as a clash of responsibilities in situations where maintaining bonds with others conflicts with personal integrity. Take for example, Sharon, a mother who has left a destructive relationship and seeks to build a new life.

1 Feeling powerless, disconnected and lonely, there is an initial concern with self-survival.
2 Survival alone seems selfish, so Sharon begins to consider the possibility of a concern for herself as well as for her young children. She is receiving welfare and has found a low-rent house.
3 Confusion mounts. Sharon is accustomed to associating feminine moral goodness with the care of dependants. This association sits uncomfortably with her desire to study in order to get a good job, and her worry about childcare problems and frail parents.
4 She meets with others similarly situated who reassure her that she need not be self-sacrificial to be a good mother and that it is ethical to include her own needs within her moral judgement.
5 Sharon's approach changes. She realizes that the parameters of care can extend to be honest to her own needs as well as to others. She enrols in study, joins a community child-minding group, and insists that her brother share the care of their parents.
6 Sharon now has a transformed understanding of relationships. She sees the interconnections between herself and those she cares for as being integral to her moral judgements. Indeed her self-chosen moral principle becomes the care of **selves-in-relations**.

Particularity

What marks the 'different voice' is its **particularity**, its attention to 'particular others in actual contexts' (Held 1987: 118). The moral self is 'thick' rather than 'thin'. The 'thick' self implies that there is substance, deep meaning and history attached to people's identity (Blum 1993: 50). Without knowing people's background, we are limited in knowing how to treat them (MacIntyre 1982, 1988; Sandel 1982; Taylor 1989, 1992). The specific details about the person/s involved in making a moral decision are not trivial, irrelevant or insignificant. As well as the self being radically particularized, so too is the other. The moral agent understands the other person as a specific individual – as a particular mother, son, colleague, headmaster – not as just a woman, boy, worker or teacher. Presenting a newborn baby with a name begins this differentiation. Moral action itself is 'irreducible particularity' (Blum 1993: 51) of the agent, the other and the situation.

Particularity contrasts with **impartiality** which assumes that moral agents are emotionally distanced, objectively neutral and adopt abstract universal principles. These assumptions disguise what Simone de Beauvoir (1980) calls 'the ethics of ambiguity', the grey areas of life where formal principles act as guidelines only and where one cannot straightforwardly decide what is just or unjust, caring or hurtful. Formal duty might decree that a woman should care for her aging sick father, but memories of a lifetime of abuse undermines this formal obligation. Without knowing the reason for this woman's reluctance, her behaviour might seem irrational, even unfair.

Those who are prime caretakers know that genuine identification with others means that abstraction and impartiality are totally inappropriate to everyday crises. If our special friend is distressed, our child is sick or best mate has cancer, we do not stand back but become engaged in the immediacy of their lives. Women's moral thinking is not context-bound in the sense of being opposed to abstract thought, its intuitive, pragmatic and emotional qualities do not 'indicate *inability* to conduct abstract thinking' (Scaltsas 1992: 17). Rather, it views the generalization of what everyone in the same situation ought to do as ignoring the particular person in question. Impartial, abstract, formal absolutes oppose the way that morality figures in our lives – there is always a content to the messy, muddled grappling with our self-understanding, crises, confusions, relationships, interpretations and choices.

Emotional judgement is particularized. Love, jealousy and anger are not abstract constructs, they vary according to whom the emotions are directed toward – spouse, friend, colleague, child, stranger – and what issue is at stake. Emotional responses are part of our judgement. Indeed feeling strongly about injustices of sexism, racism or discrimination heightens a concern for justice. Ethical practice requires a deep and thoughtful knowledge 'of all the actors' situations, needs and competencies' (Tronto 1993: 136). We cannot know everyone's details, but informed knowledge increases the likelihood of appropriate responses. While particularity is essential in the family, intimate spheres and social life, it is also pertinent in work, civic and political lives because it suggests the value of difference as 'favouring inclusiveness of moral concern and a heterogeneous moral community' (Tanner 1996: 184). Particular lives have unique stories.

Narrative

Gilligan's 'different voice' emanates from her willingness to listen. What Gilligan presents is a narrative self who is linked to others by 'a concern with relationships and response' (1983: 74) that requires a 'contextual particularity' (1983: 100). A narrative selfhood focuses on the concreteness of individuals with specific histories, identities, emotions and attachments. Individuals within 'the web of identity' (Griffiths 1995) are linked by narratives in 'the intersection of stories' whereby 'individual embroideries and idiosyncrasies' require us to be acutely attentive to the minute details of historical incidents (Walker 1989: 18). The unique offering of feminist ethics is that the honest telling, understanding and interpretation of these stories is at work in competent moral agents. Stories are part of the moral deliberation that women as lovers, mothers, daughters, sisters, friends, nurses, charity volunteers, social workers and child-minders have always done, but has been trivialized or dismissed as sentimental, domestic, private or morally immature. Responding sensitively to the narratives of different people is crucial to moral agency.

Attentiveness to particular others expresses Iris Murdoch's 'loving regard' (1970: 40) and 'patient and just discernment' (1970: 38). Attentiveness to others' needs, interests, and welfare 'requires a stance toward that person informed by care, love, empathy, compassion, and emotional sensitivity' (Blum 1993: 51). Such a focus on attentiveness posits an alternative moral **epistemology** or framework for understanding knowledge. Such a 'morally crucial epistemic mode requires distinctive sorts of understandings' (Walker 1989: 17). Emotional distance and impartial objectivity provides general understandings but not the knowledge needed to give specific persons their deserving attention. Attentive affective concern for others is the basis of an ethic of care and of fair treatment.

Ethics of justice and care

Moral voices in the ethics of care differ from the ethics of justice so their priorities warrant attention. Feminist ethics criticizes the liberal version of the justice perspective exemplified by John Rawls (1973). This critique is similar to that raised by communitarians (MacIntyre 1982; Sandel 1982; Taylor 1989, 1992; Walzer 1985). Rawls uses a social contract model, a hypothetical agreement to ensure the rationality and impartiality of the principles that people would elect in deciding on principles of justice. The assumption is that rational individuals would not agree to principles that would suppress their self-interests, but that compromise is necessary in order to obtain a mutually beneficial agreement. Ignorance of one's personal situation ensures impartiality. No one in the 'original position' knows their eventual place, class, status, natural abilities, psychological propensities or sex. Under such a 'veil of ignorance' no one is advantaged or disadvantaged. Rawls' theory of justice is linked with a theory of rational choice and has two main principles (1973: 60).

1 Each person is to have an equal right to the most extensive basic liberty compatible with a similar liberty for others.
2 Social and economic inequalities are to be arranged so that they are both (a) reasonably expected to be to everyone's advantage, and (b) attached to positions and offices open to all.

Feminist critiques of liberal theories of justice are directed primarily to the vision of the self portrayed. The individual in liberal thought is the disembodied, degendered, pre-social self with individual rights and interests. In Rawls' theory, hypothetical people are rational choosers, not moral selves with specific needs, interests and bodies. Any notion of the individual as disembodied or transcending physicality is nonsense, particularly since Western

---

Box 1.1 Contrasts between care and justice perspectives

Characteristics	Care perspective	Justice perspective
Characteristics	contextualized	generalized
	particular	universal
	informal	formal
	concrete practices	impartial principles
Conflicting priorities	contextualized content	formal abstraction
	social responsibilities	individual rights
	concrete other	generalized other
Self-identity	relational	autonomy
Moral concerns	equity and need	equality and fairness
	inclusion	balancing of claims
	fulfil responsibility	rational resolution
Moral requisites	mutual recognition	equal reciprocity
	compassion	obligations
	contextual adaptation	entitlement

---

dualistic thought defines women as nature, the body, emotions and the material, as opposed to the loftier culture, mind, reason and spirit, characteristically identified with maleness. Feminists and communitarians counter-argue that the moral self is situated historically, that identity is constituted by affective ties, affiliations to communities and social structures. Rawls (1975, 1993) has since revised his thoughts to argue that justice as fairness assumes a particular conception of the person. The care perspective responds directly to the limitations of an abstract, hypothetical justice perspective. Later we examine ways to break down dualistic antagonisms between care and justice. First, there is value in looking at the stark contrasts (Box 1.1).

Conflict of priorities

Narrow care and justice perspectives have conflicting priorities: responsibilities and relationships rather than rights and rules; adaptation to concrete circumstances rather than ties to formal abstract rules; morality is expressed as an activity of care not as a set of principles. These conflicts occur in the process of moral decision-making and in the ethical choice. In the justice ethic, personhood is linked to respecting the possession of rights. Inequality is the prime cause for moral concern, hence the need to balance claims procedurally determined from principles of fairness and impartiality. The moral agent is detached, autonomous, objective and impersonal. In the ethic of care, morality is a conflict of needs emerging from principles of equity, inclusion and a desire to minimize hurt. Emotional detachment is irrelevant, inconceivable or an anathema – the moral agent never loses sight of the personal elements which define the priorities and response. The justice perspective thinks feelings threaten the universality that is demanded of moral judgement. The care perspective views feelings to be morally central because the desires of others, their personal quirks and connections are incorporated into the perplexities of making a good ethical decision. Meeting the needs of others is primary. Whereas justice as fairness views others thinly, as part of common humanity, morally good care views others thickly, as constituted by their particular human face (Flanagan and Jackson 1993: 70). It is worth looking at another way to express contrasts between the thin and thick self. The aim is to understand and then move away from either–or scenarios.

Concrete and generalized other

We treat strangers or those we know formally differently to those we know well. Seyla Benhabib (1992) calls this the 'generalized and concrete other'. With the generalized other, we view each individual 'as a rational being entitled to the same rights and duties we would want to ascribe to ourselves' (Benhabib 1992: 158). We abstract from the individuality of the other behind a veil of ignorance, assuming a being who like ourselves has specific needs, desires and affects, but our relations are governed by formal equality and reciprocity. The significant moral categories are rights, obligations and entitlement, the corresponding feelings are respect, duty, worthiness and dignity. In contrast, the standpoint of the concrete other 'requires us to view each and every rational being as an individual with a concrete history, identity and affective-emotional constitution' (1992: 159). We assume some commonality and seek to comprehend diversity. The moral norms require that I confirm not only your *humanity* (what I share with you) but your *individuality* (how you differ from me). The appropriate moral categories 'are responsibilities, bonding and sharing, the feelings, those of love, care, sympathy and solidarity' (1992: 159). The more I know you in the fullness of your birth, family, linguistic, cultural and religious heritage, the more I not only honour your dignity as a generalized other, but acknowledge your uniqueness as a concrete other. Both the needs and well-being of the concrete other and the dignity and worth of the generalized other are significant (1992: 188).

We understand principles like, 'be loyal to friends' or 'protect children from harm' but applying these principles to a grieving friend or a confused child calls on capacities that are intimately connected with individualized care. Particularized understanding cannot be generated from universal principles alone (Blum 1993: 59), because one grieving friend may need to talk, another may need space for silence or another may want a companion to visit a graveside. Generalized principles and particular care both are part of morally responsible action. Imagine a fifteen-year-old girl who loves nightclubs. Being underage she lies to her parents about her whereabouts. A possible conclusion is that she is a liar, deceitful and untrustworthy, and should be treated as morally immature. In delving deeper into the reasons why she lies, we might find that she does not want to hurt her parents. Her concrete situation reveals complex intermeshing relationships. Yet, we cannot know everyone's full story and should not 'exclude as ethically insignificant our relationships with most people in the world, because we do not know them and never will' (Card 1990: 102). Feminist ethics reworks antagonisms so that universalism sits alongside of particularism.

Since Kant, **universalism**, understood as the totality of rules, norms and principles equally applicable to everyone, has dominated ethics. Neutrality, impartiality, rationality, abstraction and objectivity are part of the universal package that views the task of ethics as formulating higher principles. Some universal principles of respect for life and dignity cover a broad spectrum of human needs. Yet each culture has contextually sensitive understandings of ethical life. Ethics is concerned with both particularity and broad universal principles (Nussbaum 1992b). Lawrence Blum (1988) maintains that a morality of care *is* based on universal principles that we should be caring and responsible to those to whom we are connected. 'Care for particular persons can *not* be exhaustively codified into universal principles' (Scaltsas 1992: 17), however it is central to moral agency. Blum (1980: 117–21) argues that in the dominant deontological tradition, duty, the basis of morality, is seen to be opposed to feeling, thereby failing to understand that altruistic emotions like sympathy and compassion provide reasons for moral action. Gilligan refers to care as a 'universal injunction' against hurting others (1983: 90, 95, 100) and 'the most adequate guide to the resolution of conflicts in human relationships' (1983: 105). Care is a universal principle of judgement, condemning specific exploitation and hurt (1983: 74).

Overcoming dualism

While there are conflicts of priorities between ethics of justice and care, there are also inter-relationships. Overcoming dualism is important in order to counter gender stereotypes like the idea that men are suited to justice in the public world and women to care in the private sphere, or dichotomous classifications like justice is only appropriate in the public sphere and care in the domestic, or that rational ethical choices require a strict division between the body and mind. What is the relationship between justice and care perspectives? Gilligan argues that it is like the focus phenomenon, the illusion where you see a vase or a face, a crone or a beautiful woman, a rabbit or a duck, but never both simultaneously. Her idea is that the two ethics see things in competing ways. Her claim is that typically there is a gender-linked orientation which dominates moral thought.

However, if women's and men's experience have been distorted by gendered limitations, 'then adding the two perspectives together will not cancel out that distortion' (Gatens 1995: 53). Indeed, if men do not exhibit care to the same extent as women, it is an analysis of power that is needed, not an 'assertion of sexually differentiated moral perspectives' (1995: 54). Overcoming the dualism of gendered moral perspectives requires complex integration which differs from assimilation. Assimilation argues for complementarity, but assumes that justice is the proper ethic for public interactions and care for interactions with family and friends (Hill 1987; Sher 1987). Most of us utilize justice and care in our familial, work and social settings (Gatens 1995: 54). Overcoming gendered dualism is crucial to feminist ethics.

Integration of justice and care

Theorists who argue for integration take the view that justice and care are not mutually exclusive (Bartlett 1992; Friedman 1993). Some suggest that the orientations complement each other in the process of judgement (Brabeck 1993: 48; Flanagan and Jackson

1993: 73–4), or that differences between them can be bridged by a third concept like trust (Baier 93: 27), or the capacities of care and justice are found together but have a diversity of emphases (Nunner-Winkler 1993). Some examples explain integration. A universal justice perspective stresses rights. In an on-going relationship, particular needs, harms or concerns not addressed by formal rights are morally relevant. For example, you and your partner may have an agreement that you cook alternate weeks, but you have cooked every night for three weeks because your partner has an important business deadline. Strictly, this is not fair, you have a right to your week off, but to insist on this right is insensitive to your partner's pressures. Flexibility is easier to accept when you know your partner would reciprocate, otherwise self-sacrifice is oppressive. Feminist ethics demands 'non-exploitative gender and care arrangements' (Bubeck 1998: 29).

Held (1993) for example, sees justice as a skeletal moral minimum that must be fleshed out by care. Others call for justice as a corrective to care (Clement 1996; Friedman 1993; Tronto 1993). Understood fully, the ethic of justice and the ethic of care both require contextual details and general principles. Grace Clement argues that 'it is a mistake to regard either justice or care as morally primary, as they are mutually interdependent' (1996: 109). Each ethic provides a check against an exaggerated form of the other. The dangers of the ethic of care include being limited to personal relationships and being overly self-sacrificing as with traditional femininity. The universality of the ethic of justice requires that we do not restrict ourselves to personal relations but admit the equal worth of others. The dangers of the ethic of justice are its association with traditional masculinity, self-sufficiency and rights where obligations are understood as contracts. The ethic of care's commitment to satisfy needs requires us to meet obligations which we have not chosen, like to our parents, handicapped child and those we do not know who live in poverty.

Uma Narayan (1995) presents a further example of integrating care and justice. There is a fatal neglect of girls in India in terms of education and medical and nutritional aid. Cultural notions of justice distort levels of care considered appropriate for girls. Narayan argues that without the sort of justice that alters cultural meanings and material implications of having daughters, the failure of adequate care for girls means they will not grow up to become adult bearers of rights. Justice treats people as autonomous individuals, and presupposes that 'dependent individuals are nurtured to autonomy' (Clement 1996: 117). Each ethic provides 'enabling conditions' for the other ethic (Narayan 1995: 139). The ethic of care meets needs and justice is required to 'enable the powerless to seriously participate in the social and political discourse where such needs are contested and defined' (Narayan 1995: 139; also Tronto 1993: 135).

Gilligan (1988: 9) tells a story of two four-year-olds playing together. The girl said, 'Let's play next-door neighbours', but the boy replied, 'I want to play pirates'. The girl said, 'OK, then you can be the pirate that lives next door'. One suggestion is to take it in turns to play each game, leaving individual interests intact. Instead, the girl offers an inclusive solution, they both have desires met, but this leads to a game that neither had considered (Clement 1996: 39). This desire to be fair and to meet needs has massive implications for divided families, societies or politics. Inclusive approaches go beyond a complementary justice and care relationship, viewing it as a 'dialectical interplay' (Hekman 1995: 9; Porter 1991: 50). In a just society 'care-giving and care-receiving are reciprocal; the social structures of a just society ensure that both the benefits of care-receiving and the burdens of care-giving are shared equitably' (Tanner 1996: 181; also Tronto 1993: 168–9). Care and justice are interdependent in that each 'provides conditions necessary to a morally adequate version of the other' (Clement 1996: 118). Feminist ethics challenges the seeming dichotomy of care and justice, and questions 'the moral adequacy of either orientation dissociated from the other' (Friedman 1995: 70). Another way to overcome the dualism of gendered perspectives is to see a greater complexity of more perspectives (Flanagan and Jackson 1993) such as seeing how race and class complicate ethical choice (Harding 1987; Nicholson 1993; Stack 1993).

Moral response to human need

A 'just care' responds to human need. Joan Tronto (1993), keen to emphasize the ethics of care as a practice rather than as rules, highlights four elements: attentiveness, responsibility, competence, responsiveness. First, for attentiveness to occur, there is the recognition of need. Tronto's example is stark. Ignorance of the depravity of sexual slavery in Thailand, or that starvation exists alongside of capitalist indulgence is a moral catastrophe. Failure to notice needs means our 'ignorance is a moral failure' (1993: 129). Second, 'taking care of, makes responsibility into a central moral category'

(1993: 129), as distinct from conformity to obligations. Obligations are formal duties, whereas responsibilities are embedded in cultural, distinctive contexts that 'appropriately respond to actual people in actual situations' (Scaltsas 1992: 17). Third, competent care is important. Particularly in large bureaucracies, 'taking care of' is used glibly with little regard to the outcome. Welfare recipients are pushed from one bureaucrat to the next form. There are resource problems in welfare, health, education and housing which hinder efficiency. Fourth, responsiveness requires an alertness to the possibilities for abuse that arise in situations where the caregiver and receiver are of different status, like parent–child, teacher–student, or nurse–patient.

Within feminist ethics, the appropriate response is more pertinent than the right action. It is not that what is right, good and proper is not important, because it is, but to state that there is one right action presupposes a formal rule applicable in every situation. Our concrete connections influence prior ethical beliefs (Blum 1993: 52). **Moral boundaries** are the lines between what is right and wrong, good and evil, permissable and impermissible, worthy and unworthy. In the past, religion, custom, law and cultural tradition defined these boundaries rigidly, with little scope for manoeuvre except at the expense of being ostracized from one's family, church or community. A diminished rigidity is desirable, for moral choice is complicated by varying contexts. The boundaries need to be pliable. When we are sensitive to changing moral ideas, willing to adapt principle and content, it is our practical judgement that ensures a sound ethical flexibility.

Plural moral voices

Care ethics focuses on existing relationships. We need to reflect on whether the relationships are unhealthy or worthy of preservation (Tronto 1987: 660), or if they reinforce conservative gender divisions (Card 1991: 17; Gatens 1995), or they are complacent about women's failure to care adequately for other women (Spelman 1991). Care can be corrupt, insincere or coercive (Flanagan and Jackson 1993: 75) but such 'care' may be merely dutiful rather than care in an ethically positive sense. An apt example is the pressure exerted in traditional or rural cultures on the oldest (or least attractive daughter) to stay at home to care for ageing parents. Women's customary activities have not always been freely chosen commitments, so caution is needed regarding enshrining care in the image of patriarchal desires and in an identity solely derivative from mothering, nurturing or gendered experiences. Women are vulnerable to exploitation as carers, but while gender is the most significant factor, caste, class, race and ethnicity also dictate who cares. Diemut Bubeck advocates two principles of justice in care: harm minimization and equality in care (1995: 203). Public care should follow these principles, but private care follows patterns of relatedness and emotional closeness.

Some writers ask whether paradigms based on nurturant responsiveness are part of women's oppressive histories (Card 1990, 1991; Code 1987; Grimshaw 1986; Houston 1987; Walker 1989). Critics of a 'feminist ethic' suggest 'that Gilligan "heard" what confirmed the stereotypes' (Clement 1996: 3) with Western, white, well-educated women. AfroAmerican writers and writers writing on black cultures (Collins 1990: 215–17; Harding 1987; Stack 1993), refer to the deep commitment to care within these communities stemming from values within the Afrocentric religious tradition. Female essentialism assumes that women's experience has enough similarity to posit women's ethics (Houston 1987: 259). A false universalism fails to note important differences of race, class, culture, religion. Significant variations exist with differing ethical voices, emphases, virtues, priorities, experiences and moral expressions.

While Gilligan's approach has radically restructured feminist ethics, it is sensible to see that there are many moral voices, not just of gender, but of race, class, religion and culture. Susan Hekman's point is valid, that whereas traditional ethics heard a single truth of disembodied moral principles, feminist ethics listens and hears multiple voices because it 'defines morality and moral knowledge as plural and heterogeneous' (1995: 30). This book explores different moral voices, not the 'different voice'. Through 'defining the moral realm as a multiplicity of voices, we not only broaden and enrich it, we also allow subjects to speak in the moral voices that define them as subjects' (1995: 130), as Asian lawyers, migrant domestics, Aboriginal teachers, black British middle-class women, and so forth.

Feminists talk less about 'women's morality' but listen to multiple moral voices. Women's positive nurture must be valued while gendered dualisms that naturalize or romanticize women's experiences must be tackled. Gendered spheres must be reconstructed so that public life becomes sensitive to nurture and the family becomes just. Such a reconstruction is crucial for sustaining the 'just care' of society (Okin 1989, 1994, 1995). Family justice includes

'decision-making, executive action, judgements of guilt and innocence, reward and punishment, allocations of responsibilities and
privileges of burdens and benefits' (Friedman 1995: 68) and public
care includes 'aid, welfare, famine/disaster relief, other social pro-
grams designed to relieve suffering and attend to need' (1995: 69).
There are a multiplicity of moral voices, so too, moral life requires
multiple virtues and while gender influences these voices and
virtues, it need not.

Women as moral agents

To call women **moral agents** means that:

- women have full moral capacities
- their self-respect is crucial to claiming agency
- women's judgement and moral practice is ethical.

Women are 'obviously as capable as men of taking up the
subjective viewpoint, of making moral judgements, acting pur-
posefully, exercising will and controlling desire' (Frazer, Hornsby
and Lovibond 1992: 6). Women exhibit their competency to make
life and death decisions on conception, birth, abortion and care
of the dying. Moral agents deserve to be treated as morally responsible. Agency and self-respect are linked.

Self-respect

Self-respect helps to realize one's moral capacities. Even in
mutual relationships the capacity for self-respect can be nurtured or
damaged (Govier 1992, 1993; Sevenhuijsen 1998: 63). Self-respect
is embedded in a nexus of concepts like personhood, rights,
autonomy, responsibility, identity, virtue and integrity. At its core
is a valuing of self-worth. Self-respect can bolster our well-being as
a secure sense of our worth, or when it is undermined it can be
debilitating and disempowering. Developing self-respect, let alone
maintaining it, is difficult for women for whom self-sacrifice is
commonplace.

Robin Dillon (1992a) distinguishes between 'appraisal self-
respect' which we earn more or less of, and 'recognition self-
respect' which is owed to all persons. Dillon explores how to

construct a feminist conception of 'recognition self-respect' that does not disregard particularity, but takes moral account of 'the details that make me who I am' (1992a: 60), including myself *as a woman*. Self-understanding is often tortuous, fraught with guilt, hurt, embarrassment, low self-esteem, but it is a necessary prerequisite for self-respect. 'Nothing about an individual is irrelevant to self-respect' (1992a: 60). There is moral significance in everyday ordinariness including our personal inadequacies and despair, as well as our goals and achievements.

Elizabeth Spelman (1990: 1–5), in respecting differences, develops a similar argument by using an analogy of pebbles. An interest in pebbles should not be distracted by the shape or colour of unusual pebbles. Yet, Spelman asks, 'how can I disregard those features of each pebble that may distinguish it from others?' (1990: 3). Herein lies a paradox of feminism – to talk about commonality undermines differences and describing what differentiates us eclipses what we share. In undermining white middle-class privilege, Spelman advocates the need to weigh the relative importance of commonalities against our differences (1990: 4). Moral equality is the basis for treating people with equal concern and respect (Koggel 1997). For women to be considered as equally competent actors, as responsible moral subjects, stereotypical doubts as to their moral reliability must vanish.

Self-respect values a separate individuality and a connectedness to others. A feminist recognition of self-respect involves the core of Gilligan's ethic, 'that I am, in and of myself, worthy of my own care and of the care of others' (Dillon 1992a: 62). Self-determination is inseparable from relationships to others (Clement 1996: 42; Whitbeck 1984). Likewise, self-respect and care are inseparable. A respect for persons' rights and a compassionate responsiveness is central to just, caring conceptions of morality. Caring for another demonstrates respect because we view the subject as worthy of consideration, as a valid claim on our attention and then deliberate as to appropriate responses. Respect takes many forms from a mountain climber's respect for the elements, respecting an agreement, equal respect owed to all or having little respect for liars. Indigenous people and environmentalists manifest their deep respect for nature as valuable, requiring special cherishing and protecting. The respect for persons has three prongs (Dillon 1992b):

1 We are specific concrete individuals, so respect involves responding to this particularity.

2 Our self-understanding is morally significant and respect requires us to know each other in our self-defined specificity.
3 As interdependent beings, we show our respect by helping others pursue goals and satisfy needs.

'Care respect' takes account of 'the contingencies that make me who I am' (Dillon 1992b: 73). This theme is reiterated by Gilligan's grounding care in the specific context of the other (1984: 77), Noddings' situating caring as 'special regard for the particular persons in a concrete situation' (1984: 24) and Benhabib's identification of the morality of care and responsibility with 'the concrete other' (1992: 159). Care respect takes appropriate account of persons and maintains 'a constructive tension between regarding each person as *just as valuable* as every other person and regarding this individual as *special*' (Dillon 1992b: 74). Parents see each child as both equally important and equally special. In valuing differences, self-respect is affirmed.

Diana Meyers (1986) makes strong claims that a self-respecting person has due regard for personal dignity. That is, she feels resentment when others ignore her wishes and shame when she submits to degrading treatment. In later chapters we examine how these feelings relate to prostitution and pornography. A self-respecting person resists attempts to humiliate, demean or deny rights and pursues her life-plans, those interests, needs, values and wishes we intend to satisfy. 'If a person's life-plan cannot be described as her *own* life-plan, her fulfilling it does not evidence respect for her self' (1986: 85). Self-respect requires both a self-knowledge and a self-direction, knowing what is important to oneself and how best to pursue it. Many women who are poor, uneducated, or bound by religious or cultural limitations to narrowly circumscribed roles are prevented from being self-directed. It is not that these women have no self-respect, but they experience frustration at their lack of self-fulfilment. As de Beauvoir (1975) says, women have been objects, not subjects, denied the opportunity to express autonomy.

Some feminists criticize **autonomy** for being individualistic. It is helpful to appreciate that the 'autonomous self is itself a product of relationships' (Hekman 1995: 16). Jennifer Nedelsky reminds us that our embeddedness in relations incorporates oppressive forms, but becoming autonomous develops 'the capacity for finding our own law' (1989: 223) and feeling a sense of personal power.

Components of this autonomy include 'comprehension, confidence, dignity, efficacy, respect, and some degree of peace and security from oppressive power' (1989: 224). The capacity to find this personal power develops only in contexts where others nurture this capacity via respect and trust (Baier 1986; Meyers, 1987, 1989). Oppression or powerlessness in childhood, marriage, friendships, work situations and political milieus stultify autonomy. As dependency is a precondition of autonomy, so too, individuality thrives in interdependence because 'autonomy is a competency that is nurtured through relationships with others' (Clement 1996: 32).

Agency and deliberation

Ethical agents recognize moral demands and act on them. Judgement and practice is active. Selma Sevenhuijsen is particularly illuminating on what it means to judge with care. She argues for the 'necessity of viewing care as a form of social agency, which at the same time can inspire careful judgement' (1998: 70). She advocates the centrality of agency to feminist ethics, referring particularly to moral reflection as a *social practice.* Her rationale is clear. In ethics we are constantly confronted with questions of judgement and responsibility. These questions prompt us to reflect on how to act, live and lead good lives. The starting point for moral deliberation is the moral dilemmas that arise in individual and collective contexts. Sevenhuijsen describes **moral deliberation** as the process by which claims are constructed, that is, how clashes between individual claims and responsibilities for others are solved. Her notion of 'a deliberative morality' is 'open-textured, dialogic, open to criticism, self-criticism and debate' (1998: 128). Situatedness in concrete social practices raises the quality of judgement (1998: 115).

Autonomous agency is more than the potential for choice. It refers to how we fashion circumstances into coherent narratives (Benhabib 1992: 162). Intrinsic to the responsiveness of feminist ethics is the interpretation of what needs arise because of individual background. Sensitive dialogue ascertains people's needs. Moral deliberation involves attention to needs; a contextual and narrative appreciation; sensibility to nuance; and communication (Walker 1989: 19). This deliberation connects people who grapple with 'shareable interpretations of their responsibilities, and/or bearable resolutions to their moral binds' (1989: 20). Conflicting ideas for strategies for achieving goals are part of life. Disputes, power, domination and oppression are part of the dependency, suffering and vulnerability that are inevitable in everyday moral lives. It is only in active interchange of conversation, debate, and argument with others who speak their minds, and tell of their situation and needs that we come to respect the differences of others (Tanner 1996: 178). Moral agents are concerned with self and community. Autonomy is nurtured by justice in social relationships where debate and differences are given full expression.

In an important article originally published in 1985, Annette Baier asks, what do women want in a moral theory? After looking at the work women are doing, she concludes she hears 'the voice Gilligan hears, made reflective and philosophical' (1993: 20). Some men too, discontented with standard approaches in traditional ethics, affirm the importance of narrative, context and interpersonal relationships, and many are sympathetic to feminist perspectives. Feminist ethics benefits from drawing on this work. Feminist ethics has its roots in women's experiences, but its positive alternatives offer much to reflective men. Rethinking feminist ethics is ongoing (Koehn 1998). This chapter explores the theoretical groundwork to feminist ethics. The next chapters look at practical dilemmas in which feminist ethics provides distinctive perspectives. Some writers support the ethic of care and responsibility, others integrate this ethic with that of justice and rights. Others criticize it, ignore it, or reflect the multiplicity of voices that become apparent when race, ethnicity, culture, class, religion, literacy level and standard of living impact on our moral identities. All writers of feminist ethics are committed to the pursuit of right action, social justice and moral goodness.

Summary

- Feminist ethics places personal experience, context, care and good relationships as central features of morality.

- Narrative notions of self-respect place interlocking stories within the social embeddedness of moral life.

- Multiple moral voices reflect differences in values, priorities and principles.

- There is a dynamic interplay between justice and care, rights and responsibilities.

- Women as moral agents exhibit self-respect, judgement and ethical practice.

Further reading

Clement, G. (1996) *Care, Autonomy, and Justice. Feminism and the Ethic of Care*, Colorado and Oxford: Westview Press.

Cole, E. Browning and Coultrap-McQuin, S. (eds) (1992) *Explorations in Feminist Ethics*, Bloomington: Indiana University Press.

Held, V. (ed.) (1995) *Justice and Care. Essential Readings in Feminist Ethics*, Colorado and Oxford: Westview Press.

Larrabee, M. J. (ed.) (1993) *An Ethic of Care. Feminist and Interdisciplinary Perspectives*, London and New York: Routledge.

Tong, R. (1993) *Feminine and Feminist Ethics*, Belmont, CA: Wadsworth.

Chapter 2

Intimate Relationships

Chapter outline

This chapter begins by affirming the importance of positive intimate relationships to our well-being. It shows how the emotions
influence personal relationships and why some women sacrifice
personal interests in order to care for others' needs. Friendships
rely on mutuality and the chapter looks at:

- differences in women's and men's friendships
- how passionate friendship searches for others like ourselves
- duties within friendships.

The chapter then examines special moral ties in the family. Some
ties are healthy, others are destructive. Obligations in families
depend on the just or unjust treatment of family members. To
decide how to treat others decently, the chapter concludes by
examining a feminist ethics approach to:

- trust
- dealing with conflict
- expressing anger
- discerning oppression in intimate relationships
- guilt and conflicting interests.

Particular relationships

Intimate relationships are essential for happy human life. The
deprivation of connection through solitary confinement or the

institutionalization of children and the elderly threatens human-ness. Intimate relationships differ from non-intimate relationships. The latter include contractual relationships with a house-builder; client–expert relationships such as victim and lawyer; professional relationships between doctor and patient or teacher and student; formal relationships with a bank manager; or anonymous ex-changes in shops. Non-intimate relationships are characterized by formality, impersonality, procedures, contracts, financial exchanges and an emotional distancing. This is not to suggest that a doctor or a teacher cannot be friendly, approachable and personable, even adopting informal approaches at times and becoming emotionally affected by their contacts, but professionals maintain distance.

In contrast, intimate relationships occur with people with whom we are very familiar, and usually relate informally and casually. They are relationships that confirm the importance of bonds, ties and a closeness to others. They are non-voluntary in the case of our fam-ilies and colleagues, and voluntary in the case of lovers, spouse and friends. In including colleagues as intimate relationships, I refer to fellow-workers who also are close friends. Not all intimate relationships are affirming, rather they range from those relation-ships that are oppressive, destructive and harmful to those with minimal effect, through to those relationships that are liberating, enriching and fulfilling. Whatever their nature, all intimate rela-tionships are particular. For example, our mother might be a birth mother or a social mother to someone who is adopted, fostered or sharing the parenting or a step-mother. She may be a belligerent alcoholic who harassed us and undermined our integrity, or we may feel quite removed from our mother, or she may be inspira-tional, a constant source of love and encouragement. Orphans, refugees and indigenous children taken from their families may never know their mothers. Whatever our feelings are toward our mother, this is an irreplaceable intimate relationship.

Friends have distinctive characteristics. Sally might be like Jade, but she is not Jade. Sally is fun to be with, but is more selfish than Jade, so she is not as sensitive when a good listener is needed. The moral topics which trouble us and touch us deeply are the quality of our relationships in 'kinship, love, friendship and sex' (Benhabib 1992: 184). This chapter examines the moral significance of the particularity of persons. Our lives are intricately involved with others. Our identity emerges in social narratives with intimate others. People of significance are part of our history, and we figure in their stories. Relationships that have been trivial and significant, destructive and fulfilling, hurtful and compassionate, profoundly influence our self-identity.

Particular personal relationships

When feminist ethics values the particular, it significantly challenges the emotional distancing of traditional impartial ethics. According to Seyla Benhabib, universalistic moral theories defend 'the experiences of a specific group of subjects as the paradigmatic case of the, human' who are invariably white, propertied, professional men (1992: 153). Clearly, fairness, reciprocity and universality are necessary to moral standpoints, but morality should not be exclusively based on a 'generalized other' who abstracts from individuality in relationships governed by formal norms of equality, rights, obligations and entitlement. This standpoint is inappropriate in dealing with our favourite granny or only brother. The standpoint of the 'concrete other' requires us to view each 'individual with a concrete history, identity and affective-emotional constitution' (1992: 159). Granny is a dear, but she has had a tough life and often talks about it. We try to comprehend her needs, motivations and desires. Granny needs a lot of time and patience in listening to her repetitious stories. She reciprocates. Granny loves eating with the family at the weekend and, in return, she baby-sits. Norms of friendship and love are appropriate to interactions of bonding and sharing and our emotions are sympathy and solidarity. Benhabib's moral theory recognizes general dignity and concrete identity (1992: 164), thereby breaking down dualisms.

In facing the 'otherness of the other' we confront the distinctiveness from ourselves, whether this includes differences in gender, race, class, welfare or work status, abilities, personalities, sexual preference, marital status, presence or absence of children. The equality of agents requires an attention to difference. **Intimate relationships** are particular, partial and refer to specific familiar relationships. It is precisely because someone is my child or neighbour that I am prompted to act for reasons derivative 'from connections of feeling, familiarity, love' (Herman 1991: 780). When someone we love is hurt, ill or needs our help, we do not respond as an impartial emotionally distanced observer, but we respond to that person as lover, mother, sister, friend, close neighbour. If our friend is distraught because the doctor has just told her she cannot have children, we will be a better friend to her if we know how desperately she wanted children, what her attitudes toward adoption are, what sort of support she needs.

Ethics encourages partiality, the specific response to distinctiveness. If my object of affection is a particular woman, then 'loving and delighting in her are not completely commensurate with loving and delighting in another . . . the loss of the old friend is a distinct loss, the gain of the new friendship, a distinct gain' (Badhwar 1987: 14). My responsibility to be a good friend or a loving daughter depends on an intimate knowledge of how to fulfil the requirements of friendship or family obligations. Such requirements differ according to the degree of intimacy. Where these are healthy intimate relationships, the requirements are to care, listen, be responsive, honest, keep promises and confidences, challenge each other's views, lend possessions, provide emotional support and be available. Later, we discuss those intimate relationships that are unhealthy, and thus demand less of us.

Partiality does not preclude impartiality. 'Because the demands for impartiality are so highly contextual, considerable reflection and sensitivity are needed for the agent to judge that treating So-and-so as special . . . is permissible' (Baron 1991: 837–8). We do not unfairly favour one child over another, but we treat each one specially. This is impartial partial ethical behaviour. Partiality varies according to the bonds involved: parent–child, grandmother to grandson, aunt to niece, best friend, oldest friend, ex-spouse. These particular relationships affect how we act towards specific persons (Blum 1986). 'Indeed the moral dimension of these relationships is bound with this particularity and the different way we respond to them' (Porter 1995: 36). The care of our healthy sister involves different considerations from that appropriate to our invalid mother. Responding to this particularity is fundamental to ethics. The more we know a person in a deep sense, the more we know how to respond meaningfully to their needs. Reacting with attentiveness to contexts is more important than trying to be morally right according to inflexible codes.

The importance of the emotions

In formalistic ethics, the emotions distract from the rigours of objectivity. In feminist ethics, the **emotions** are crucial to responding sensitively or appropriately to people's situations. Certainly emotions are subjective in the sense that the person feeling angry, fearful, excited or joyful holds the emotion and is responsible for the actions that result directly from it. Simultaneously, 'all emotions have a conceptual, rational basis which enables us to judge any particular emotion as rational/irrational, appropriate or inappropriate in particular contexts' (Berenson 1991: 67). The 'possession of various emotions and desires – care, concern, love, but also anger, revulsion, indignation – is not just immensely useful to seeing the moral landscape, it is a *necessary* condition of doing so' (Little 1995: 118). Mary Little takes torture as an example where someone can discern its painfulness and another the fact that it is evil, that is, that torture is repulsive, the pain is a reason not to torture. Little acknowledges the salient features of a situation as constituting a justification for some response whereby one has become 'morally aware' (1995: 126) and the emotions are part of this awareness.

Love is an intense emotion. A love relationship is very precious, it makes life meaningful and influences perceptions of life, so that anything which threatens this relationship is viewed with hostility. The unique irreplaceable aspect of this love relationship makes sharing it difficult. Imagine a man called Joe who is witty, loyal and empathetic. If Tess loves Joe, she does so because he has unique attractive qualities. Tess does not love the qualities separated from Joe (Berenson 1991: 68). Whereas we can substitute qualities, we cannot substitute persons. Even though Joe is low-spirited since not getting his promotion, it is Joe who Tess loves, not James. James is wonderful, but he cannot replace Joe. The qualities we once loved in a person may change over time, altering our feelings for the person. As we mature, the qualities we admire change, different personalities have different appeal. The person we lived with, loved, married or is a parent of our child may change, or we change, or both, altering this once intimate relationship.

'Loving someone without ever feeling jealous would throw in doubt the very genuineness or depth of the love felt' (Berenson 1991: 74). What is at stake with jealousy of our prime relationship is our concept of self-identity in relation to the beloved. When this relationship is threatened there is a loss of self. Love in a full sense 'is a mutual revelation of otherness' (Berenson 1991: 71). With different people, there are different degrees of revelation. Obviously, we would hope that with our spouse (married and de facto) there is the fullest revelation of self that encompasses the sexual, spiritual, emotional and friendship levels. Yet, even with close friends we reveal different types of things, being afraid to express thoroughly our fears, dislikes or anxieties with some, and yet pouring out our innermost self to others. Some of us have families with whom we can express ourselves honestly, others of us have to hide our sexual preference, lifestyle, new family forms or political and religious beliefs. The emotions are a significant part of intimate relationships and contribute to disfavour or fulfilment.

Mutuality

Mutuality is a reciprocal exchange that bolsters well-being. The give and take of mutuality assumes equality. While many men have fraternities, clubs, pubs and old-boys networks to sustain their interests, many women, particularly those raised in fundamentalist religious settings or traditional gender socialization, are reluctant to assert personal interests. Typically, they define feminine moral goodness as **agape**, the other-regarding love that prioritizes **self-sacrifice** over self-love. For these women, the interests and needs of their children, husband, ageing parents and in-laws are more important than their own desires. These women view themselves relationally as wife, mother, daughter and their autonomous self-identity is obscured, as becomes vivid when the last child leaves home. A femininity that idealizes sacrifice victimizes women.

Barbara Andolsen argues that feminist ethicists have good reason to be critical of self-sacrifice. She advocates '*agape* as a full mutuality marked by equality between the sexes' (1994: 154). This mutuality implies that all parties in loving relationships display both receptive and active qualities. That is, if I am sick, have just failed an exam, cannot find employment or am confused, then my partner, friend or family should care for my needs knowing that if s/he is similarly down, I ought to reciprocate, and that as soon as my spirits are raised, my actively caring qualities will be manifest again. Mutuality is more than instrumental or calculative exchange. The receptive and active qualities are not always in equal proportions. An important aspect to this feminist interpretation of mutual love is not merely the openness to the exigencies of life such as ill health, unemployment, grief and disappointment, but to the receptivity, vulnerability and dependency on love from others.

> **Box 2.1 Qualities of enduring relationships**
>
> The results of four combined studies of 2,483 individuals in enduring relationships reveal twelve common characteristics (Rice 1993: 75–87).
>
> 1 Commitment to making the relationship work well.
> 2 Honesty, trust and fidelity is important to sincerity.
> 3 Responsibility shared ensures dependability.
> 4 Adaptability, flexibility and tolerance are signs of adjustment to changes.
> 5 Unselfishness in helping each other is part of being generous.
> 6 Communication involves listening, self-disclosure, confiding, stimulating exchanges, responding, respecting other's views, arguing fairly.
> 7 Empathy and sensitivity includes being warm and compassionate.
> 8 Admiration and respect, being proud of achievements, respecting differences and property and expressing appreciation builds partner's esteem.
> 9 Affection demonstrates verbal and physical care.
> 10 Companionship allows enjoyable time to be spent together, sharing interests.
> 11 Ability to deal with crisis and stress and problem-solve is necessary given inevitable life problems.
> 12 Spirituality and values when shared cement agreement on goals in life.

Friendships

Friendships represent an important paradigm of mutuality as equality. Friendships are marked by mutual regard. Reciprocity prevails when friends are confirmed as having worth. Being affirmed as valued enriches mutuality. When **friendship** is understood as a 'practical and emotional relationship marked by mutual and equal goodwill, liking, and pleasure' it can exist 'between siblings, lovers, parent and adult child' as well as between unrelated persons (Kapur 1991: 483). Friendship shapes and confirms our sense of life and selfhood. Without it, life is empty and our identities are not affirmed as valuable (Friedman 1993). Friendship is an intrinsic aspect to pleasurable happiness. Where there is a mutual sharing of experiences, uncertainties and alternative ways to approach moral dilemmas, friendships also give us new insights into experiences beyond personal boundaries. Lorraine Code (1991), reflecting on the epistemic significance of knowing others, suggests that the autonomous reasoner learns not just through detached impartial self-reliance, but through attachments to friends, parents, teachers.

Mutual respect cements friendships and positive intimate relationships. This respect incorporates the general respect for justice and rights and the compassionate responsiveness for particular interdependent beings. Indeed, 'caring for another is a way of respecting her' (Dillon 1992b: 69). 'Care respect' (1992b: 77) breaks dichotomies because respect confirms common humanity and care responds to our distinctive individuality. When we demonstrate respect we make someone feel valued. The ethical dimensions of 'care respect' generate rationales for action. Care for a new friend, old friend, best friend, hurt friend differs. 'The more experienced we are in sensitive, reflective, contextualized judgement the better our care' (Porter 1996b: 68). Given that many people live in family situations where abuse and discord is the norm, where they feel cheated by 'the system', those in authority have let them down or family members have hurt them deeply, most people value friends for their acceptance and affirmation. They let us be ourselves. Good friends affirm 'trust, honesty, respect, commitment, safety, support, generosity, loyalty, mutuality, constancy, understanding' (Rubin 1985: 7).

Women and men's friendships generally differ. Our experiences of growing up as a girl and as a young woman influence friendships. Research seems unequivocal in showing that at every life stage, women have more friendships than men and the differences in quality are marked (Rubin 1985: 60). Women confide readily in each other, relying on the emotional support gained. There are 'three main qualities typical of women's friendships – unique supportiveness, genuine affection, and responsive particularity' (Porter 1996b: 65). First, supportiveness is crucial wherever everyday life is a struggle. For working-class women this may mean helping out with the children to accommodate shift work. In close-knit working-class and ethnic communities women rely on relatives and neighbours to care for children, exchange clothes and appliances and lend emotional support. As Simone de Beauvoir expresses it, the value to these relations is the 'moral ingenuity' and the 'truthfulness' whereby 'women help one another, discuss their social problems, each creating for the others a kind of protecting nest'

(1975: 55). Mutual support enables women to confide in each other when they are tired, poor or worried. For middle-class women it may include keeping the courage to fight workplace discrimination. For girls it is the shared intimacy of discussing new experiences, exchanging clothes, wondering about sex.

Second, women show affection for each other. Janice Raymond uses the term *gyn/affection* to express the embracing affection for women that allows for personal growth (1986: 15). This is an attraction where 'women affect, move, stir, and arouse each other to full power' (1986: 9, 229). This passion is a fascination for the companionship of those who lift us when we are low, and who help us move toward personal growth. Third, women's friendships respond to particularity. Accustomed to meeting people's needs, women are not ashamed to cry with a friend who has miscarried, or screech for joy at a friend's promotion. Intimacy requires partiality, special attentiveness, responsiveness and favouritism (Friedman 1991: 818). The more intimately we know our friends' characteristics, needs, failings and strengths, the more we identify with their joys and sorrows.

Men who write on friendships confirm the difficulty many men have with expressing intimacy (Jackson 1990; Nardi 1992; Strikwerda and May 1992). They write of comradeship or mateship developed through war, and of shared activities like playing sport or drinking in pubs. Obstacles to achieving intimacy in men's friendships include a masculine cult of toughness and aggression and the association of emotional closeness and feelings with femininity. Black women writers stress the significance of community relationships, not only among women but also between men and women. Patricia Hill Collins (1990) speaks of the centrality of women in AfroAmerican communities, of woman-centred networks of resilient bloodmothers and 'othermothers', grandmothers, sisters, aunts, cousins, or close friends who are there for anyone's children when necessary. She talks of a personal accountability among AfroAmerican women to all the children in the black community (1990: 129).

Passion for friends

There is a spaciousness in women's friendships that allows a light-heartedness in enjoying each other. Janice Raymond posits a strong argument that 'friendship begins with the affinity a woman has with her vital Self' (1986: 5). We are fascinated with the company of those who bring us out of ourselves when we are low, help us to appreciate our potential and who tap deep into our personality. To talk of a friend as 'another self' presupposes self-love, self-respect, self-regard. Self-trust enables us to perform as cognitive agents who are responsible for the type of friends we are, and how we demonstrate our commitment to friendships and other intimate relationships. This 'self is the I of relation and dialogue as well as the I of self-understanding and independent action. . . . The self is the I that listens and speaks, that wonders, feels and responds – that accepts or rejects, confirms or disconfirms, persists or desists' (Govier 1993: 117). Worthwhile relationships, based on thoughtful connections, develop self-integrity.

Raymond's idea that there can be no genuine friendship between women that 'does not come from a strong Self' (1986: 162) is important to feminist ethics. It contradicts de Beauvoir's statement that 'women's fellow feeling rarely rises to genuine friendship. . . . Their relations are not founded on their individualities' (1975: 558). Raymond's point is that in order to appreciate what we share in common with other women, we need to know what we believe, think, desire. We know the personality and character traits we admire and enjoy, or despise and avoid. This does not deny confusion or uncertainty, or being persuaded differently, but it does rely on a healthy self-regard. 'Until the Self is another friend, it is often difficult for women to have confidence in their power of making and sustaining friends' (Raymond 1986: 222). What is embraced is the dual injunction to be true to one's own needs while caring for others. Again this breaks down the dualism of self–other.

Often it is through friendships with people with similar aspirations, goals and values that we discover more about our self, which is why it is when 'the search for others like my Self begins' (Friedman 1988: 132) that we find people who become close friends. The enjoyment or significance of things we value the most, like a candle-lit dinner, listening to music, going to a play or walking on the beach depends on the company we share these experiences with. Through shared intimacy, we realize self-affirmation and self-discovery, even though they are not always welcome bits of knowledge. As Marilyn Friedman aptly summarizes, '"a passion for friends" is also a passion for one's *Self*' (1988: 136). Close friends long to know the truth of each other – their upbringing, background, work experiences, crises, hopes, desires, fears. Developing a deep knowledge requires time and reflection, which is why best friends are often the friends we have had for the longest stretch of time.

Duties and friendships

Friendships involve bonds of deep moral significance that cannot be reduced to formal duties but are based on past trust and intimacy (Blum 1980: 69). We trust our friends to be honest with us, fair and supportive, and similarly, we treat them well because the bond is special. A mutuality of trust, affection and intimate self-disclosure is built over time and 'this mutuality is the basis of special responsibilities' (Annis 1987: 352). We listen, keep confidences and promises, borrow and lend possessions and give emotional support and enjoyment. Friends welcome laughter, encouragement, practical assistance and time. Our friendships differ. We rank the importance of friendships for different reasons – there are friends we have known the longest, shared the most trying experiences, have the most in common with, are the most reliable, or enjoy their companionship the most. As interests and values change or our friends themselves change, friendships alter.

Valuing friendships differently leads to a ranking of responsibilities toward different friends. These responsibilities are neither strictly defined nor mechanically applied but depend on sensitivity. Michael Stocker argues that the moral nature of adult friendship 'is shown by the constitutive fact that friends care for and are concerned with the well-being of friends' (1987: 63). When we disappoint our friends by not giving them the attention they deserve, break a promise, are ridiculously late for dinner or are not sensitive to their current needs, we invite their censure. Nevertheless, it is characteristic of friends to demonstrate **benevolence**, 'the disposition to be generous in good times, helpful in bad times, and forgiving in the face of injury', as well as justice, 'the disposition not to cause injury, to be honest, and to judge fairly' (Kapur 1991: 499). Benevolent friendships foster integrity and autonomy. Without integrity we cannot act as friends. Without autonomy we do not have the independent facet that individuates us and makes us unique, as an object of attraction for others and as an agent who is attracted to others.

Meaningful friendships accept responsibilities. There are general duties owed to all persons that respect the essential humanity of another, like promise-keeping, telling the truth, showing gratitude, asking for forgiveness, making reparations and acting justly.

Again context and the specificity of the relationships makes a difference. A promise to visit our mother in hospital is more important to fulfil than a promise to take our nephew to the park, but a quick visit to the park might be fitted in after hospital. General duties are owed to all persons, but friendship involves special duties that are grounded by the friendship, in fact we 'violate a special duty of friendship' by not according friends special care and attention (Stocker 1987: 65). Care and attention includes affection, listening, empathy, openness and time. Attentiveness is so important that failure to fulfil such duties justifies a breaking of friendship. 'A poor friend is close to not being a friend at all' (Card 1988: 123). While we might not owe anyone friendship, we certainly owe our friends, that is, we ought to act like friends.

The ethics of gratitude is part of this obligation, the requirements which can be messy when there are relationships between persons who are unequal in power. As Claudia Card (1988) explains, those who are powerless may develop a misplaced gratitude for ordinary decencies that should be shown to everyone, or for less abusiveness than was possible. This latter example is the case when a woman loves a man who is physically violent to her. Often she is pathetically grateful if he is not as violent as usual, or perhaps is drunk but does not hit her, or he brings her flowers the day after violating her body. This is misplaced gratitude. Gratitude highlights differences between obligation and duty. Bonds of obligation to friends and kin are based in our knowledge of the histories of these people. As the woman who has been subject to domestic violence may grasp, her obligations to the man she thought loved her diminishes as his abuse of her personhood continues, until her perceived obligations halt abruptly. Persistent undermining of her self-respect suggests she should end this relationship. **Obligations** are the bases of duties, 'the discharge of which can fulfil an obligation' (Card 1988: 121). The obligations we owe in friendships are informal. Whereas with formal obligations to pay a loan from a bank, once the debt is paid, the obligation is discharged, living up to informal obligations tends to reaffirm the special relationship involved, strengthening the friendship.

Sisterhood

Strong ties are part of 'sisterhood'. Second-wave feminism built on an assumed 'victim mentality', where women oppressed by men believed that through banding together, a protective bonding would emerge. The concept 'sisterhood' was useful for women in consciousness-raising groups who discussed shared roots in patriarchy, men's domination, gender roles, reproduction and sex. What shared assumptions disregarded was the ways in which women's oppression differed according to culture, class, ethnicity, religion and colour. Most white middle-class educated women are privileged compared to their black or Asian working-class, poorly educated 'sisters'. A superficial notion of sisterhood limits feminist politics, naturalizing and sentimentalizing female friendship.

María Lugones is critical of the notion that sisterhood in feminist discourse is sometimes a metaphorical ideal and sometimes a metaphor for actual relationships among women (1993: 406). She explains sisterhood as 'egalitarian kinship bonding' (1993: 407) that does not necessarily incorporate a deep respect. She criticizes the concept on the basis that white family structures have often been oppressive institutions, lacking extended kinship support. Further, white/Anglo feminism has not been effective in including egalitarianism across differences. Among Latinas, 'sister' is used only for siblings and for close friends. While 'compañera' connotes egalitarianism, it is that of companionship in common political struggle. In the AfroAmerican community, the word 'sister' conveys a sense of community, status and affection. The slave experience fragmented families, and through racist insults deprived blacks of dignity. It became a political act to call people 'brother' and 'sister', an act of resistance and of respect (1993: 409). When white women appropriated this term as a resistance to male domination, its roots as a confrontation to enslavement and racism erased the differences between women.

Lugones advocates 'friendship' as an important part of building a feminist ethos, because it creates bonds across differences. Friendship embraces plurality, a commitment to understand friends' varying realities. Consequently, self-knowledge is enhanced as we come to understand ourselves as differently situated in race, ethnicity, class and experience. Feminist history explores women's friendship circles, finding a particular 'women's world' of love and ritual that exists 'within, or perhaps beneath, patriarchal relationship' (Stanley 1992: 161). Establishing a lesbian history involves recovery and reconceptualization, suggesting questions of essentialism, difference, womanhood and selfhood (1992: 162). Friendships substitute, complement or overlap with family bonds.

Family relationships

To develop into morally competent individuals, we require nurture. The networks of dependence that develop are not like the clothes we outgrow, but are ties that bind and shape our moral identities and visions of the good life. In healthy families, the dependency that is part of interdependency involves caring, sharing and mutuality within childhood socialization. Our sense of self unfolds within a web of narratives. In unhealthy families, dependency contributes to emotional immaturity, where interdependency never occurs.

It is in families where we first learn to live moral or immoral lives in concrete relations as a daughter or a son to a particular father, mother, social parent or welfare institution. Special moral ties emerge in families that give relationships like parent–child, sister–brother, grandson–grandfather moral weight. 'There are unique joys and tensions, social expectations and responsibilities that are attached to these relationships' (Porter 1995: 6). For example, a child who is disrespectful to a loving parent should feel shame because courtesy is fitting in all relationships. An affluent brother who fails to take in his homeless sister fails to fulfil reasonable family expectations of concern for one's kin. A grandmother who refuses contact with her granddaughter because of her outlandish dress style breaks family traditions for the younger generation. A father who is cruel to his son and deprives him of affection distorts moral ties, for parenting requires sensitive kindness to vulnerable dependants.

Family networks change with mobility and people often value voluntary relationships rather than difficult family members. Decent families of all forms are committed to care, to instil a sense of belonging and communicate intimate affection. Not all families are geared toward constructive socialization. Consequently, many of us spend much of our adult life dealing with guilt, fear, repression, suppressed emotions or hostilities, and 'other sins of intimacy' (Herman 1991: 788), trying to rid ourselves of unwanted socially constructed personhood. Unfortunately, within many families, relationships of domination and subordination, power and yielding to the controller prevail. Jessica Benjamin (1990) explains how domination involves those who exercise power and those who submit to it. In traditional families, men as 'household heads' expect deference and may lash out when it is not forthcoming. Within gendered power relations, the economic dependency of women

leaves them vulnerable to abuse. While domination refuses to valid-
ate the personhood of the other, submission does not necessarily
imply consent. Submission may be based on fear, ignorance or a
lack of alternatives. Yet not all power is violent, destructive or controlling. Parents potentially wield positive power to influence their
children's development.

An ethical goal within families is to foster a balance between
the family as a connected unit and the separate individuality of
its members. Moral choice is part of maintaining this balance and
the range of significant ethical dilemmas covers abortion, affairs,
balance between work and family commitments, bisexuality, incest,
coping with violence, custody, division of labour, divorce, finances,
stealing, lying, who gets leisure time, and the list could continue.
Sound ethical responses to moral choices include retaining one's
autonomy and accountability for the consequences of decisions
made; trying to be inclusive to all family members; being flexible
and negotiating with relevant persons; being faithful, loyal and
reliable; being truthful, honest and trustworthy; being prepared
to forgive, acting fairly, expressing affection, minimizing hurt and
creating a sphere of secure intimacy (Porter 1995: 51). We all make
good and bad choices. Sometimes we only grasp the stupidity of
our decisions in retrospect.

Case study. One daughter's response to her mother

María Lugones (1997), brought up in Argentina, explores her failure to love her mother and the white/Anglo women's failure to
love women across racial and cultural boundaries. Growing up,
she identified a love for her mother as demanding her services,
and thus equated servitude with love. Further, not wanting to be
like her mother, she perceived her separation as a lack of love.
When she came to the USA, she learnt 'that part of racism is the
internalization of the propriety of abuse' (1997: 150), while being
ignored, ostracized, rendered invisible, stereotyped, left alone or
interpreted as crazy. Change came when she saw that this was similar to how she treated her mother. She discovered that only through
'travelling to her "world"' (1997: 152) could she identify with her.
As a '"world"-traveller' (1997: 154), she has the distinct experience
of being at ease in different worlds, in terms of language, norms,
bonds, shared history. Travelling to someone's world identifies with
them. Eventually, seeing herself in her mother's world 'meant
seeing how different from her I am in her "world"' (1997: 159).

Family obligations

The question of what we owe to family members is increasingly complex in a world where 'families' are so diverse. One child may have a birth mother and an adopted, foster, step or social mother, as well as gay, non-related uncles, numerous step-siblings, and a father seen infrequently. Who owes who, what? Annette Baier (1993) raises an extreme example to make a powerful point. She refers to war orphans who grow up without parental love and become adults who fail to keep their word, as well as children who did experience loving affection but grow up breaking promises. Baier asks who has failed in their obligations? Does the fault lie with the parents, or in the failure to educate parents, or with those who care for orphans and refugees? Baier suggests that it would be confusing 'if the obligation to lovingly rear one's children were added to the list of obligations' (1993: 23). Yet evidence is clear that children are more likely to learn morality in conditions where they are 'lovingly' raised as opposed to merely 'conscientiously' raised. Baier asks then, 'do we have an obligation to love' (1993: 23)? To answer this, she turns Rawls' response around. Rawls examines how just institutions produce adequate support across generations and how a sense of justice will arise in children. He writes, 'the parents, we may suppose, love the child and in time the child comes to love and trust the parents' (1973: 463). Baier, in questioning these assumptions, responds that 'the virtue of being a *loving parent* must supplement the natural duties and the obligations of justice if the just society is to last' (1993: 23).

As Sara Ruddick argues, many moral dilemmas of family life revolve around 'fragile obligations that seem beyond consent' (1995: 210). The recognition of familial obligation construes it as an inevitable consequence of relationship. Children have to be fed, the ill nursed, dependants nourished. Radical inequalities accompany the disproportionate assumption of responsibility. Ruddick explains how 'theories of justice tend to idealize equality, transcendence of difference, and the ability to give or withhold consent' (1995: 210). It seems tempting to turn to ethics of care to accept given obligations but this 'threatens to render care private and familial while at the same time excusing families from the demands of justice' (1995: 211). Justice is in tandem with care.

Justice in families

Susan Okin develops substantial arguments on justice, gender and the family. She argues that within family structures that have a strict

gender division of labour, 'women's self-conceptions, life opportunities, and access to political power' are considerably more con-
strained than those of men (1989: 93, 1994: 26). Such constraints
are particularly conspicuous where girls are raised in fundamentalist, orthodox or religious households or highly traditionalist families. There is an ethical urgency for injustice in the family to be
addressed. Yet this is no easy task, for the family is the site 'where
things both good and bad are frequently hidden from public view'
and where both affection and naked power occur (Okin 1994: 27).
Okin's strong argument is that it is difficult to imagine how families that do not live according to principles of fairness can play
a positive role in the moral education of citizens in a just society
(1989: 17–24, 195–6; 1994: 33).

Sociologically, there is much evidence that men and women are
differentially positioned in relation to paid work, power, leisure
and opportunity to pursue personal goals. Such injustices signal
that entitlements and responsibilities are based on a morally irrelevant contingency, namely, one's sex. While many men are becoming more involved in child-rearing (Balbus 1998), the prevalent
expectation that women should be the exclusive or prime nurturer
is not a fair one. Okin acknowledges that some individuals who
have a concern with justice have grown up in abusive or unfair
families. Yet, if Okin is right, and the family is a place where there
is a learned acceptance of injustice, it is difficult to presume that
the family is a good place to learn to treat others as equals, to be
just, fair, meet others halfway, share the household labour, and
treat family members with respect and equal dignity. For family
justice, material provisions of subsidized childcare and parental
leave are needed, as well as a fairer division of household labour,
and changed attitudes that grant equal dignity to all family members.

Treating others decently

Acting ethically means we treat others decently, considering the
well-being of others as an ethical concern. This concern reflects
on human frailty as well as strength, that despite our intentions to
be friendly, agreeable, entertaining, pleasant and kind, we fail. We
make mistakes in the way we treat others. Some of these mistakes
are trivial and easily excused, others are more serious and hurt
deeply. People who are ridiculed, humiliated, lied to, verbally harassed, disappointed, or physically, psychologically or sexually abused

by those with whom there is some intimacy, whether voluntarily as
a friend or lover, or non-voluntarily through family ties, are victims
of betrayed intimacy. Victims carry scars, many for a lifetime, never
fully recovering a sense of personal dignity and worth.

Acknowledging wrong-doing and asking for forgiveness is difficult and fraught with tension. When a wrongdoer acknowledges
their ill-treatment to others, feelings of shame, remorse, embarrassment, regret and humiliation are typical. If their action was
morally unjustifiable, asking for forgiveness is a way of accepting
moral culpability, and for attempting to repair the relationship.
This benefits both self and the other, through restoring the quality of the relationship. Forgiving limits the resentment toward the
person who has wronged us, but this depends on the context and
degree of harm inflicted. Those who have suffered extremely
through domestic violence, incest or rape may find it difficult, if
not impossible, to forgive, wanting to start a life away from their
abusers. Moving away may be the only way to relearn to trust others.

Trust

Trust is crucial in intimate relationships. Baier defines trust as
'reliance on others', a 'competence and willingness to look after,
rather than harm, things one cares about which are entrusted to
their care' (1986: 259). But, she also asks, 'who should trust whom,
with what, and why?' (1993: 30), especially when people lie, de-
ceive, distort, disappoint or betray our confidence in them. Trust
is a dependency on the goodwill of another, we allow ourselves to
be vulnerable. We fall asleep in trains, hoping no one takes our
bag. We put our faith in pilots, drivers, doctors. We rely on friends
to mind our children, animals or home. Sometimes there is a risk
with our confidence, we are not sure how our children will relate
to a new friend who is baby-sitting, a locum doctor is in the surgery, or our friend is a gossip despite being lovable and we are not
sure if we can trust her with our confidentiality. We trust someone
to whom we are prepared to hand the care for something we
value. The care may be for something intangible like a private fear
or hope.

Trust means we are prepared to be vulnerable in the sense of
believing that others will not harm us, even when we are unsure of
others' motivations. We know trust is morally decent if we have
full confidence in the reasons for the trust. For example, imagine

an old lonely woman who confides in her single daughter a secret from youth that ties them together in a tangle of guilt and which pressurizes the daughter to avoid other relationships in order to protect her mother. This is not a morally decent trust. Consider a couple who have joint custody of their children due to the prime caring they both undertake. They trust each other's abilities to care for their children, despite their personal differences. Knowing they both truly care for the children cements the trust.

As parents, trust is crucial. A trustworthy parent cares for a child's needs for nutrition, shelter, clothing, health, education, privacy and loving attachment to others. Barbara Herman writes, 'what my son has reason to trust is that I am committed to his well-being: that among the things that matter to me most and that will determine how I act is that he do well and flourish' (1991: 782). Herman continues that it is not that she cares exclusively about her son's interests, for her friends, spouse, students and her own claims also press on her attention, as well as complete strangers' needs, but because her son knows she cares for him, he can trust her to consider his well-being as fundamental to her multiple commitments. Similarly, when we trust a child to a separated spouse 'it is all aspects of the child's good as a developing person which are entrusted to the other parent's care' (Baier 1986: 238). Both parents want the child to be healthy, happy, well-educated and fulfilled, even if both differ on how to achieve their goals. When children approach adulthood, and when parents become dependent through old age, the trust changes to a 'mutual trust and mutual vulnerability between equals' (1986: 243).

Trust indicates binding obligations between equals and non-equals, such as teacher–pupil, confider–confidante, worker–co-worker and professional–client. Our obligations indicate what it is reasonable to expect from each other. Baier talks of an appropriate trust and distrust (1993: 28). She is convinced that a morality of love is part of all its variants, like parental love, children's love for their parents, love of other family members, friends, lovers, co-workers, figureheads because 'love and loyalty demand maximal trust of one sort, and maximal trust worthiness' (1993: 28). Yet, it is foolish to be naive and trust someone who does not value our goodwill. As it is appropriate to trust someone who wants the best for us, 'judicious untrust worthiness, selective refusal to trust, discriminating discouragement of trust' (1993: 31) is necessary because not all trust relationships are good. A daughter misses school and relies on her brother to cover for her, big businesses and crime syndicates rely on each other to carry out dubious dealings, a spouse trusted with the housekeeping money repeatedly gambles it.

People we trust usually are loyal. **Loyalty** involves faithfulness, constancy, dependability and devotion. 'Loyalty is based on a *deep attachment* to something, and it requires proof of the attachment. Morality is active. We prove our loyalty by *being loyal*' (Porter 1995: 78). Loyalty explains the devoted care, usually by a mother, daughter or daughter-in-law, to those who require constant attention. Such a devotion may not always be a direct choice, nevertheless, loyalty to one's own is strong and, for women, generally accompanies some sacrifice to career, leisure or flexibility of time. Loyalty to intimate relationships means we are prepared to do things we would not do for someone we knew less well, like shifting furniture on a hot day or coming at inconvenience to help get a car started. Loyal people are reliable. Reliability is part of having your word trusted. Loyalty and reliability are demonstrated in practical instances.

Conflict in relationships

No matter how much we want our intimate relationships to be meaningful, brimming with mutual enrichment, enjoyable, loving and loyal, personal crises occur. Relationships have inevitable ups and downs, sometimes fall flat, sour, disappoint or alienate. When trust is violated, it is difficult to rebuild, because we are unsure of our standing with those who have severely hurt us. Admittedly there are degrees of hurt. Even with something like truth, there are direct lies, distortions of the facts, misleading information, unintentional untruths, withholding of truth and glossing over the truth. The impact of relationships in crisis increases in proportion to the value of the relationships and the degree of pain. Some friends are better friends and mean more to us than other friends who value us differently. Some family members experience a special relationship with other family members. Within interpersonal relationships, ethics deals with how we should treat our family, friends, spouse and close colleagues. Responses like anger, confusion, fear, guilt, humiliation and shame are deep emotions which morality sometimes requires us to feel. These are not necessarily harmful or negative emotions, rather they play an important role in responding ethically.

Anger

Anger is a morally legitimate emotion which helps to identify wrongs like racism, sectarianism, sexism, workplace discrimination, capitalist exploitation. Anger prompts individuals to become involved in social movements to eradicate injustices against races, cultural groups, women, ethnic minorities, gays and lesbians or welfare recipients. While there is a legitimate place in morality for strong emotions, they need to be kept within moral limits and this is not always easy. Understandably, Jewish people who witnessed the Holocaust or who lost loved ones, black writers on slavery and feminist historians want to keep anger alive in order to learn from the past and identify extreme evil and injustice. In Aristotle's *Ethics*, he writes, 'those who do not get angry at things that ought to make them angry are considered to be foolish' (1977: 1126a4: 161). For Aristotle, working out the appropriateness of anger is part of thinking about how we should live as ethical agents. Admittedly, for Aristotle, the 'those' he refers to are free men (not women or slaves) and the emotions typically are viewed as interfering with the fluid functioning of reason.

Elizabeth Spelman argues that 'while members of subordinate groups are expected to be emotional, indeed to have their emotions run their lives, their anger will not be tolerated' (1989: 264). Women are permitted to be jealous, sad and cry but their anger is likely to be branded hysteria. Blacks, as depicted by whites, are full of the emotions heard in the plaintive music of the blues, but not anger. Spelman asks why anger is appropriated by and for dominant groups when the emotions are considered to be the province of subordinate groups? She insists that judgements are constituent of emotions so that 'being angry involves judging that some wrong or injustice has been done' (1989: 265) hence it is an appropriate, reasonable emotional response. To be angry is to judge someone as blameworthy, as being in the wrong.

Take, for example, a housewife waiting for her partner to return from the pub to put their children to bed so she can go to her night-class. The man walks in too late for her to go and she explodes in fury at his indifference. 'A man's telling a woman how "cute" she is when she is angry signals his desire to undermine the moral and political agency of the angry woman' (Spelman 1989: 267). However, 'subordinate groups have the right to be angry – that since they are oppressed, exploited, or otherwise treated unfairly, their anger is a justified response to their situation' (1989:

267). Often circumstances in friendship, marriage, work situations or self-respect call for people to be angry. Spelman argues further that the systematic denial of anger – of a woman subject to domestic violence, a worker being paid poorly, an ethnic group facing discrimination – is a mechanism of subjection, part of the politics of the emotions. 'Where power and/or inequality mix with intimacy, questions of exploitation and abuse are raised' (Herman 1991: 788). Such questions do not treat persons as ends who are worthy of respect and value.

Discerning oppression

In intimate relationships, the closeness is so valued that it is hard to admit to debilitating or oppressive aspects of the relationship. Yet we all know times when a man we love gets moody and aggressive, a woman we love gets over-sensitive and snaps, our best friend tries to dominate, or the closest workmate never takes initiative in organizing social events. Sarah Hoagland (1990) maintains that it is crucial to perceive oneself as ethically separate and related in order to acknowledge difference, such as being black or white in a racist society and male and female in a sexist society, and 'to assess any relationship for abuse/oppression and withdraw if I find it to be so' (1990: 111). The ability to say, I will not let my friend, lover or spouse, dominate, be aggressive toward me, be rude, insulting or demeaning enhances my ethical self. 'To pursue the feminine (whose essence is *agape* and unconditional loving), to pursue this sense of female agency, is to pursue oppression' (1990: 112). We should be concerned with others but not persistently at the expense of our own desires.

Likewise, Barbara Houston is concerned with the gendered distribution of benefits and burdens of caring. The problem of self-sacrifice is real, particularly for those who have been victimized or exploited and do not experience mutuality in their relationships. Houston's point is that there are 'undesirable caring relations' and 'to keep caring morally decent' we need 'recourse to other values such as autonomy, justice, mutuality, and respect for persons' (1990: 118). When women associate femininity with self-sacrifice, autonomous self-respect is inhibited and oppression is not discerned.

Guilt

Special relationships are characterized by powerful personal connections. For many women, the desire to maintain connections is paramount to their everyday lives. The women in Gilligan's studies (1983, 1988) talk of several commitments that simultaneously require a response, and the moral problem is to discern how best to meet these requirements. Sharon Bishop argues 'that there is moral guilt that arises directly from failures of concern which break connections between persons' (1987: 16). To maintain our well-being we need another's attention, and the failure to give due attention can induce loss of self-esteem in one person and shame in another. Feelings of compulsion in intimate relationships are not bound by strict obligations but more the sense that certain dispositions are constitutive of these relationships. The failure to act in ways that express these attitudes indicates a ruptured relationship that needs repairing, otherwise people feel betrayal or guilt. Guilt arises when someone's actions damage a connection. The more women feel ultimately responsible for maintaining connections, the more guilt they are likely to experience, even when the blame lies elsewhere or should be shared, as is typically the case in separation and divorce. Connectedness is significant, regret and remorse are reparative responses. 'They signal that one wishes things had been different' (Bishop 1987: 21).

Conflicting interests

Whatever our intentions, we let people down, we equivocate unduly, are hesitant, bewildered and make wrong decisions. Our relationships make varying claims on us and our interests and priorities clash. Ethics suggests how we should respond to these claims in morally decent ways. Monika Keller (1984) uses an example of two young friends who have a special arrangement to meet on a particular day each week. One friend knows the other really wants to discuss some things, but a new child moves into the neighbourhood and invites the protagonist to a movie. The old friend does not like this new person. Keller (1984: 146) points to three norms of healthy intimate relationships: contractual norms of promising; norms that acknowledge the particular intimacy of each friendship relationship; and general norms such as sympathetic concern and altruism. Accompanying these norms are three fundamental principles of fairness and reciprocity with a duty to keeping a promise; truthfulness that informs the reluctance to lie even when an obligation is violated; and **beneficence**, a responsibility to help someone in need.

Even in close friendships, conflict arises in trying to determine what should take priority. Our young friend knows there is the regular promise of time spent with the old friend, they both treasure shared time and there is something important the older friend wants to discuss. Our protagonist values their reciprocity and would be disappointed to miss out, so does not want to lie, but does want to help the new neighbour. Here, a contextualized moral judgement absorbs all the minutiae of the dilemma in order to make a decision that minimizes harm to another. All the subtle particularities of the situation are meaningful criteria for practical decision-making, including the friends' needs and feelings (Keller 1984: 153). Any violation of these obligations toward the friend by lying, betraying confidences or failing to be loyal, lead to a guilty friend who feels shame for acts that are inconsistent with ideals of friendship.

Most of us live busy lives with many competing interests and obligations. Herman (1991) suggests two models of practical concern. First, there is the 'plural interest model'. When there are many people we care about, we need to balance interests. Tensions exist between trying to satisfy the most interests or the most important. 'But a human life is not the resultant of a "bundle" of competing interests' (Herman 1991: 784). Second, there is the 'deliberative model'. Our attachments and connections lie in a deliberative field where reasons for responding, knowledge of the particular persons, grounds of obligations and prudential rationality need to be considered. Destructive as well as fulfilling relationships lie in this field. At the core of the self is the desire for recognition: sexism and racism undermine self-identity as Cynthia Willett (1998) demonstrates by weaving accounts of the self from AfroAmerican and slave narratives. Our intimate relationships and emotional attachments are vital. Sometimes they harm us and we break away from destructive connections. Usually, we look to intimate relationships to make life meaningful. The ethical basis to these relationships results in manifold choices and obligations.

Summary

- There is moral significance in particular relationships.

- Emotions help us to respond to people's specific situations.

- Friendships represent an important example of mutual regard.

- Specific duties and obligations accompany a commitment to intimate relationships.

- Treating others decently is part of acting ethically.

- Conflict in relationships can be handled through careful deliberation and dialogue.

Further reading

Friedman, M. (1993) *What Are Friends For?: Feminist Perspectives on Personal Relationships and Moral Theory*, Ithaca and London: Cornell University Press.

Porter, E. (1996) 'Women and friendships: pedagogies of care and relationality', in C. Luke (ed.) *Feminisms and Pedagogies of Everyday Life*, New York: State University of New York Press, pp. 66–92.

Raymond, J. (1986) *A Passion for Friends. Toward a Philosophy of Female Affection*, London: The Women's Press.

Rubin, L. B. (1985) *Just Friends. The Role of Friendship in Our Lives*, New York: Harper & Row.

Chapter 3

Professions

Chapter outline

In the professions, a feminist perspective informs work practices. Workplace sexism, discrimination and oppression should not be tolerated. Equal opportunity, affirmative action and disability rights aim to rectify gendered injustices. With many women in caring work, the chapter distinguishes between:

- social expectations of women's care
- the informal care women voluntarily do
- paid carework.

The rest of the chapter looks specifically at how feminist ethics applies to:

- health care with its moral dilemmas and difficult choices
- social work with a rationality of caring and principles of empowerment
- legal equality with family law and custody
- business ethics with an ethic of economically sustainable flourishing.

Sex, work and professional ethics

Literature on professional ethics in the workplace is concerned with the study of morals – what is right/wrong, good/bad – and normative ethics – prescribing what people ought to do in work contexts. Public debate on workplace ethical issues is dominated by lawyers, medical professionals, organizational psychologists, philosophers and theologians. Few adopt specific feminist perspectives. This chapter examines how sex and gender influence work ethics, 'care in context', and work situations where feminists contribute significantly, namely health care, social work, law and business. These areas of professional expertise require higher education, receive reasonable salaries with full benefits and reflect status.

In professional work, a feminist perspective is a distinct way of seeing, knowing and understanding that informs the specific practices of work. Practice is informed by feminist ethics rather than guidelines derived from a feminist perspective (Wise 1995: 107). Women are active agents, 'the sex of the knower *is* epistemologically significant' (Code 1991: 8). It is not that there are essentially feminine ways of knowing, but our gendered social location and the experiences we have as a result of being a man or a woman influence the ways we come to know and experience life. A feminist epistemology challenges the subject–object dichotomy. The professional worker is a participant, the recipient of care or attention is not an 'object to be known' but someone whom the professional listens to, understands and communicates with (Sevenhuijsen 1998: 61).

Professional workers act on behalf of others. Respect for persons underpins professional practice. 'The pledges grounding the ethics of the various professions bind those agents to act for the benefit of the client' (Koehn 1994: 117). In trusting the professional as teacher, nurse, lawyer, doctor or social worker, the client believes that the professional is able to provide genuine help and is committed to doing so. Accountability is central to good professional practice. Professions have different work cultures with principles suitable to ethical functioning. Given the complexities of professions, rules, laws and norms help workers to identify ethical dilemmas like workplace theft, sexual harassment, responsibilities to customers, conflicts of interest, the need for confidentiality and members of staff who are disabled or have AIDS. Despite different practices, all professions presume the importance of accountability, autonomy, fairness, honesty, kindness, loyalty, preventing harm, respect, trust, worker rights.

Each profession has a code of ethics to contribute to the status of an occupation; establish and maintain professional identity; guide practitioners about how to act; and protect users from malpractice or abuse (Banks 1995: 89). Professional ethics are needed because in entering the workforce, an employee enters a complex set of relationships with employers, co-workers, clients, other related agencies, companies and businesses. Each relationship involves duties required to accomplish tasks and maintain standards and rights like fair pay, giving commands to others or compensation for work done (Johnson 1985: 23). Employers have conflicts of interest that leave them susceptible to bribes or privileged information that is open to abuse. Professional ethics protects the competency of professionals given the power they wield.

Sexism and discrimination

Sexism is rife at work. Marilyn Frye (1983) came to understand that viewing sexism as irrelevant markings of the distinction between the sexes, exhibited in school subjects or employment patterns misses the locus of systematic sexism. In a sexist context, sex is very relevant. Sex-marking behaviour delineates two repertoires of behaviour so that there are different ways of greeting, storytelling, order-giving and -receiving, negotiating, gesturing, encouraging, challenging and asking for information, depending on whether the relevant other is a woman or a man. Sexism characterizes the structures which create and enforce uncompromising patterns of sex-marking which divides humans into dominators and subordinators by sex. Sexual harassment is discrimination. It makes employment, advancement or job retention dependent on returning unwelcome advances. Legislation against sex discrimination protects gays and women employees and is particularly important in non-traditional occupations like the military, train drivers, air pilots.

Discrimination is not always wrong. In a movie about black basketball players, it is not unjust only to employ black athletes. However, it is unfair discrimination not to employ a qualified person for a job because they are woman, brown, Asian, Muslim, homosexual or disabled. It is wrong because it is the qualifications and experience that is relevant to employment not one's sex, skin colour, ethnic background, religious beliefs, sexual preference or physical ability. Clearly if the job demands heavy physical labour, being fit and well-abled is part of the necessary qualifications. The technological era alters this requirement of physical strength with increasing numbers of tasks reliant on services, computers and mental skills. Sex may be a relevant category of discrimination. There are good reasons why only women should be employed in refuges or as medical and counselling personnel with female rape victims.

Aristotle argued that justice requires that equals be treated equally and unequals be treated unequally. Men and women are unequal in reproductive capacities, hence have different needs regarding work leave. Once a child is born and the woman has regained strength, then men and women may have equal needs regarding the desire to bond and care for the infant, and both should be eligible for parental leave. Indirect sex discrimination, like the fact that more women are employed on fixed-term contracts, abound and restrict the conditions of employment like pensions, holiday and sick pay rights. Figures show around 40 per cent of all staff in higher education are now employed on fixed-term contracts, affecting teaching, administration, library and computer staff (Rubin 1998: 12). Lesbians, gays and bisexuals may suffer prejudice by other colleagues, be disproportionately at risk of being harassed or accused of harassment and discriminated against in promotion or contract renewal by homophobic management.

Oppression at work

Oppression is real. Iris Marion Young is concerned with nonprofessionals who experience five faces of oppression: exploitation, marginalization, powerlessness, cultural imperialism, and violence (1990: 65).

- Exploitation occurs when there is a steady process of transfer of the results of labour of one social group to another.
- Marginalization occurs to people whom the system of labour cannot or will not use. The underclass experience feelings of uselessness, boredom and lack of self-respect. Marginality happens to racial, cultural or class groups that are subject to discrimination.
- Powerlessness occurs to those who lack the authority, status and self-integrity that professionals possess. For employees, workplaces are rarely organized democratically, rather workers are subject to hierarchy and rigid rules.
- Cultural imperialism involves the universalization of a dominant group's culture which is established as the norm, thereby rendering the particular perspective of one group invisible, yet marking it as the Other.
- Violence includes the full range of shocking acts like assault, harassment, intimidation and ridicule that degrades, humiliates and stigmatizes another.

'As a group women are subject to gender-based exploitation, power-lessness, cultural imperialism, and violence' (Young 1990: 65).

Another form of oppression at work is the threat to autonomy, when a boss or someone to whom workers are accountable asks them to do something that in good conscience, they disagree with, that is, it goes against what they believe they ought to do. A nurse is asked to perform an abortion she thinks is morally unwarranted, a lecturer is asked to spend more time on research than on teaching, a salesperson is asked to put a sale ticket on an item that is not reduced in price, a teacher disagrees with the principal about how to treat a disruptive student. Workers committed to caregiving often define work differently from the bureaucracies that employ them and these differences in priorities compromise workers' autonomy. The nurse who is well attuned to a patient's needs may disagree with treatment a physician decides. In paid work, autonomous care requires 'giving caregivers credit for the knowledge they gain through their close interaction with clients, and recognizing that the bureaucratic rules that typically govern caregiving institutions cannot do so adequately' (Clement 1996: 65).

Equal opportunities

Equal opportunities and sex discrimination legislation exist because of deeply entrenched prejudices. All humans have a legitimate expectation of justice. In work contexts, justice involves the morally appropriate treatment of people that ensures that what is done to workers is what ought to be done. The United Nations Universal Declaration of Human Rights (Article 23, paragraph 1) states that, 'Everyone has the right to work, to free choice of employment, to just and favourable conditions of work and to protection against unemployment' (in Chryssides and Kaler 1993: 239). Furthermore, it also states (Article 23, paragraph 2), 'Everyone, without any discrimination has the right to equal pay for equal work' (1993: 239). Any differentials must be justified according to measures like qualifications, experience, merit. 'Valuing diversity means treating people equally while incorporating their diverse ideas. Discrimination means treating people unequally because they are or appear to be, different' (Treviño and Nelson 1995: 52). Equal Opportunities departments are often attached to Human Resources to ensure that people feel appreciated and that issues like discrimination, hiring and firing, discipline, general relationships and performance evaluation are handled sensitively (1995: 37). Workers

often perceive Human Resources to be distanced from the realities of everyday work lives, failing to appreciate that personal
concerns of health, morale, alcoholism, drug abuse, debt, children,
divorce and separation impinge on workers' ability to perform
adequately. Work rarely caters well with workers' crises.

Affirmative action

Affirmative action accepts that groups like women or ethnic
minorities have been discriminated against or disadvantaged in
the past, and hence that deliberate measures to compensate are
in order. The arguments are twofold: for retributive justice to
compensate for the shortcomings of history; or distributive, since
employers continue to discriminate against women, their prospects
are unlikely to be very good. Some argue that despite being a short-
term measure, it creates problems of 'reverse discrimination'
(Richards 1982: 137–51). A major counter-argument is the undermining of women's achievements and the merit problem. When
a person is perceived to be appointed or promoted 'because she is
a woman' then she is not taken as seriously as if she was appointed
in a competitive context of merit and achievement. Often a back-
lash against further employment or promotion of women occurs.
Affirmative action is a form of positive discrimination, a preferen-
tial treatment aimed at redressing the injustices, prejudices and
inequalities of the past. It often involves monitored quotas. It looks
toward a just future where such action will be unnecessary.

Disability

Feminist ethics validates the importance of dependency, vulnerability and special needs. Anita Silvers searches for a form of justice which embraces difference, with 'energizing . . . inclusive moral
and social practice' (1995: 33). Her argument is that disability tests
which paradigm of justice resists marginalization, repression or
other negative consequences of difference. Silvers draws on Lawrence Blum (1991) who argues that it is by feeling about disabled
persons as they might themselves that we can attend morally toward
them. For Blum, the possibility of interpersonal moral argument
lies in engaging with uninviting perspectives so as to acknowledge
their importance. It is possible to acknowledge someone's perspective while also recognizing that it is impossible to imagine one's
self as the other person. This is as relevant for disability as for skin

colour, employment status, class and political allegiance. Not all disabled persons are entirely dependent on others, nevertheless dependence is a moral issue. How should we respond to those people who are dependent? For individuals with disabilities, their dilemma lies not in their personal differences, but in their marginalization. In everyday life, a person who is mobile through a wheelchair may suffer enormous social exclusion in not having access to lavatories, transport, places of work, theatres and other places of entertainment. Inclusivity, justice and care are intrinsic to feminist ethics.

Caring in context

Whereas care accorded to women via the sexual division of labour may 'slide into paternalism, authoritarianism, and dogmatism' (Jaggar 1995: 189), professional care has a 'distinctive moral commitment to serve a client good' (Koehn 1994: 179). The public caring professions are expanding. Public care is not based on an emotional involvement, however it responds informatively to needs. Professional care is rarely applied mechanically, 'moral sensitivity, imagination, and intuition' feature (Bubeck 1995: 221).

Celia Davies qualifies 'caring work' as 'committed attending' of physical, mental and emotional needs of another through 'giving a commitment to the nurturance, growth and healing of that other' (1995: 18–19). She calls the unpaid emotionally intense care with family and friends 'caregiving work'. 'Carework' refers to paid jobs in the health and personal services sector as well as in the informal economy of care assistants, domestics and childminders. 'Professional care' is the public caring work undertaken by those formally trained such as nurses who acquire knowledge through education, develop emotional attachments to patients, remain alert to others' needs and create a comfortable ambience (1995: 21–3). Grace Clement defines 'care work' as: care which occurs in the context of a personal relationship between care-giver and recipient; the care worker promotes the well-being of others; and is motivated by a feeling of concern for the recipients of care (1996: 56).

Diemut Bubeck calls carers 'good practioners' because 'care has features of both *poiesis* (making) and *praxis* (action), according to Aristotle's distinction' (1995: 218). Care is an art and moral action. Carers with good intentions are good at meeting needs. Only through knowledge, talking and listening can carers discern genuine needs. 'Asking, telling, repeating, mutually clarifying, mulling over, and checking back are the most dependable, accessible, and efficient devices for finding out how it is with others' (Walker 1991: 769). Meeting needs is imperative for everyday requirements and for those who have no voice or are silenced.

Gender differentiation in care

Caring is embedded in deep traditional gender differentiations – typically men show they care by the work they do, and women demonstrate care for others (Tronto 1989: 172). Disentangling traditional feminine scripts from transformative caring is crucial. Tronto argues that care is linked not only to gender but to race and class, and refers to practices aimed at 'maintaining, continuing and repairing the world' (1993: 104), particularly through the work of cleaning up after bodily functions. In 'modern industrial societies, these tasks of caring continue to be disproportionately carried out by the lowest ranks of society: by women, the working-class, and in most of the West, by people of colour' (1993: 113).

Men care in intimate relationships, with children, elderly parents and in the paid caring professions. Men who spend time with young children frequently are unwilling to change nappies, toilet-train or bath children. Men too are confronted with gender-symbolism that caring responsibilities are not expected from them or that they are 'not real men' for engaging sympathetically in the attentiveness required of good care (Sevenhuijsen 1998: 80). Many men repress their emotions, inhibiting their capacity to empathize. Caring 'requires high degrees of empathy to enable us to discern what morality recommends in our caring activities' (Held 1993: 30).

Caring as a feminist practice

Care is 'a distinctively human way of engaging with others that produces morally appropriate action' (Jaggar 1995: 181). Deciding what is right lies at the core of ethics. Lorraine Code, in talking of 'moral practice', suggests that while sometimes 'traditionally female' values like trust, kindness and responsiveness are worthy principles for practical deliberation, in other circumstances efficiency-maximizing and autonomy-promoting values are more appropriate (1991: 108). Values and principles invoked must be appropriately responsive to the context (Held 1984: 35). Ethics adapts to subtleties and requires balance to avoid extremes. Giving spare cash to a homeless person is one option, other times it is more meaningful to assist in a homeless shelter or teach life-skills to homeless persons. Some practices minimize oppression and marginalization, others promote empowering relationships and alliances. Alison Jaggar maintains that 'attending to an individual's immediate needs for food, shelter, comfort, or companionship is likely to distract from moral scrutiny of the social structures that create those needs or leave them unfulfilled' (1995: 195). Jaggar is not arguing that immediate needs are morally insignificant. She supports care's insistence on personal engagement as a corrective to insensitivity. However, to improve women's lives, moral practices that problematize structures that keep human need unfulfilled are essential at familial, local, national and international levels.

Selma Sevenhuijsen defends caring as a feminist practice, for its moral repertoire allows 'more discursive space for values associated with trust, respect for differences, and the encouragement of self-respect' (1998: 84–5). These values are not unique to feminism. Their feminist distinctiveness opens spaces for reflection and deliberation by women and listens to and interprets the deliberations expressed by care-providers and recipients. Different styles of ethical reasoning reflect the moral considerations of women; how class, family background, socialization and politics makes them reluctant to care or prompts their caring responsiveness to see, hear and responsibly meet needs. Seeing what is important 'is a *task* to come to see the world as it is' (Murdoch 1970: 91). Margaret Little explains 'that the seeing *itself* is a task – the task of being attentive' (1995: 121). The task of feminist practice is not simply to gather information, the morally aware person does not have a list of items to check for, but 'the required attentiveness is a background disposition for relevant details to come into your consciousness – for them to emerge as salient, to come to the forefront of your attention' (1995: 122). Caring demonstrates appropriate responses.

Practical reasoning identifies morally desirable or permissable practices. Each pupil, patient, client, elderly person differs in a myriad of morally relevant ways requiring 'intricate skill and intelligent practice' (Bowden 1996). Jaggar argues that in some plausible sense, the ethics of care is feminine, but this does not establish it as a morality that is necessarily suitable for feminism (1995: 184). Throughout our intellectual heritage, women have been associated with affect, desire and emotion and men with control through reason (Lloyd 1984; McMillan 1982; Tuana 1992). Care's focus on particularity may be a liability given that feminist ethics is concerned with ways in which male-dominant social structures restrict life chances. Rather, it is more plausible to suppose that justice and care are 'logically compatible' and 'logically indispensable to each other' but that this is no easy synthesis (Jaggar 1995: 185–7; Porter 1991: 168–70). Judgement is best ensured by practical care about people (Blum 1988; Walker 1991). For a nurse, this is not merely caring deeply about discharging well the duties of a nurse or promoting the interests of a patient, but of caring about the actual specific patient. This means welcoming personal uniqueness, often only understood through voicing disagreement and arguing. Subjects are empowered because their considerations are included in deliberations (Sevenhuijsen 1998: 135). Nancy Fraser calls this a 'politics of needs-interpretation' (1989) where open debate discusses what needs should be met. We turn to specific examples of professional care.

Health care

Framework for health caring practices

The practice of health care ethics requires guidelines for conduct that have a broad application (Henry 1995: 4–7; Randall and Downie 1996: 21). Consensus exists as to the main principles.

- **Nonmaleficence** means to do no harm.
- **Beneficence** means to do good, be kind and positively care for others.
- **Respect for autonomy** means allowing people to make choices as self-determined, responsible and capable persons.
- **Justice** involves fairness and equity, both to staff and clients.

Health care extends Carol Gilligan's notion of caring as 'an activity of relationship, of seeing and responding to need, taking care of the world by sustaining the web of connection so that no one is left alone' (1983: 62). It also builds on Nel Noddings' interpretation which assumes that personal relationships are 'ontologically basic' and that the caring relation is 'ethically basic' (1984: 150). That is, relationships are crucial to our selfhood and caring is fundamental to morality. When health workers are imaginatively attentive, they experience the world through 'the eyes of the cared-for' (Noddings 1984: 13) who may be depressed; facing cancer treatment; dying; in pain; suicidal; or suffering post-natal depression. The positive effect of someone empathizing is an awareness of self-worth that emanates from experiencing a caring presence (Bishop and Scudder 1996: 122).

Health care encompasses more than nursing, but nursing provides clear examples of 'a practice with an inherent moral sense' and it is 'the practice of caring that fulfils that moral sense' (Bishop and Scudder 1996: 1). Anne Bishop and John Scudder advocate an approach to nursing ethics that directly addresses practising nurses who take seriously the moral intent of nursing practices. By practice, they mean practical ways of fostering the good, that is, the well-being of persons. They maintain that the integral relation is between 'the good sought, the ways of fostering that good, and the personal concern for the other' (1996: 20). Clement also writes, 'the good in competent practice and the moral good are the same' (1996: 25). Nursing as a caring practice presupposes the autonomy, attention, efficiency and effectiveness of the nurse needed to develop practical wisdom and fulfil the moral sense of nursing. Not all nurses are women, but there is a tight relationship between caring, nursing, women and ethics (Bowden 1996; Kuhse 1997). Ironically, nurses are the subordinate members of the health care team, yet closest to the patient, and those with ultimate authority have minimal patient contact (Clement 1996: 63).

Patricia Benner develops the idea of practice further. She believes that nursing as a caring profession should determine the circumstances under which their practices can thrive, despite being undermined by inequities and sexism. She argues that it is important to understand 'how practical communities develop shared distinctions and meanings that are carried forward in living traditions' (1994: 140). The articulation of humane practices has all the demands of clinical knowledge, 'that is, they are transitional, contextual, dialogical, particularistic' (1994: 141). Caring depends on the person, context and intent, so Benner argues that distinctions between public and private caring matter. Public practices have a reciprocity that is formalized by payments not expected with the care given in home privacy, but neither can be simplistically compared. All care is grounded in common meanings of skilful practices. In the health sphere these practices have specific ways of knowing what maximizes well-being and Benner mentions supporting life functions, promoting wholeness, care of the body, focused attention, systematic listening, coaching, fostering a healing relationship, decreasing the sense of alienation that accompanies illness, humanizing the coldness of the technology and domesticating an alien environment (1994: 144–5). Perhaps of most significance is the need to preserve dignity and personhood, expressing a respect for another person's body that might be shrivelled, scarred or ugly in illness.

Sevenhuijsen (1998) offers five concepts for a feminist approach to health care: social participation, autonomy, equality, justice and solidarity. First, health care needs to be situated in the broad context of its contribution to meaningful social participation. Health, illness and fragility are integral to human life, so care should be part of the economic arrangements which structure social policies. Second, good health care contributes to choices which enhance people's self-respect. An elderly Alzheimer's sufferer might not know when she needs to shower, but she might know where she likes to sit after a wash. Third, equality involves norms of access and voice in deliberations that shape interests; equal opportunities that pay attention to diverse needs; and equal rights that account for multicultural differences. Fourth, justice in health care is a commitment to structure public life on responsible values. Fifth, norms of solidarity shape commonality based on diversity.

Palliative care ethics

Palliative care, when one knows that all one can do is to alleviate suffering, is difficult for the patient, the carer and loved ones. All involved know that pain, suffering and death are inevitable. **Compassion**, 'the capacity to feel with others, to enter to some extent into their predicaments and share their emotions' (Randall and Downie 1996: 12) has an *affective* aspect where we feel with others; a *cognitive* aspect where we have particularized insight into the situation of others; and a *conative* aspect where we are moved to act on behalf of others (1996: 12–13). The use of drugs in palliative care is controversial. It is legally permissible for drugs to be used that may shorten life only if the following rules are obeyed: the patient must already be dying; the drugs must be 'right and proper' professional practice; and the motive must be to relieve pain, not to shorten life (1996: 54). Killing is prohibited, but letting die is permissible in certain circumstances. Nursing homes, intensive care wards and neonate units have professional codes on when it is essential to resuscitate and when it is ill-advised. Legal norms are safeguards against reckless actions but do not deal with the intricate ethical questions 'of how to deal with dependency, responsibility, vulnerability and trust; the importance, but also the fragility of intimacy and connectedness' (Sevenhuijsen 1998: 3). Such intricacies are part of the debates on euthanasia, sometimes called mercy-killing. Watching a loved one suffer is heart-breaking. While no one wishes for their loved ones to die, there is relief with a timely death.

Choices in childbirth

As modern technology progresses and scientific attitudes permeate medicine, pregnant women are viewed as passive tools of the medical profession, their bulks waiting to be released. The exceptions are in countries where midwives take an active role in attending to the needs of pregnant women, and where the process of childbirth is based on 'principles of care which stress respect for individual autonomy' so that health is 'women-centred' (Frith 1996: 4). In conjunction with these principles, motherhood is accepted as 'a moral relationship, where a woman takes on certain moral obligations towards a particular child' (Draper 1996: 33). Encouraging patient choice is an ethical imperative to confirm women's moral agency. Consent expresses patient autonomy to accept responsibility for one's decisions and not blame others for the consequences. Freedom and ability to exercise autonomy are necessary. Heather Draper (1996: 20) outlines four criteria to **consent**:

- voluntariness, to ensure one is free from coercion
- information, so that one can be informed and discuss options
- competence, the foundation for autonomy
- decision, the conscious process of choosing, not just an acquiescence that agrees without reflection.

Consent in childbirth, as in other aspects of health care, prevents **paternalism**, when someone's capacity to make their own judgement is ignored. The prevalence of male gynaecologists unconcerned with women's preferences is a worry. Informed choice is a fundamental right of a woman having a baby in order to retain autonomy and bodily integrity. Two obstacles obstruct women's empowerment in terms of being able to make informed choices: the low information base with which many women embark on pregnancy; and an alleged reluctance to take responsibility for making difficult choices while in a trying pregnancy or in labour (Lewison 1996: 38). Where there are language problems with an ethnic minority community, these problems are more visible.

Moral dilemmas in health care

The moral dilemmas in health care are relevant to all, for none of us know when we may become ill. There is an intensity in medical ethics, due to five main reasons (Evans 1990: 2–4).

1 Litigation against practitioners concentrates the minds on what they ought to do.
2 The move toward greater freedom of information and openness leads to a sharper awareness of individual rights.
3 The explosion of high technology medicine and drug therapies means difficult choices must be made.
4 The scarcity of resources requires sensitive allocation.
5 AIDS, with its confidentiality, compulsory screening and assisted deaths, introduces new ethical dilemmas.

Scarce resources must be allocated and used so as to maximize benefit and be distributed justly. Distribution raises questions. Should a smoker with lung cancer be treated the same as a non-smoker? Is it fair that the financially comfortable can buy private treatment, and others remain on seemingly endless waiting lists. Should all premature babies be given expensive intensive care? Who should decide? Another dilemma is sex-selectivity. Ultrasounds are clear and knowing whether or not medical staff should reveal the sex of the foetus is difficult when some women are prepared to abort if the expected baby is not the desired sex. There are legitimate grounds to discover the sex of the foetus with inherited diseases carried to one sex. When should one tell the whole truth? Should you always tell someone who is dying how close they are to death? The conflict between a worker's conscience and the expectations of the job are conspicuous in abortion, premature births and euthanasia. The debates these questions raise must be ongoing, ever sensitive to relevant changes.

Trust constitutes a central moral dilemma because those in a position of trust make decisions that affect the vulnerable. In the patient–carer relationship, there exists an inequality of power, for

---

Box 3.1 Notification of child abuse

Megan-Jane Johnstone, an Australian researcher, examines
the ethical issues involved in reporting child abuse to nurse
registration authorities (in Walker 1998: 43). When she looked
at mainstream bio-ethics literature, she was struck by the
conspicuous absence of material on child abuse. Fundamental
issues surrounding the notification of child abuse include:

• what constitutes harm
• what skills are needed to make proper assessments of
  dangerous situations
• a definition of what constitutes reasonable suspicion
• an exploration of the legal and moral obligations of nurses
  in mandatory and voluntary notification of child abuse.

In making recommendations on how ethical issues can best be
addressed, she is critically examining the role of Nurses Boards
in regulating the conduct of nurses involved. Her intent is to
place 'the issue of child abuse firmly on the bio-ethics agenda'
(in Walker 1998: 43).

---

the patient has to trust the carer who has the knowledge, skills
and resources. Respect for patient autonomy is necessary, allowing an autonomous patient the extent to which they want to participate in decisions about their treatment, and involving relatives
as much as possible in the case of patients unable to make decisions. Professional carers are morally responsible for how the truth
is communicated to the patient. Confidentiality should be assured,
so that information is only used for the purposes intended.

Social work

Rationality of caring

Feminists challenge services in the welfare state. The responsibility for caring for children, the ill, disabled and elderly, as well as
the emotional needs in families is part of the cultural expectation
of femininity. When there are deficiencies in the welfare state, it
is assumed that women will cope with these inadequacies. This
assumption sits uncomfortably alongside the fact that public

care-giving services are perceived as social rights of citizens in the welfare state. Yet public care often lacks the qualities that transform 'services' into 'caring' (Waerness 1987: 209). In order to develop models for caregiving work, Kari Waerness expounds caring as both a labour and an emotion. There are feelings of concern that one acts upon. Caring for dependents differs from the informal care within reciprocal relationships. Both categories present different problems for women striving for autonomy and independence.

Waerness explains her idea of 'rationality of caring'. Given that reason and emotions, instrumentality and expressiveness are often polarized, her notion is radical. It challenges the notion that women who care are less rational than men who achieve other goals. Waerness supports 'a social actor who is *both* conscious and feeling', a 'sentient actor' (1987: 219). Caring is not instinctual, but must be learned, and the process of learning teaches us about the 'rationality of caring'. Scientific rationality depends on an outsider's search for predictability and control. The rationality of caring relies on an insider's thoughts and adaptable actions. Expertise is based on practical experience and personal knowledge. Waerness concludes that this versatile knowledge is reasonable caregiving. Her research into home-helps shows that the most satisfying aspect of these jobs is their personal attachment to clients. Even when helpers understood the formal requirements of their duties, 'they gave priority to doing what seemed right according to the rationality of caring' (1987: 222), and this meant staying longer than their hours paid or doing extra tasks that went beyond their job specification. It is morally preferable to be dependent on family than on the state, yet many elderly people prefer public to private support not because 'the elderly do not value family commitment, but that they seek genuine rather than distorted care' (Clement 1996: 102), preferring a kind professional to a dutiful cold relative.

Principles of the social worker

Within social work, ethical dilemmas arise where a choice must be made between unwelcome competing alternatives like between the rights of an adolescent youth and parents, or between a senile parent and an indifferent child, or the social worker's duty to an agency or a client. Given that these dilemmas affect basic aspects of human welfare – a living income, housing or shelter, ethical ways to deal with the enormity of the complexities are needed. Sarah Banks (1995: 26) lists as key principles of the social worker:

- individual uniqueness
- recognition of users' feelings
- sensitivity to users' feelings
- acceptance
- non-judgemental
- user self-determination
- confidentiality.

These principles respect the individual person as a self-determining being. This is not easy; there is a temptation to make the decision for a reckless youth, a drug addict or a homeless alcoholic. Banks (1995: 35) suggests four major ethical principles for social work: respect for a promotion of individual's rights to self-determination; promotion of welfare or well-being; equality; and distributive justice.

Empowerment

Empowerment actualizes these principles. The provision of emergency housing for refugees, women subject to domestic violence, or youth abused in families is vital, but to help culturally alienated persons, battered women and frightened youth, more than temporary measures are needed. To empower someone is to help them understand that they are not alone in their oppression, there are structural reasons that impact on them as individuals and 'enable them thereby to take back some control in their lives' (Wise 1995: 108). Sue Wise suggests that collective self-help is the most fruitful way to achieve such empowerment through encouraging people with similar socially structured problems to share experiences, thereby appreciating the shared nature of their problems. Collective empowerment creates non-exploitative egalitarian relationships that focus on need and foster well-being through co-operative means. Often needy people are difficult to work with, unwashed, angry, disillusioned, hungry, desperate. Respect for their integrity is hard at times. Powerlessness, power, control and conflicting requirements must be dealt with. Needs have to be prioritized. A feminist-influenced ethic of anti-discrimination (Wise 1995: 116) goes beyond the potential corruption of power that is implicit in making decisions on the basis of one angry, upset person's needs, to empowering that person in the community of other like-minded angry upset people.

All social work requires counsel that might include advice on teenage pregnancy, unemployment, a mother leaving her violent partner, a retrenched worker, homeless youth, refugees' rights. Effective counsellors demonstrate characteristics like goodwill, recognition of personal power and the vulnerability of the client, self-respect, willingness to admit mistakes and a sense of humour (Corey, Schneider and Callanan 1988: 28–9). Confidentiality is central, there is an ethical responsibility to protect clients from unauthorized disclosures of information while ensuring clients' right to informed consent in having access to files. Trust is crucial. Cultural awareness understands that cultures have different views on privacy, power and vulnerability. Counsel should empower.

Keith Pringle (1995) writes on men in social welfare who are committed to anti-sexist, anti-racist, anti-homophobic approaches (Clarke 1993; Langan and Day 1992; Thompson 1993). Bob Connell's (1995) work addresses racism, heterosexism, ageism, disabilism, classism and sexism. Pringle states the importance of men working toward anti-oppressive practices not to 'colonize the efforts of women' (1995: 31). He advocates the need for men to 'develop services to assist men to play a constructive rather than a destructive part in families' as well as pushing for changes in the structures governing the way lone mothers are treated (1995: 76). In breaking down gendered barriers around caring, he looks to lone fathers, men caring for adult dependants and gay men caring for partners as exhibiting qualities not associated with dominant masculinity. He views the halting of men's violence as 'the priority task for men involved with social welfare' (1995: 211). Zero tolerance of male violence is an ethical strategy.

Case study. Sensitivity to lesbians and gays

Social workers make moral judgements and respond to moral preferences. Ann Hartman and Joan Laird (1998) write of the particular ethical challenges of social workers who work with lesbians and gay men to ensure values like client self-determination and anti-discrimination. Fact sheets are structured to list husband, wife, children, consequently excluding these groups. Attention to AIDS addresses ethical issues of confidentiality, the duty to warn, advocacy for health care and the right to die. Laird writes of her personal journey in the late 1970s that made her aware of the need for ethical sensitivity (Hartman and Laird 1998: 268–9). She admits her shock when a lesbian client wanted to become pregnant through artificial insemination. The child is now a talented, thoughtful young man. Another client came out as a lesbian and chose to leave her two children. Again Laird was aghast. These experiences taught her that 'moral and responsible practice requires that we truly listen to clients' (1998: 271), particularly those whose experiences differ from our own. A heterosexual practitioner usefully informed young boys who were confused by their mother's new lesbian relationship that she had grown up happily in a lesbian family. Moral practice in social work is about creating a fair, caring society.

Law

Feminist approaches to jurisprudence, or the theory of law cover areas such as sexual harassment and discrimination, pornography, rape, divorce, abortion, violence, custody, marital property. Catherine MacKinnon (1987b) argues that men's domination is systemic and hegemonic, built all-pervasively into social structures and institutions. Gendered inequality and women's oppression define the need for a feminist critique of power. Carol Smart calls the law a 'gendering machine' (1995). In sexual assault and rape law, initiatives to make the police more sensitive, prosecutors more responsive and judges more receptive make the law less sexist, but 'is it empowering in the feminist sense' (MacKinnon 1987b: 139)? What is not dealt with is why women are raped. Similarly laws against spouse violence do not address 'the conditions that produce men who systematically express themselves violently toward women' (1987b: 139–40). MacKinnon's argument is that 'the law sees and treats women the way men see and treat women . . . the state, in part through law, institutionalizes male power' (1987b: 140–1).

MacKinnon proposes a radical view on rape. Whereas a feminist like Susan Brownmiller (1976) sees rape as an act of violence, a displacement of power and physical force onto sexuality, MacKinnon maintains that a feminist view sees 'sexuality as a social sphere of male power of which forced sex is paradigmatic . . . coercion has become integral to male sexuality' (1987b: 141). A major problem with this view is that many women experience sexual relationships with men in a domination-free context of equality and loving reciprocity. However, MacKinnon draws attention to the legal implications whereby the law adjudicates levels of 'acceptable force', so that 'rape is a sex crime that is not a crime when it looks like sex' (1987b: 143). The law urgently needs to consider the impact of masculinity on judgements, process, procedure, adjudication and legislation.

Elizabeth Kingdom explicitly distances herself from MacKinnon's views. She works with the law to reconceptualize 'women's rights in terms of women's capabilities, capacities and competences' to identify 'the benefits and drawbacks for feminists which a formal declaration of rights may carry' (1991: 42, 131). Such reconceptualizations appeal to moral status and workforce ability. Kingdom argues that if feminist campaigns are to be successful, 'they require the formulation of specific objectives which are at least potentially assimilable into law' (1991: 45), and can be translated into strategies to achieve them. Many of these objectives pivot around equality. Kingdom (1991: 119) suggests that objectives directed toward equality in terms of equal pay, labour market status and prevention of discrimination require incorporating:

- the moral principle of gender equality
- formal legal equality, as it is defined in Acts of Parliament
- substantive equality, as found in domestic, economic, financial, political or other relations between men and women.

Kingdom argues that feminists should make decisions on how to intervene in legal issues because there is 'no single principle in relation to feminist politics of law' (1991: 149). Instead, calculating the specific feminist issues, strategies, tactics and possibilities relies on contextualized ethical judgements.

Legal equality

Since the mid-1960s the equal treatment paradigm informed the feminist legal community. It proposed that once women were given equal opportunities and treated the same as men they could compete as equals in the market. This necessitated equal participation of girls in education, pressure to work in the labour force and anti-discriminatory legislation. Adherents of a liberal view are concerned with the elimination of laws that treat women differently from men because of their sex. Any differences are assumed to be the result of unequal treatment and sex-stereotyped socialization. Mary Frug (1992) writes of the shifting vocabulary of strategies of difference from 'equal versus special treatment' to 'equal versus equal achievement' to 'assimilation versus acceptance' to 'difference versus anti-domination'.

The principle of equal treatment 'required that a husband have an equal right to make the decision whether or not to terminate his wife's pregnancy' (Krieger 1987: 55). Maternity and paternity were treated the same. Elizabeth Wolgast (1980, 1987) maintains that differences between men and women need to be treated respectfully and that for there to be 'equal rights' there needs to be 'special rights'. A disabled person requires suitable access to exercise the right to work, so equality is effected only by the special provision of ramps, adequate space for wheelchairs, toilet facilities, lifts. Similarly without special rights that take into account reproductive needs, women are discriminated against. Protective legislation facilitates human welfare.

Sevenhuijsen (1998: 85) signals three problems with the liberal equality view. First, logically, while the argument that equal treatment produces equal results sounds plausible, it is circular. If the expected equality in results fails, this leads to assertions that people are not equal, implying biological notions of sexual difference. Second, making equality the main principle marginalizes other questions like how to deal with oppression, violence, vulnerability and plurality. The opposition between equality and difference is used to judge behaviour. Third, feminism fights for reevaluations of 'the feminine' and a reshaping of images associated with sexual difference. The inability of the liberal equality framework to deal with ethical issues of difference led to the search for a woman-centred jurisprudence of equality.

'The inclusion of formerly excluded groups who see things differently – the "giving of a voice" in the jurisprudential assembly – is critical in the evolution of civil rights law. It is at times only by their inclusion that results previously seen as "just" are instead viewed as anomalous' (Krieger 1987: 49). A feminist jurisprudence considers equality in relationships. Lizbeth Hasse, a lawyer, argues that along with a reconstruction of legal rules, there needs to be 'a reinvention of forums for judging moral issues' (1987: 294). At surface level, hurdles to women's participation in society and their control over their bodies have been dismantled formally on the grounds of equal citizenship with equal rights to property, privacy and personal choice. The ideology of equality can perpetuate disadvantage, not merely to women but to other oppressed groups, because the rhetoric of formal equality 'assumes a much greater sameness than is essentially the case, and only manages to further

---

Box 3.2 Gender, lawyers and morality

A study of 36 American attorneys reveals gendered differences
in response to their notion of morality; what constitutes a moral
problem; the importance of justice; and their definition of
justice (Jack and Crowley Jack 1989). They were questioned on
hypothetical and real-life dilemmas. On the basis of responses,
the authors formulated four positions.

1 More men adopt a 'maximum role identification' (1989: 99),
  with moral responsibility seen to lie in legal institutions with a
  detachment from clients.
2 This position revealed a 'disagreement between the world of
  personal morality and imperatives of professional role' (1989:
  106).
3 Those in this position expressed sentiments of reluctance and
  regret with a 'recognition of moral cost' (1989: 110) that
  accompanies personal responsibility.
4 Primarily women 'demonstrate a very high degree of care
  reasoning' (1989: 125) even when it runs counter to
  professional role demands.

Judith Miller (1990) responds to position three favourably as
having the potential to rethink lawyers' role to infuse professional
ethics with the critical concerns of feminist ethics. She asks,
'how can we legitimize feeling bad about beating the widow on
behalf of the insurance company, even while recognizing the
importance of doing it' (1990: 165)? She wisely acknowledges the
irony that women's banishment from public life has necessitated
their cultivation of ethical values that public life now needs.

---

crystallize a given set of power relations' (1987: 288). Differences
are masked, or seen as insignificant. People have 'to be *similarly
situated* before the equal treatment challenge will be triggered'
(1987: 288).

Feminists demand a responsiveness to difference whether or not
these emerge through sex, experiences, skin colour or social location, while acknowledging the enormous problems in accommod-
ating such changes. An extreme example is the long-term battered
wife, who, as a last resort, kills her husband. To articulate a defence, a lawyer can appeal to the ineffectiveness of the law to deal
with violence against women. A battered wife who gets no response
from the police might take the law into her own hands because
she sees no alternative but to fight back. The lawyer who presents

the 'battered-wife murder defence' can base her argument on claims about the status of women in a male-dominated legal system where a wife is considered the husband's property and the privacy of married life is sanctified by law so that 'the only rational response for the battered wife is to kill her husband' (Hasse 1987: 290).

Custody

Who should have parental authority when a relationship splits? Sevenhuijsen demonstrates implications of the appeal to principles of equality in divorce law and custody. Liberal feminist lawyers criticize the 'maternal preference' argument because it maintains traditional ideas of femininity and thus advocate joint custody on the grounds that it accords natural equality between women and men and could increase men's responsibility to children because duties derive from rights (Sevenhuijsen 1998: 197). When people are treated as legal entities, 'legal discourse constructs parents as degendered "persons" who can appear before the law, in this capacity, according to their genetic ties with specific children' (1998: 189; also 1991). This implies that men and women are free and equal. Fatherhood is reinstated as a legal institution of authority with no attention given to who provides the daily nurture. Sevenhuijsen argues that parental rights provide an example of the limitations of equal rights reasoning for feminism.

A feminist revisionist liberal argument 'states that to award rights to men as fathers in situations where women are responsible for children's care is in conflict with the principles of justice' (Sevenhuijsen 1998: 204). Sevenhuijsen supports the 'primary caretaker principle' in custody conflict, the principle that the parent who has been responsible for the daily care of the child should be able to lay greater claim to the right to legal custody. It allows for continuity of care, for men who have been prime carers, or a woman who prefers to have her children brought up by the father. These allowances are more useful than formal attempts to apply justice, as distributive rights do not absorb what is at stake in custody politics. Child-rearing is not about formal absolute contracts, but about the diverse ways to encourage the well-being of vulnerable children. Sevenhuijsen advocates a feminist perspective to custody that implies a collective responsibility to make the authority over children less contested and asks, 'what is the best way to deal with dependency, vulnerability and responsibility?' (1998: 108–9).

Family law

Martha Minow and Mary Shanley (1996) examine legal theories about the family and argue that neither contract, community or rights are adequate foci to incorporate paradoxical features of family life that family members are individuals defined by relationships; and that family relationships are shaped by social practices and state action. First, contract appears liberatory to advocates of gender equality but its crudity cannot deal with complex family life. Contract theories of the family, pre-nuptial agreements, marriage or pregnancy cannot guarantee an equal relationship between the contracting parties nor address the dependencies that arise in intimate relationships. Contract is based on self-possessing individuals linked by agreement (Pateman 1989). Reducing genetic material or babies to marketable resources, or implying that gestation is no different from other forms of waged labour diminishes the richness of the socially constructed nature of families.

Second, community-based theories regard families as important expressions of personal and social relationships. The feminist controversy lies in the disagreement as to which norms and values communities should endorse and the law enforce. Such controversy extends particularly to whether the law should make divorce more difficult or whether same-sex marriages should have equal legal protection to heterosexual marriages. Community-based theories lack an 'easy accommodation for pluralism' that contract allows with private agreement and rights allows with individual freedoms (Minow and Shanley 1996: 16). Third, rights-based theories to family law promote pluralism as well as individual freedom. Rights inhere to the family as a unitary entity entitled to protection from interference and inhere to individuals. Yet the rights associated with family life to marry, divorce, receive child support and procreate do not merely involve individuals but the claims of particular relationships with moral requirements.

Minow and Shanley propose relational rights and responsibilities as the framework for an adequate theory of family law whereby the individual is simultaneously a distinct individual and a person in relationships. A woman who has agreed to bear a child for someone else is both an agent of choice and someone who has developed a relationship to the child. If she wants to keep the child, the court should not 'reduce the case to the enforcement of a contract nor regard the fact of childbearing alone as determining parental claims' (Minow and Shanley 1996: 22). Similarly when same-sex or heterosexual couples separate, custody, visitation rights and financial support of children should consider both parents as separate persons and as individuals-in-relationships. Relational rights 'arise out of relationships of human interdependence' (1996: 23). A legal theory that incorporates interdependence and social shaping ensures that contractarian models of the market do not unduly influence public life or intimate relationships, and that a search for common values does not curtail privacy or pluralism. Legal theory must respect sexual equality, relationships and changing family forms.

Business ethics

Business ethics are situated within a context of capitalist structures where private ownership, competition and the profit motive is paramount. While there is nothing wrong with any of these features in themselves, excesses overstep reasonable moral boundaries and then become immoral. Private ownership that dislocates and dispossesses subsistence people from their native land to make way for cash crops is wrong. Colonialists' activity of taking over Aboriginal people's land is wrong. Competition between two small shops is healthy, giving customers a range of items for sale, but when large stores dominate a neighbourhood, forcing smaller retail places to close, something is lost in terms of community loyalty as well as the impossibility of competing against large business magnates. Some profit is essential to be able to live well, but when greed takes over, or workers are exploited and not paid a fair wage, or unethical, devious or illegal means are used to increase wealth, or pollution is a by-product of manufacture, then economic immorality escalates. Feminists are concerned to foster an 'ethic of flourishing' in ecologically sustainable communities (Cuomo 1997).

Within capitalist society, business ethics are crucial. The responsibilities of business corporations are the moral responsibilities to the workers, the communities in which they operate and to society at large (Chryssides and Kaler 1993: 230). Moral responsibilities include the just treatment of workers, community welfare and social benefit. Responsibilities to workers include fair wages, sickness benefits, employee safety, pensions, paternity leave, holidays and ecological and sustainable economic considerations. To customers or clients, confidentiality, product safety and truth in advertising is owed, because fairness, honesty and a respect for persons is intrinsic to ethics. Corporate resources should be used ethically. This incorporates the honest use of information, the judicious use of finances and the careful maintaining of reputations. To shareholders, integrity is owed. A market economy thrives on advertising. The ethics of persuasion are often dubious. Advertisements are couched in glamour, seduction, mystery where images of luxury are visually displayed for items that bear little resemblance to the message portrayed. Advertising that does not give full information does not grant due respect for persons. Accountability is the crucial measure.

Ina Praetorius, in exploring questions of economy and business ethics from a feminist angle, defines economy as 'all the measures taken worldwide to provide what human beings need (starting from birth), and the production, distribution and utilization of the means of living' (1997: 58). Her starting point is the birth, care and education of humans. Women's contribution to the economy is absolutely necessary, involving organization, traditions and systems of exchange. Most of this work 'is economics that is not limited to market-conditioned transactions of exchange, but rather includes all measures taken to satisfy needs and desires' (1997: 63). Yet it is true that most women, men and increasingly children need 'to have access to money and markets, because a number of vitally necessary goods and services are only available through money and markets' (1997: 58).

What feminists challenge is the dualistic understanding of economy as being about men and money versus women's unpaid work. In traditional cultures, women tend livestock, cultivate fields, process grain, gather fuel, fetch water (often for miles) and care for children, yet they are known as the 'invisible economy'. The new business paradigm of 'interconnectedness' (Treviño and Nelson 1995: 37) links the ecological system with the world community. This paradigm is central to feminist perspectives. Some management consultants, keen to change corporate structures, suggest quantum paradigm shifts. Danah Zohar (1997) marks some features of new corporate leadership that reflect feminist ethics with an emphasis on relationships, integration, trust, ambiguity, context, imagination, co-operation.

Technological ethics

Technology plays a major role in all professions. The intrusion on personal privacy is a worry. It is not the fact of data information, because files have always been kept for medical and dental records, bank statements, law reports. The difference lies in the massive amounts of information that can be stored by computers and hence a stronger chance for manipulation of data, unauthorized access and an invasion of privacy. The reliance on computers is substantial, paralysing work when they fail. The legal liability of software poses a substantial concern for programmers. For example, a software firm develops a medical diagnostic system and sells it to a hospital. A doctor uses it and misdiagnoses a patient. The patient is harmed as a result of the treatment recommended by the computer diagnosis. Who is liable? Is it the programmer, doctor or hospital (Johnson 1985: 40)?

Surveillance technology, crowd control weapons, prison control systems, torture techniques and military technology are fearful means of technological and political control. The world of the internet and the immediacy of email 'conversation', originally created for military use, is real for most of us in the Western world who use the 'cyberhighway' for work, information or communication purposes. However, there are real ethical concerns with its immediacy. A woman's labour and the birth of her son was advertised and displayed on the internet. Why? While purporting to reveal the autonomy of the woman, it was orchestrated to fit medical and internet time controls. Voyeurs can enter the world of teenage girls who agree to allow a camera to roam over their mundane and titillating bedroom romps. An eighteen-year-old couple sought sponsorship to have their loss of virginity filmed on the web. A further concern is the blurring of boundaries between body and machine, physical and virtual realities (Shilling 1993) that permit 'cybersex', arrange transgendered dating, where play-acting on the screen becomes a substitute for actual sex, or where young girls or boys arrange to meet older men who have devious unethical motives. Chat-lines may be used by shy or introverted individuals as a substitute for actual social contact. The dehumanizing propensity of an escalating use of technology remains a concern. Donna Haraway (1997) explores new territory between feminism and technoscience. Haraway's book is titled: *Modest_Witness@Second_Millenium.FemaleMan_Meets_OncoMouse.*

Summary

- Professional practice, informed by feminist ethics, is based on the willingness to make empathetic connections.

- Professional care is an art, a practice, a skill and a form of reasoning.

- Nursing is a practice with an inherent moral sense with tight connections between care and ethics.

- Feminist social work seeks to empower people to take control of their lives. It responds to individual needs by linking individual experience with social structures.

- Feminist law builds on equality with rights and responsibilities situated in accounts of interdependence.

- Businesses have moral responsibilities to workers, clients, the society and the global community.

Further reading

Bowden, P. (1996) *Caring. Gender-Sensitive Ethics*, London and New York: Routledge.

Bubeck, D. E. (1995) *Care, Gender and Justice*, Oxford: Clarendon Press.

Hugman, R. and Smith, D. (eds) (1995) *Ethical Issues in Social Work*, London: Routledge.

Chapter 4

Politics

Chapter outline

This chapter seeks to demonstrate how political decisions ought to be ethical decisions. Many feminists respond by being active in community politics, while smaller numbers seek electoral representation to formal politics. All feminist politics attend to the differences of women. Feminist visions to include women as full citizens require:

- open dialogue and inclusive political judgement
- attention to diverse identities and group difference
- electoral representation of women's specific and general needs.

Much of politics concerns the allocation of resources. This chapter seeks to show how interpreting needs from a feminist perspective is an attempt to:

- translate justifiable needs claims into social rights claims
- provide the rights to participate as equal citizens
- show that justice and care provide the enabling conditions to fulfil human capabilities.

The chapter concludes with suggestions for how feminists might work in coalition across intense differences of political belief, religion, ethnicity, class.

Politics and ethics

Some readers may think it peculiar to have a chapter on politics in a book on ethics. These readers may be familiar with typical ideas that politics is about power, state legitimacy and public resources. All of this is true, but the way in which politics is practised is influenced enormously by ethics. Ethics is conspicuous in ways in which governments, communities and civil societies choose certain priorities, treat people, are inclusionary or exclusionary, utilize resources and respond to people's needs. These responses are political and ethical. In fact, for democratic polities, what is political should be inseparable from what is ethical.

Political ethics critically reflects on good and bad decisions and right and wrong actions in the polity. Ethics draws on citizens' capacities to make decent judgements, to review these in the light of changing circumstances and differing needs of others and to act decently. Normative political theory examines how citizens ought to respond to questions of equality, justice, freedom, representation and legitimacy. This chapter surveys key ethical controversies in politics. Feminism's ethical appeal lies in 'a call for us to re-imagine our form of life so that we can "see" differently' (Cornell 1995: 79) and discover which political contexts do justice to feminist ethics. Feminist ethics is political in breaking gendered patterns of domination and in working toward visions of political judgement and social justice. It insists on women's full citizenship.

Power

Power is intrinsic to politics. Feminists adopt broad definitions of 'politics' beyond the institutional mechanisms of government, many regarding everything that involves power struggles as political. Cross-culturally, men are the centre of cultural value, wielding authority or legitimate power over women. Men hold most positions of power as household heads, and in government, business, industry, finance, education, the police and military. The connection between authority and masculinity consolidates power structures with gender (Connell 1995). Unsurprisingly, many feminists view politics as 'power structured relationships' (Randall 1991) which permeate social, public, intimate and institutional life.

Positive power is enabling, such as a parent's exercise of direction to a child to encourage necessary school revision. Negative power is controlling and ranges from older men's domination of conversation to systematic abuses of marginalized groups. Within political theory, central questions of obligation, freedom and equality presuppose power. People who experience powerlessness may not feel equal in their capacity to influence choices and to act as free political agents. The feminist concern with gendered power is in exposing the domination, submission, repression and oppression 'that frustrates truly free and autonomous self-development and self-determination' (Porter 1997b: 393). Feminist ethics differentiates between power and domination, or enabling and controlling dimensions. Admitting the constraints of power means refusing to accept abuses of power, or unfair differences in treatment or unjustified arbitrariness of public decision-making.

Making feminist politics

Feminist politics has its dynamism in women's lived experiences and accepts that women have some interests in common and many that differ. Universal sameness marginalizes differences, hence some feminists are critical of assuming any essential experiences for all women. Yet, 'if women cannot be characterized in any general way, if all there is to femininity is socially produced, how can feminism be taken seriously? What justifies the assumption that women are oppressed as a sex?' (Grosz 1994: 93). The political basis of feminism lies in a defence of women as a category with specific bodies and sexually specific experiences that are influenced by gender socialization and subordination. 'The strategic deployment of generalizations about women are necessary to the feminist political project' (Jones 1993: 13) as long as interpretations are contested (Bacchi 1996: 13).

One can speak as a woman without assuming a monolithic essence for the subject 'woman' as 'the site of multiple, complex and potentially contradictory sets of experiences' (Braidotti 1992: 185). Rosi Braidotti's **'embodiment as positionality'** sets the epistemological boundaries of communities of feminist knowing-subjects empowered in their entitlement to speak and be heard. The validation of women's experiences is the basis from which feminist political voices speak. The idea that the women's movement speaks for all women is rightly shattered by writers of colour writing on racism, imperialism and postcolonialism. For example, racism involves multiple variables, and 'black women's particularity is transparent because of racism; any failure of white women to recognize *their* own particularity continues that racism' (Aziz 1992: 297). Feminist politics incorporates women's varying experiences, differing identities and multiple complex subjectivities.

Small-scale political activities at local, community and neighbour-hood levels strengthen women's self-esteem. For example, when working-class women claim 'private' space from the kitchen table to mobilize women for campaigns around public policy issues that affect them they subvert the public–private divide (Lister 1997: 123). Participation in informal community-based politics is easier for women than in formal politics given their constraints of time with children returning from school, and/or nursery. The sexual division of labour 'engenders democracy' (Phillips 1991), present-ing real obstacles to women's participation as political citizens. Yet for many women, it is their identification as 'mothers' with 'family interests' that provides the impetus to political involvement, fight-ing for practical community resources. Globally, women carry the communities in crises times like miners' and dockers' strikes or during 'The Troubles' in Northern Ireland. African and Afro-American women's activism is based around protection of the extended family. Women in Latin American countries occupy public spaces to protest against the disappearance of husbands and sons (Roberts 1995).

Community politics fosters public goals as an ethical choice. Feminist politics requires a commitment to goods like childcare, playgrounds, safe public transport, adequate housing, support networks, employment prospects, health care. Such a commitment shifts the priorities from individual rights and freedom to com-munal solidarity. Feminism values those concerns historically associ-ated with women, like nurture, care of the environment and the pursuit of peace. Many feminist campaigns centre on communal problems of education, rape, paedophilia, domestic violence, por-nography, media stereotypes, health. Thus it is tempting to view women's nurture as a basis for political involvement. Jean Bethke Elshtain (1981) asserts the primacy of family values in an 'ethical polity'. Diemut Bubeck (1995) argues for the importance of care as a resource for political citizenship. Ruth Lister situates women as political actors at the interstices of the public and private, giving expression to the urgency of care and the need for justice, making public the experiences of sexual oppression and domestic violence, constructing 'notions of "intimate citizenship"' (1997: 153). 'A women friendly polity' roots its democracy in women's experiences and transforms the practice of citizenship to fit these varied experiences (Jones 1990: 811). Feminist ethics appreciates the political relevance of family responsibilities for women's effective access to political power, their positions in civil society and the labour market (Frazer and Lacey 1993: 75).

Others point to the danger of consolidating women's political marginalization because women's incorporation into the political order as wives and mothers and their subordination to men limits their representation and participation (Pateman 1992). Women's engagement in informal politics is important, but women must enter the formal political arena also to present a 'politics of presence' (Phillips 1995). Any idealization of women's nurture is uncritical of gendered stereotypes. 'Conformism is often a prerequisite for nurturance in the close-knit community', where subversives or outsiders pay a price 'for the majority's bonds of membership' (Sypnowich 1993b: 493) and where those who challenge communal traditions are cast out as whores or traitors.

Sara Ruddick (1992) plots a personal journey from maternal thinking to peace politics, a transformation of 'womanly' stances into feminist liberatory standpoints. She traces three stages. First, a representation of maternal peacefulness presents 'maternal thinking *as if* it were already peaceful in order to discover and reveal the peacefulness' hoped for (1992: 145). Ruddick refers to attentive love, concrete cognition, tolerance for ambivalence and ambiguity, receptiveness to change and recognition of the limits of control. Despite parental abandonment and assault, she discovers 'women and men who are powerless, powerfully and passionately engaged with vulnerable and provocative children, making "peace"' (1992: 146). Second, she discerns flaws in this representation that mystify ideology. Preserving traditions is part of reproduction and some mothers 'support violence against the "enemy" who seem to threaten their "ways", community or state' (1992: 147). Others are racist, sectarian or bigoted and shield their family and neighbourhood from the perceived 'enemy'. Others encourage their children to embrace state violence. 'Maternal peacefulness is an empowering myth' (1992: 148). Third, there is a transformative encounter between feminism and women's politics of resistance to an awareness of others' suffering, a 'compassion for the different "other"' (1992: 152), naming abuses, subverting divisions between private care and public justice, demanding policies that provide economic means to sustain others.

Mary Dietz (1985) also criticizes maternal thinking as a model for feminist politics, given the inequalities of power associated with

---

Box 4.1 Women in public life

A United Nations study of public life concludes that only a
critical mass of 30.35 per cent of women in politics makes a
significant difference to influencing the political culture and
facilitating alliances (United Nations Division 1992: 5). This study
found that the distinction women tend to make is their attention
given to the needs of other women, children, elderly, disabled
and disadvantaged. In the 1970s several Scandinavian parties
fostered the principle of having at least 40 per cent of women
represented at all ranks of elected politics. In 1980, parties in
Norway and Sweden proposed legislation that would commit all
parties to this minimum of 40 per cent. Consequently, in 1992 in
the Lower House, women constitute 33.7 per cent in Denmark,
35.8 per cent in Norway, 37.8 per cent in Sweden, and 38.4
per cent in Finland (Gardiner 1993: 46). Evidence is clear that
quotas, the arrangement of reserved seats for women's committee
delegates on significant bodies, and the gender-proofing of policy
proposals are necessary for increasing the political representation
of women. Yet in polities where there is an absence of a broad
feminist consciousness, where gender parity is not accepted as
a desirable political goal, quotas alone are insufficient. There
must be a breakdown of the gendering of status, power and a
masculinist organizational structure.

---

the mother–child bond and the increasing numbers of women who
choose to remain childfree. Later, Dietz (1992) sets out a feminist
vision of citizenship where the virtues, relations and practices are
political, participatory and democratic. Democracy transforms 'the
individual as teacher, trader, corporate executive, child, sibling,
worker, artist, friend or mother into a special sort of political
being, a citizen among other citizens' (1992: 75). Democracy
offers an identity based around mutual participation of speech and
action of 'self-conscious political thinkers' (1992: 78). As long as
feminists focus solely on socio-economic concerns that affect
children, women and families, they will neither articulate a truly
political vision nor address citizenship in its entirety.

Overcoming dualisms between liberal and feminist political ethics

Political values influence political ethics. For example, liberal individualistic ethics centre on universality, abstraction, impartiality and

rationality geared to agreeing on procedures that meet individuals' rights. Liberal politics assumes that particularities of family, sex, race and class are personal matters which will be ignored in public in order to ensure equality. Equality is defined as sameness, because difference and equality appear irreconcilable. Difference is reduced to otherness, negating sexual difference, embodiment, instability and unpredictability. In liberal politics, particularity is transcended in pursuit of the general will. Men and women are subsumed under a single umbrella of 'general human subject' who supposedly possesses universal rights and duties. Distancing from specificity is thought to enhance neutral objectivity because loyalties and dependencies impinge on personal freedom.

Feminist ethics presents the individual not as unattached, 'but as constituted by an ensemble of "subject positions", inscribed in a multiplicity of social relations' (Mouffe 1993: 78). As members of families, churches, work, social life we participate in plural forms of identification. Identity is formed through cultural, historical, civic and political interactions where responsibilities are integral to moral judgement. Situatedness raises 'the quality of judgement' (Sevenhuijsen 1998: 59) in permitting an intimate knowledge of people's needs.

The feminist challenge to the universalism of 'woman' comes primarily from postmodern deconstructionism and from black writers whose identities are marginalized or ignored by the category 'woman'. Deconstruction breaks down old categories, it has 'an ethical impulse to attend to difference' (Frazer and Lacey 1993: 203, 204). This impulse is a commitment to be open to 'unassimilated otherness' (Cornell 1991, 1992). Black feminists contend that 'white' is a racial category of privilege which contributes to the exclusion of black women from citizenship (Afshar and Maynard 1994). Other challenges are directed at tendencies to homogenize groups regarded as 'other', like the creation of 'a composite, singular, "third-world" woman who is denied all agency' (Mohanty 1988: 62). In turn, many black women homogenize white women as being middle-class, denying the reality and cross-over of race, gender, class (Aziz 1992). Women from South Asian descent do not classify themselves as black, and women from Northern Ireland or the former Yugoslavia define themselves by differences of religion and culture.

Anne Phillips comments that the movement from universal grand theory to historically grounded local theory leads towards complaints of conservatism, that the central theoretical categories of gender, patriarchy and women are crucial in opening challenges. She poses the important question, 'when people query the universalizing pretensions of previous traditions, do they thereby limit their radical potential?' (1992: 13). Feminists consistently resist polar oppositions 'between what is abstract, impartial, gender-neutral, and what is specific, relational, engendered' (Phillips 1992: 13). Phillips urges feminists who challenge the universalism of traditional political or moral thought not to react in the opposite direction, but to realize that they are 'most persuasive not in counterposing the particular to the general, the sexually specific to the universal, but in emphasizing the interplay between the two' (1992: 27). This interplay overcomes dualisms. It conceptualizes 'our political existence as individuals and as citizens, as embodying particularity and universality, diversity and commonality so that neither is sacrificed to the other' (Porter 1997a: 94). Accordingly, feminist political ethics draws on insights from liberalism, socialism, communitarianism, republicanism. Its concern is to overcome binary oppositions that stultify political ethical agency like mind/body, reason/emotion, abstract/concrete, knowledge/opinion, self/others, universality/particularity.

Dialogue and deliberation

New visions of political ethics require dialogue. Open dialogue occurs when the public sphere is viewed as a meeting ground of action and interaction, where opinions are exchanged through debate. Public deliberation on ethics includes how to incorporate citizen's similarities and differences, or deciding which values deserve to be common values (like the respect for others) and which should remain open (like how to demonstrate such respect). We cannot presume consensus and agreement on fundamental political issues, hence argument, debate and working through diverse values and options are integral aspects of ethical agency. Selma Sevenhuijsen argues that a principle task of collective citizenship is 'judging', distinguishing between good and bad and being accountable (1998: 15). In democratic contexts, judging 'takes place at the intersection between equality and difference' (1998: 15), whereby judgements simultaneously recognize the radical alterity of subject's individuality and diversity while considering and treating others as equals.

Feminists agree that within political spaces where dialogue, open communication and interpretative ethics prevail, space exists for situated political judgements and actions (Bickford 1996; Code 1995). They differ on how best to achieve open dialogue. Lorraine Code, in advocating a **deliberative morality**, refers to it as 'open-textured, dialogic, and open to criticism, self-criticism and debate' (1991: 109), leaving scope for trial and error. Without dialogue, there can be no real appreciation of the richness of diversity. Too often, fear of the unknown stultifies the search for what people have in common. Seyla Benhabib advocates **discourse ethics** which does not aim at consensus but communication and mutual understanding 'with others with whom I know I must finally come to some agreement' (1992: 9). This is the type of communication adopted by a friend who says, 'But let me see if I understand your point correctly' (1992: 52), or the admonition of the parent to the child, 'What if others threw sand in your face or pushed you into the pool, how would you feel then?' (1992: 53). In ordinary moral conversations we try to come to terms with others' views. A mutual understanding of differences is a prerequisite to reciprocity in listening and speaking.

Elizabeth Frazer and Nicola Lacey support a **dialogic communitarianism** (1993: 203) that assumes democratic institutions provide access to political processes for all citizens, admits the importance of dialogue in deliberating on public goods and places collective life at the heart of politics. Susan James discusses ways in which the family is important to the political sphere by developing self-esteem, because accepting the validity of one's voice as being worthy to be heard is a fundamental 'requirement of citizens – having a voice of their own' (1992: 60). In order to be confident to voice one's views in the polity 'one must esteem oneself as a woman, black, white, Bengali, worker, mother, Hindu, old-age pensioner, republican or whatever' (1992: 63). Self-esteem is sustained in sensitive respectful practices. Dialogue is strategic to feminist ethics, building on the belief that a conversational approach requires disagreement and contrasting stories (Weiss 1997).

Diverse citizenship

'Citizenship' evokes a host of powerful concepts like respect, dignity, political inclusion, rights. Nancy Fraser and Linda Gordon use the expression 'social citizenship' which extracts themes from differing traditions of political theory: themes of social rights and equal respect from liberalism; norms of solidarity and shared responsibility from communitarianism; and ideals of participation in public life from republicanism (1994: 91). Elizabeth Meehan takes social rights, together with civil and political rights, to 'form a triad, which must be regarded as interlocked if we are able to speak of the existence of equal citizenship' (1993: 2). Kathleen Jones defines citizenship 'as a practice of embodied subjects whose sex/gendered identity affects fundamentally their membership and participation in public life' (1990: 786). Political actors are affected by gender-defined practices, including the significance of the 'body' in the 'body politic'. Feminist political ethics defies dualistic notions that relegate bodies to the domestic realm. Citizens, with embodied identities, participate in diversity.

Diversity as a political principle

Intrinsic to an embodied feminist ethics and to working alliances (Jakobsen 1998) are the differences of race, ethnicity, colour, class, sexual preference, education, employment, dis/ability. For many feminists, diversity is the guiding principle for an inclusionary politics which validates experience, identity and social location. Political life is constituted through resolving the tensions of 'different skills, resources, qualities, claims on each other and the community, and opinions about the good' (Flax 1993: 112). Feminism's aim is not 'parity, equivalence, or disinterested treatment under the prevailing standards; rather, it starts from, and affirms, the *difference* between men and women' (Sypnowich 1993b: 490). This assumes a struggle against appropriating the Other into a system of meaning that denies, minimalizes or trivializes difference. 'Ethical difference' aspires 'to a nonviolent relationship to the Other and to otherness in the widest possible sense' (Cornell 1995: 78).

Yet diversity often threatens the safety of what is known and familiar in situations of sectarianism, racism and sexism. With those who perceive diversity as divisive, there is a closure, a cutting-off of options where 'difference is understood in terms of inequality, distinction, or opposition, and sexual difference modelled on negative, binary, or oppositional structures' (Grosz 1994: 91). Valuing diversity undermines status quo beliefs and dualistic practices. Yet many 'differences are born out of oppression' and are not liberatory (Sypnowich 1993a: 105). Furthermore, 'all differences are not equal nor do they deserve the same political consideration' (Flax 1993: 111). Determining this consideration is contentious. Differences that undermine people's dignity cannot be supported. Differences that occur through poverty have more urgency than those dealing with sexual preference unless the latter affects one's ability to meet material needs. It is possible that because of one's sexuality, discrimination in housing and jobs contributes to material deprivation. Sometimes it is important to disentangle 'the differences that are inevitable from those that are chosen, and from those that are simply imposed' (Phillips 1992: 23). An inclusionary feminist politics validates differences between women and men; in groups of women and groups of men; and within ourselves. It understands the interaction between class, race, ethnicity, sexuality and gender and that it is not the differences that are problematic, 'but the reluctance to sincerely try to understand these differences that results in misnaming, misapprehensions or ignoring the differences' (Porter 1997a: 89). There is a healthy balance between respecting difference and elevating identity politics.

Identity politics

Sometimes individuals, but more often groups use specific identities as the basis for political activism, usually to draw attention to injustices they suffer as a result of being single mothers, black or Asian in a white country, disabled, poor or unemployed. Most of us hold different combinations of identities that overlap and vary in significance. Identity politics appears an attractive route to many feminists, yet it has two potentially positive and two negative dimensions (Porter 1997a: 86). First, on a positive angle it is empowering, in that claiming aspects of identity that have been marginalized such as one's first language allows the expression of something that has been suppressed. Naming and claiming an identity as one's own is liberating. Agency is reclaimed as being intrinsic to political processes. Second, it permits alliances to develop by allowing differing identities to work together in order to further the political struggle. For example, some women in Northern Ireland who have suffered at the expense of terrorist disruption and army surveillance make enormous personal journeys to work in coalition with privileged women who have not been so personally affected by 'The Troubles', for the sake of a mutual concern for lasting peace.

Positive aspects of identity politics sit alongside negative dimensions. First, its exclusionary nature can alienate, privileging one identity and excluding all others. 'The cost of a "home" in any identity is the exercise of a power to include the chosen and exclude the other' (Aziz 1992: 304), contributing to an isolation from those who are differently situated. Second, identity politics can be narrow-minded, asserting identity as an end in itself, losing sight of the bigger picture and the dynamics of claiming an identity. Singularity involves more than dogmatism. In conflict over issues of race, bigotry, ethnic 'cleansing' or indigenous land rights, singular politics focuses on fixed demands, whatever the resulting cost and violence. A politics entirely rooted in particular experiences is dangerous, because it 'gives rise to a self-righteous assertion that if one inhabits a certain identity this gives one the right to pressure others into particular ways of behaving' (Weeks 1993: 202). Also, 'deferring to special categories of experience can function as a reverse "othering", as an excuse not to engage in discussion' (Spivak in Burman 1994: 161).

The practicalities of differences are complex. How can we accept diverse identities and find mutually acceptable decisions? In political contexts, agency outweighs identity because the requirement of collective responsibility asks us sometimes to stand back from self-proclaimed identities (Sevenhuijsen 1998: 30) to enter imaginatively into others' experiences. Nira Yuval-Davis, in discussing dialogue between Serbs and Croats, and Palestinian and Israeli Jewish women calls this 'rooting' and 'shifting', the idea being 'that each participant brings with her the rooting in her own membership and identity but at the same time tries to shift in order to put herself in a situation of exchange with women who have different membership and identity' (1994: 192–3). The process of shifting neither negates one's roots nor homogenizes the other, but attempts to empathize with another's background.

The resolution and recognition of difference is an urgent contemporary problem, driving nationalism and multiculturalism as well as feminism (Flax 1993). Writers other than feminists note that it is not just the need for recognition that is at stake, but for race, culture and gender, 'the withholding of recognition can be a form of oppression' (Taylor 1992: 35, 36). The politics of equal dignity was supposed to ensure universal treatment through equal rights but the politics of identity addresses the distinctiveness that universality ignores. The quest for public recognition of collective identities underlies a fundamental demand for 'equality of respect'

(Galeotti 1993: 597), the ethical basis to full political inclusion. Yet if difference and plurality are prioritized over commonality and unity, the political capacity to deliver specific and general interests is lost. Identity politics should not hide in separateness but listen to and respect others' voices. An individual right to celebrate differences runs parallel to the responsibility to respect others' differences.

Group difference

To overcome any limitations of individualistic assertions of identity politics, and to reclaim the positive meaning of difference, Iris Marion Young (1990, 1993) defends the importance of group difference. Oppressive notions of group difference define 'it as absolute otherness, mutual exclusion, categorical opposition' (1990: 169). Young explains that in objectifying ideologies like sexism, racism, anti-Semitism and homophobia, 'only the oppressed and excluded groups are defined as different' (1990: 170), thereby undermining the significance of distinction. Political processes of decision-making should ensure specific representation of disadvantaged social groups. Mechanisms to represent oppressed groups (Cockburn 1996) and holders of power should demonstrate listening by permitting a group veto on issues affecting the group directly (Young 1993), like reproductive rights for women, voting and citizenship rights for refugees, welfare payments and training for single mothers. Adequate representation is the only hope for achieving a political co-operation that respects the cultural specificity and needs of different groups, and which compensates 'disadvantaged groups, institutionalizing means of ensuring that their voice and perspective will be heard' (1993: 142). The ethical basis for this representation is to foster just policies that facilitate different understandings of needs. In an inclusive politics, public spaces should be open and accessible and people's differences respected 'though perhaps not completely understood, by others' (Young 1990: 119).

Phillips asks, what is 'the dividing line between pressing one's own selfish and sectional interest and organizing around your needs as a disadvantaged or oppressed group?' (1993: 81–2). The answer depends on ethical political conduct and whether one is a member of a privileged or disadvantaged group. Phillips sees difficulties establishing political identity, retaining accountability and minimizing group closure to widen solidarities. For example, if three community consultative committees are set up around issues of race, disability and women, rarely do all groups manage a balanced group representation. Tokenism is inadequate. Yet even selecting a committee member from the category 'black people' is complex because life experience, culture, history, opportunities for education and degree of self-conscious political identity vary, as does identification with colour, as pride or shame. Intragroup differences are important, denoting the ways in which race, gender, class intersect (Crenshaw 1997) with varying degrees in the lived realities of a racism that marginalizes and victimizes (Aziz 1992: 296). The writings of black feminists stress both the struggle and the agency in women's lives.

Representation and difference

Women's needs should be represented by women. The unequal representation of the sexes in politics is unjust 'because of the enormous impact of political power on other spheres of our lives' (Okin 1995: 132), but 'the sex of the representatives matters only if we think it will change what the representatives do' (Phillips 1994: 14). Do women have unique interests, needs and rights that cannot be represented by men? Ideally, in a world where domestic tasks, children, nurture, leisure, paid work and public decision-making were shared, issues of education, childcare, family and welfare would be men's as well as women's interests and thus could be represented by anyone. While women remain the prime carers in society and underrepresented in positions of power and influence, then 'it does matter who the representatives are' (Phillips 1994: 19).

Few men have experience of the daily care of the very young, sick, old or handicapped; are subject to rape, domestic violence, sexual harassment; juggle demands of waged work and parenthood; or single parenthood in poverty. So women need to be present in politics, because their experiences bring different perspectives. These experiences are political in the double sense of constructing an identifiable set of interests that can be expressed in public and creating a group that shares those interests (Jones 1990: 799–800). Granting the representation of women's experiences as

---

Box 4.2 Women in global politics

Women's participation in politics is a reasonable measure of how democratic a nation is. Globally, women constitute less than 5 per cent of the world's heads of state, heads of major corporations and top positions in international organizations (United Nations 1991: 6). Women hold an average of 10 per cent of parliamentary seats. In 1993, women held more than 20 per cent of parliamentary seats in only 11 out of 170 countries. In numeric descending order they include: Seychelles, Finland, Norway, Sweden, Denmark, The Netherlands, Iceland, Cuba, Austria, China, Germany. At a ministerial level, in 1990 women had 4 per cent of positions, and in more than 80 per cent of countries women hold no ministerial positions at all. Those who do are responsible primarily for health, welfare, education, culture and women's affairs (Karl 1995: 61). In the EU, women hold 16 per cent of government positions and 31 per cent in the Nordic countries. After the 1994 elections to the European Parliament, women represented 25.7 per cent of elected representatives (European Network of Experts 1994).

---

mothers, carers of dependants, lesser paid, usually lesser qualified citizens, political influence is of ethical significance. 'Meaningful citizenship must incorporate particularities of culture, ethnicity, religious difference, class, income, and gender' (Porter 1998a: 26–7) in order to respect ethical autonomy and encourage political agency.

The statistics in Box 4.2 do not prove women's incapacity to hold powerful positions. Explanations include explicit acts of discrimination against appointing women; subtle forms of excluding women like refusing to adjust times and expectations to the needs of families; and long-term effects of socialization into positions of subordination. Marilee Karl (1995) lists global influences of domestic violence, education, fertility, finances, literacy, low self-esteem, status. Other factors include differential employment, remuneration and work-related rights; cultural traditions; and the triple burden of childcare, domestic duties and paid work. Structural explanations exist like the reluctance of political parties to preselect women, inadequate childcare, unsociable hours, negative attitudes towards public women and insufficient support from women. These responses are ethically damaging to women's political agency.

Politics of needs

The 'politics of need interpretation' (Fraser 1989: 145–6) is a struggle over competing needs, determining what is required to satisfy these needs and the translation into actual rights. For example, welfare practices construct women's needs according to understandings of women as unpaid care-givers, welfare beneficiaries and dependants. The interpretive nature of needs can be illustrated by childcare. Feminists maintain that day-care needs should be met by parents, the state, employer or local community; social conservatives insist on children's need for a mother's care; and economic rationalists claim the market should meet demands. Even the terms sexual harassment, date rape, wife-battering and labour market segmentation express the politicization of needs, resisting established boundaries of the political, economic and domestic (1989: 172).

Feminists seek to translate justifiable needs claims into social rights claims. Substantive rights to collective self-determination require a context devoid of poverty, inequality and oppression. Interpreting needs is intrinsic to ethical judgement that listens to people's stories about 'what they need to live well' (Sevenhuijsen 1998: 60). Morality exhibits itself through sensitive interpretations of people's needs. Feminist politics is based on the ethical urgency of contextual moral reasoning, on the support not exploitation of caregiving (Manning 1992). A polity that takes needs seriously cares about creating a good society.

Human rights

Part of fulfilling needs is ensuring people's rights. There will always be competing claims about rights, hence the necessity for sound political debate. Political justice aims to provide everyone with the **rights** to participate in social life as equal citizens. Rights can be particularized to incorporate the needs of specific groups both in counteracting injustices that undermine citizenship and in affirming diversity, and may include affirmative action programmes, disability discrimination legislation, multicultural language policies (Lister 1997: 85). While differences are important, human needs and rights address universal ideas of human dignity and self-respect. Certainly rights discourse specifies particular needs but the basis to rights is not individualistic. Human rights are fundamental because they protect a condition of human existence which cannot be eliminated without destroying what is essential to being human. 'Our human dignity is at stake when our rights are infringed or neglected, but whereas human dignity is a constant value, what gives human beings dignity is always changing' (Sypnowich 1993b: 500).

Rights provide the ethical framework for a dignified empowered life. They enable the 'meaningful exercise of one's capacities as well as the adequate satisfaction of one's needs' (Narayan 1997: 53). Uma Narayan stresses the centrality of human vulnerability, for dignity is at risk when humans are left without protection or the means to satisfy basic needs, and rights '*minimize such vulnerabilities*, as attempts to ensure a minimum amount of *social dignity* to all members of society' (1997: 54). For while liberty rights protect us from others, rights also confer claims on others. Elizabeth Kiss (1997: 5) notes the ways in which rights institutionalize obligations, create a framework for co-operation and imply moral connections like the right to vote, a fair trial, open association and free education.

Political, civil, social and economic rights are prerequisite to human agency, 'grounded in the nature of human beings' (Gould 1988: 209). Indeed, citizenship rights enable people to act as agents. Agency is the basis for a claim to equal rights and to recast women as full actors. Citizen agency requires a personal belief that one can act and the activity demonstrates agency. 'Agency is not simply about the capacity to choose and act but it is also about a *conscious* capacity which is important to the individual's self-identity' (Lister 1997: 38). We need self-confidence to participate in political life. Collins uses the image of 'a journey toward self-definition' through which 'Black women's power as human subjects' is validated (1990: 106–7) and Morris (1991) writes similarly with regard to disabled women's agency. Representation for women in Western Europe, North America and Australia conveys the extent of women's participation in or exclusion from Western democracy. In the Third World, civil and political liberties 'together with broader political representation are valued mostly for the way they guarantee a political space to demand social and economic rights, better living standards and basic services; they are a means to an end' (Pankhurst and Pearce 1996: 42).

Box 4.3 Abuse of women's rights

Women Aid International target women who have suffered human
rights abuse and overwhelming need. Their literature (1998) cites
United Nations facts that 'women are half the world's people
who do two-thirds of the world's work. They earn a tenth of the
world's income and own a hundredth of the world's property'.
Also, 'two-thirds of the world's illiterates (900 million) are
women'. Rural women in the Third World shoulder the burden
of growing and processing food, searching for and carrying fuel
wood and fetching water, often over miles. Eighty per cent of the
world's almost 50 million refugees and displaced persons are
women and children. Examples of human rights abuse are
numerous. Since the Taliban took control of two-thirds of
Afghanistan, Afghan women and girls are barred from receiving
education, public paid work, speaking in public, leaving the
home unaccompanied or possessing a passport. Women found
with lipstick have their lips mutilated. They are forced to wear
the all-enveloping burqa. Women educate children in
underground schools and throw back the burqa when they
think no one else can see them. War widows, unable to earn a
livelihood, are driven to begging. Prostitution amongst beggars
has escalated. Reports exist of sex offered for subsidized food or
essential medicines. In the former Yugoslavia, 'rape camps' were
part of an appalling 'ethnic cleansing', directed particularly
against Muslim women in Bosnia-Herzegovina. In the Eastern
European Republics and in Central Asia, wars, economic
dislocation and ethnic conflicts mean inadequate food, medical
supplies, money to repair buildings, minimal water and electricity.
In Bangladesh, men throw acid over women who refuse their
advances, permanently destroying their chances of ever appearing
attractive.

Justice

Actualizing women's rights is intrinsic to justice. Justice and care
are unopposed. 'Justice is not uniform; care is not unprincipled'
but both 'have to respect principles *and* to deliberate about their
application' (O'Neill 1989: 22). Social justice attempts to recon-
cile 'radical pluralism and universalism' (Lister 1997: 102). Indeed,
justice teaches us how to 'tolerate differences between subjects and

others without domination' (Flax 1993: 123). Justice has universal scope and it 'embraces and acknowledges difference' (Phillips 1992: 19). Compassionate identification 'demands a searching analysis of differences in order that the general good be appropriately realized in the concrete case' (Nussbaum 1992b: 241). Ethically responsible politics are accountable for priorities, policies and actions in 'a world of justice *and* mercy, autonomy *and* caring, particular ties *and* universal aspirations' (Elshtain 1993: 173).

A commitment to justice demonstrates a care for people's rights. Adequate attention to justice enables the powerless, marginalized, excluded and oppressed to participate in political discourse through addressing causes of injustice (Young 1990). Justice and care provide 'enabling conditions'. In some cases, like the disastrous neglect of girls in Third World nations, only improvements of justice and rights will provide for adequate care. In other cases, improvements in the attentiveness to suffering and need might provide the grounds for more adequate practices of justice that institutionalize welfare, medical, housing and education rights.

Amy Gutmann shows how cultures contain different ethical standards, so for example, polygamy can be unjust for members of one culture and 'just for members of another culture whose understandings of marital responsibility and kinship are radically different' (1993: 173). According to cultural relativism, social justice distributes goods according to cultural meanings, but dominant understandings do not alone determine justice or dissolve multicultural conflicts. Political relativism acknowledges 'that disagreements over social meanings should be publicly discussed, negotiated, and adjudicated', but 'its weakness lies in its silence regarding standards, other than social agreement, by which to judge the justice of procedures or their results' (1993: 182).

Gutmann advocates a '**deliberative universalism**' (1993: 193) that meets the ethical challenges of cultural diversity. This notion accepts core universal principles and the need to publicly debate how conflicts on social justice can best be addressed. The preconditions to this notion being workable are mutually respectful persons who are prepared to admit to the need to change their views in the light of reasoned argument and to 'collectively discovering a just resolution that is presently unseen' (1993: 199). As Sypnowich argues, human rights neither involve a relativism about justice nor an uncritical acceptance of the status quo, 'rather, human rights develop from the margins, in the face of injustice, as instruments of critique and change, progressively enriched in the opportunities afforded by new political orders, new technologies, and new conceptions of justice' (1993b: 500). Quality of life is a key moral concern.

Human capabilities

It is possible to respect and question context, local traditions and specific needs. Martha Nussbaum cites an American economist at a conference who defends the embedded way of life in rural India. 'His example: just as in the home a menstruating woman is thought to pollute the kitchen and so may not enter it, so too in the workplace a menstruating woman is taken to pollute the loom and may not enter the room where looms are kept' (1992b: 203). Nussbaum notes how an Indian economist condemns this example as morally objectionable because it degrades women and inhibits their freedom. Indeed, appeals to tradition continue to defend the suppression of women's rights. At another conference, Nussbaum hears the example of Japanese men who, when they return home from work, do not want to bother choosing what to wear or eat, they want their wives to decide for them. In view of racism, sexism, colonialism, many fear neglecting the radical otherness of cultures, not wanting to be accused of Western cultural imperialism. Unintentionally, 'political correct anti-essentialism' converges with oppression and sexism. Genital mutilation, cannibalism and slavery have all been justified in terms of cultural respect.

Nussbaum defends **essentialism** 'as the view that human life has certain central defining features' (1992b: 205). She defends a historically sensitive account of basic human needs and functions that underlie the moral sentiments needed to live decently; compassion and respect. Her suggestions presuppose humans who are 'both capable and needy' of an ethical 'quality of life' (1992b: 216). Yet without a notion of what it means to function ethically, we cannot say how well a country is or is not doing in facilitating human capabilities. Without an account of the good, we cannot say what is absent in those who are marginalized or excluded, there is no adequate way of accusing embedded traditions of being unjust. Nussbaum lists ten basic human functional capabilities (1992b: 222):

1 Being able to live to the end of a complete human life, as far as is possible; not dying prematurely, or before one's life is so reduced as to be not worth living.

2 Being able to have good health; to be adequately nourished; to have adequate shelter; having opportunities for sexual satisfaction; being able to move from place to place.
3 Being able to avoid unnecessary and nonbeneficial pain and to have pleasurable experiences.
4 Being able to use the five senses; being able to imagine, think, and reason.
5 Being able to have attachments to things and persons outside ourselves; to love those who love and care for us, grieve at their absence; and feel longing and gratitude.
6 Being able to form a conception of the good and engage in critical reflection about the planning of one's own life.
7 Being able to live for and with others, to recognize and show concern for other human beings, to engage in various forms of familial and social interaction.
8 Being able to live with concern for and in relation to animals, plants and nature.
9 Being able to laugh, play and enjoy recreational activities.
10 Being able to live one's own life and nobody else's; in one's own surroundings and context.

Case study. Fulfilling capabilities in traditional locations

Nussbaum examines how it is possible to balance a sensitivity to local traditions with a commitment to human capability. She uses Mary Chen's (1983) examination of a literacy campaign directed at women in rural Bangladesh. The women Chen worked with had low status in terms of human functioning. Also, they were less well nourished than men, less educated, free or respected. The development agency Chen worked with went into the village holding the conviction of the importance of literacy, despite the women's lack of desire for change. She did not conclude that local traditions should be the final moral arbiter. The development workers founded women's co-operatives where the agency workers joined with local women in discussing the needs of the village, the role that literacy played in women's lives elsewhere and 'showing concrete examples of transformations in empowerment and self-respect' (Nussbaum 1992b: 236). The women opened up and told their stories of the impediments to education that their traditions imposed. Over time, a gradual transformation happened. Once literacy was perceived as a skill that might be deployed in their particular context, it became of enormous interest and led to significant changes. Women took over the tailoring industry, earning wages that give them stronger claims to food and medical care. The dialogue between the development workers and the local women 'presupposed the recognition of common humanity, and it was only with this basis securely established that they could fruitfully explore the concrete circumstances in which they were trying, in the one case, to live and in the other case, to promote flourishing human lives' (1992b: 236–7).

Working across differences

It is morally and politically important to work across differences. In order to do so, there needs to be an underpinning commitment to valuing difference and to open dialogue. Habermas's (1971) notion of a '**communicative ethic**' highlights the role of open, free, unconstrained, accessible and public deliberation as the ethical basis of democratic political legitimation. Feminist political theorists draw critically on this framework to articulate diverse voices, particularly the right to be heard and the incorporation of one's viewpoint into political decisions. Only through debate can we realize 'the ethical impulse to recognize each other's claims by listening attentively to them, respecting the difference of others whom we identify as in some deep sense having the same moral status as ourselves' (Frazer and Lacey 1993: 207).

Diana Meyers develops the idea of 'empathic thought' that asks, 'how can I *best* respond to your needs?' (1993: 227). This response assumes that every person is unique, and the task of moral reflection is to respond to the particularity of persons. 'Empathic thought' is interactive in inviting 'deliberators to articulate their capabilities and their values' (1993: 228). Dialogue permits glimpses into what possibilities exist. Consciousness-raising is an example of developing transformative politics through dialogic processes. Multiple experiences are exchanged, claims and perceptions of others are acknowledged, personal justifications are given, the importance (negative and positive) of practical traditions are raised, and new interpretations emerge, generating new ideas, language and frameworks. Transformative politics keep feminist ethics dynamic.

Ethnic boundaries

For many, ethnicity defines difference. As Floya Anthias and Nira Yuval-Davis (1992) explain, within structures of dominance, ethnic positioning interprets the world based on shared resources like culture, language, territory and collective status. Ethnic boundaries are not static, marriage and cultural drifting redefines identities. Some are born into the collectivity, others marry into it, some drift in and out depending on context or socio-political changes. Where boundaries are rigid, belonging implies that membership is exclusive. Ethnic, gender and class divisions involve differential access to resources and processes of inclusion. Exclusion, oppression and domination of ethnic minorities are exhibited within everyday language and are embodied in official documents, state practices and legislation (Anthias and Yuval-Davis 1992: 17). Divisions assume natural inequalities, and provoke practices of exclusion which structure disadvantage (1992: 111). Such exclusions and privileges result in different experiences for men and women, middle-class and working-class, racially dominant and racialized women.

Representations of ethnicity present notions of sexual difference and biological reproduction that effect opinions on female capacity, suitable waged labour and expectations of mothering. These effects are particularly pertinent in ethnic cultures that are organized around cultural expectations relating to sexuality, marriage and the family. Indeed this pivotal focus on reproductive roles in ethnic discourses explains the central role of common origin, that 'outsiders' generally only join the national collectivity through intermarriage, consequently 'women reproduce biologically, culturally, and symbolically their ethnic and national collectivities' (Yuval-Davis 1996: 17). Symbolic representations have major ramifications for feminist ethics. The opportunity to exercise deliberative reflection, judgement and accountability cements moral agency. While some women are active in national or ethnic struggles, 'in general, women are symbols of the nation while men are its agents' (Lutz, Phoenix and Yuval-Davis 1995: 9).

Interdependence

Politics is constituted through our differences from each other and our interdependence on each other. We possess different skills, resources, qualities, claims and ideals. No one is self-sufficient. The traditional expectation of men's ability to support wives and children privileges independence and makes it a primary virtue of citizenship, thereby 'judging a huge number of people in liberal societies as less than full citizens' (Young 1995: 547). This includes many women, children, frail old people, those with physical and mental disabilities, the sick, injured and dependency workers whose dependency marginalizes them. Ethical politics, as Onora O'Neill (1996) explains, is directed toward a plurality of others; connected others; and vulnerable others. She argues that even just social relations intensify vulnerabilities – affections which emotionally sustain also reject cruelly, officials who secure support expose corrupt inefficiencies, food aid supplements nutrition but increases dependence. Connected lives are acutely vulnerable lives. Differences must be accommodated within a context of striving to achieve the good(s) for all (Flax 1993: 112).

While rainbow coalitions of people with varying identities form to solve similar issues, feminist identity politics stress the need for some common denominator. A term like 'unity in diversity' emphasizes 'that political struggles do not have to be uniform, nor do they have to be united' (Lutz, Phoenix and Yuval-Davis 1995: 15). Consensus is rarely possible, compromise is vital, and solidarity to be worked at through dialogue, debate and reasoned argument in order to create an inclusive politics of coalition-building. 'If there is no connectedness between the two realms, "us" and "other," then how is it possible to form strategic coalitions across class, race, and national boundaries?' (Udayagiri 1995: 166). Coalitionary politics break down when people do not trust each other or learn to sustain working relationships in contexts of disagreement (Narayan 1988: 33). Coalitionary politics are sustained through dialogue and due recognition given the specific positions of participants. Examples are the Women's National Coalition formed during the transition to the new South Africa where women with deep animosities could identify common concerns (Basu 1995) and the Northern Ireland Women's Coalition (McWilliams with Kelly 1997) formed to participate in the multiparty peace talks, and elected to the new Assembly, crossing community, class, region and sectors.

Dualism constructs difference as antagonism. Feminist political ethics abandons dualistic thinking and practices. Equality and difference are compatible, making borders become permeable so that 'different women become visible as the different sorts of women they are, but with the potential to act in solidarity through their differences' (Jones 1990: 812). Equal citizenship embraces plural differences. An inclusive feminist politics incorporates universal equality and particular difference, obligations to those we care for and a commitment to rights for those we do not know. In demonstrating pluralism, dignity is restored to the political. Feminist ethics transcends, overcomes or disrupts boundaries.

Summary

- Feminist ethics is political in wanting to disrupt gendered patterns of domination and work toward inclusive forms of political participation and social justice.

- Social, civil and political rights are part of equal citizenship.

- Differences must be adequately represented.

- An aim of political justice is to provide everyone with the rights that enable them to participate as equal citizens.

- Working across differences, in coalitions, requires a commitment to valuing pluralism and open dialogue.

Further reading

Lister, R. (1997) *Citizenship. Feminist Perspectives*, London: Macmillan Press.

Phillips, A. (1993) *Democracy and Difference*, Cambridge: Polity Press.

Sevenhuijsen, S. (1998) *Citizenship and the Ethics of Care. Feminist Considerations on Justice, Morality and Politics*, trans. L. Savage, London and New York: Routledge.

Shanley, M. Lyndon and Narayan, U. (eds) (1997) *Reconstructing Political Theory. Feminist Perspectives*, Cambridge: Polity Press.

Chapter 5

Sexual Politics

Chapter outline

This chapter briefly explores diverse sexualities like:

- lesbianism
- queer or transgressive sexuality
- a redefined heterosexuality.

Sexual difference refers not only to various expressions of sexual pleasure, but to women's desire to become empowered as embodied subjects. The chapter's main purpose is to examine sexual politics, the ways in which sexual relations are influenced by inequalities of power. Sexualized violence exacerbates sexual politics and makes people (mainly women) appear as mere sex objects. Examples of sexualized violence include:

- female genital mutilation
- pornography as explicit representations of sexual behaviour that degrade and harm
- women who regard themselves positively as sex objects
- prostitution as commercialized sexual abuse.

The aims of the chapter are to criticize sexualized power and to respect the complexities of sexual lives.

Diverse sexualities

Sex! The idea, fantasies, misconceptions, fears, desires and reality pervades everyday life. A sexual presence is felt in the workplace, media, leisure as well as in the bedroom. Sexuality is complex and culturally diverse. The person who is single by choice, chance or misfortune might or might not crave physical intimacy, satisfaction of need and fulfilment of longing. Some people engage in recreational sex without commitment. Others have several regular partners, with perhaps one more primary. A few are promiscuous. Most people practise serial monogamy with smaller numbers maintaining one life-partner. Feminists have different sexual experiences of being single, celibate, lesbian, bisexual or heterosexual. Given this variation, the controversies on sexuality within feminism are lively (Soble 1997). However, there are a number of agreements, namely that **sexual politics** is about unequal power relations; sexuality is a crucial part of our embodiment; treating anyone as if they are nothing but a sex object is wrong. This is not a chapter on sexuality, but on sexual politics.

Feminist ethics is concerned with how unequal power relations undermine the moral integrity of persons. To accommodate diversity and resist abstract constructions of otherness, feminist ethics deconstructs dualisms like sex/gender, nature/culture, domination/submission and hetero/homosexuality. Sexuality is not purely natural, biological or instinctual, but is profoundly affected by cultural interpretations, socialization into gendered positions of masculinity and femininity and the power relations that correspond to these positions. The boundaries between sex and gender are blurred. Theorists like Susan Bordo (1993) and Moria Gatens (1996) elucidate the neglect of the body as a product of dualistic thought that divides human experience into body and mind. 'The female body becomes a metaphor for the corporeal pole of this dualism, representing nature, emotionality, irrationality and sensuality. Images of the dangerous, appetitive female body, ruled precariously by her emotions, stand in contrast to the masterful, masculine will, the locus of social power, rationality and self-control' (Davis 1997: 5).

Sexual politics

What are 'sexual politics'? Aristotle's view is that relations are political when one rules and another is ruled, when relations are grounded on inequalities of power and status. Aristotle believed that one demonstration of a man's courage is his command over a woman, whose courage is exhibited in her obedience. In 1969, Kate Millett's *Sexual Politics* explained how women are subordinated by control of their sexuality. Feminist challenges in the 1960s and 1970s, particularly those from socialist or Marxist views exposed splits between private and public, home and work, the needs of capitalism and labour, of patriarchy and domestic labour, affirming that 'the personal is political'. Consciousness-raising groups helped women to understand their sexuality and oppression. Relationships that are political are marked by inequalities of wealth, power and skill. Who controls is a key issue in human relations (Rothenberg 1984), from a boss firing someone to friends deciding which film to see. Gendered power differences generally are the most extreme in traditional families where male dominance accompanies economic privilege and female dependence strengthens her subordination, regardless of a woman's participation in the paid workforce.

To talk of sexual politics is to say two things. First, that sexual relations are influenced by the inequalities of power and privilege that divide women and men in their daily lives. The historical status of women and children in men's proprietorial attitudes are most obviously legitimized in marital rape exemption clauses (Kelly 1988). The greater a man's perceived right to sexual access, the more likely it is that he will consider some aggression as legitimate. Second, that relationships of any sort that use gender as a qualifier in situations where it is not relevant to do so are marred by the inequalities and advantages that accrue to men because of their sex. Men assume sexual access to women by their approach or remarks. Some men view sex as an entitlement, justified by 'uncontrollable instincts'. Men often sexualize all relationships with women in an attempt to control them.

To overcome the inference that biology is destiny, feminists drew a distinction between sex as biological and gender as culturally constructed. This was an important stage in feminist thought in order to counter biological determinist assertions that gender was as natural as sex. More recently, feminists have questioned this distinction. Once the invariability of sex is contested, then the possibility of sex being culturally constructed as well as gender is real. It does not make sense to define gender as the cultural interpretation of sex if sex itself is a gendered category (Butler 1990). When Simone de Beauvoir writes, 'One is not born, but rather becomes, a woman' (1975: 295), she is not only referring to the passive imposition of the construction of gender, but to the active transformative aspect of being an agent. Gender identity is a relationship between sex, gender, sexual practice and desire. Judith

Butler (1990, 1993, 1997) provides a radical refusal of gender difference, arguing that distinctions between female or male bodies are social artifacts. We appropriate cultural prescriptions on sex. Butler gives examples of 'gender trouble' (1990) represented by Madonna, female body-builders or male transvestites.

Sexual liberation

Sexuality for feminists can be a pleasurable fulfilment of agency, an awkward repression, an indifference or a violent humiliation. Sexual liberation can be understood 'as the struggle to recognize the pleasure of multiple sexualities' (Kemp and Squires 1997: 318). The contraceptive pill radically altered women's sex lives, from swinging single women to women with many children. 'The sexual revolution brought about an unprecedented cultural sea change' in women's lives (Viney 1996: 94). It altered sexual behaviour and attitudes to what was permissible. ' "Sex" was the new gate-way to freedom and equality, the way to establish one's individual identity' (1996: 94). Women, wanting to be autonomous sexual persons, found that men were delighted with their new sexual assertiveness and availability, but in the climate of permissiveness, an emphasis on physicality was divorced from emotional bonding. Also, sexual equality was not happening in women's economic lives. Women remained in low stratas of lower-paid work. The politicization of women and gay men during this time contributed significantly to the battle against sexism and heterosexism.

Celebrating diverse sexualities is part of the struggle to combat anxieties about sexuality which accompany homophobia and violence against women. Lynne Segal (1994) argues that a central reason why left and feminist radicals need to revive their enthusiasm for sexual liberation is because the political and religious right continue to oppose it. Certainly trends indicate a decline in men's control over women's sexuality. Women's sexual autonomy, fertility rights and knowledge about their body enhances the possibilities for responsible pleasure. Sexual pleasure is a significant expression of moral agency. The conditions for equal agency lie in the fashioning of 'new concepts and practices of gender based upon the mutual recognition of similarities and differences between women and men' (1994: 318).

Cybersex, where people live out their fantasies through communicating with another on screen, or observe others participating in sexual activities, allows for interactions that do not fit traditional gender hierarchies. Anonymity permits pretence, fantasy, imaginative exchanges. However, simulation is a poor substitute for reality. Some cybercontacts arrange to meet. The reality of meeting cyberpartners often is shocking. The person they thought was a young slender, long-legged black woman may be an obese old white man. Already, dangerous liaisons have resulted with innocent curious schoolchildren meeting paedophiles.

Sexual difference and embodiment

The body is important to feminists in the struggle to gain fertility control (Dreifus 1978), in critiques of patriarchal power relations (Firestone 1970; Mitchell 1971), and in critiques of scientific and philosophic dualism that see the female body as needing to be tamed and controlled by disembodied objective male scientists who view menstruation, lactation, PMT, menopause and female passion as dangerous, unruly, emotionally precarious and closely tied to nature (Keller 1985). Ideal body image as projected by fashion models results in anorexia nervosa and bulimia as women, girls and increasing numbers of men strive for culturally desired appearances. Women's experiences with the body are well documented in terms of beauty (Bartky 1990), fitness (Radner 1995), eating disorders (Bordo 1993) and cosmetic surgery 'rage' (Davis 1995; Wolf 1991). Feminist embodiment (Diprose 1994) encompasses dynamics between nature and culture, sex and gender, expectations and subversions.

In talking of the 'female feminist subject' who is confronted by multiple differences of class, race, lifestyle and sexual preference, Rosi Braidotti places 'sexual difference as positivity' (1993: 3) as a central strategy to fight for the equality of the sexes. 'Embodied subjectivity' is central to a feminist theory of **sexual difference**. What is at stake is desire, 'the desire to become and to speak as female feminist subjects. . . . What is being empowered is women's entitlement to speak' (1993: 6). It is not the content of women's utterances that is paramount but their entitlements, not a model of becoming but women's desire to become. Desire is not merely libidinal, but ontological, the desire to be. For Braidotti, 'the redefinition of the female feminist subject starts with the revaluation of the bodily roots of subjectivity' (1993: 6). The foremost

location is one's own embodiment, 'a starting point for the epistemological side of the "politics of location"' (1993: 7). The embodied
subject marks the overlapping points 'between the physical, the
symbolic and the sociological' (1993: 7).

While 'woman' as female sexed subject identifies with cultural
understandings of gender, the starting point of feminist consciousness is a resistance, a becoming. Teresa De Lauretis (1990)
defines this recognition between Woman and real women as the
recognition of an 'essential difference' between representation
(Woman as cultural image) and experience (real women as agents
of change). Sexual difference refers to differences among women
and within each woman. Part of embodiment is the physical expression of sexuality. Embodied sexuality is ethical in involving
agency, choice and responsibility to others.

Lesbian sexuality

Some women have always felt attracted to other women, other
women are lesbians as a political position in fearing men's inability to participate in a relationship of equality. Adrienne Rich (1980)
talks of a '**lesbian continuum**' that includes the range of 'woman-
identified experiences', the different forms of primary intensity
between women that include the sharing of a rich inner life, bonding against male oppression, and giving and receiving practical and
political support as well as sensual and sexual experiences. Her
rationale is that the term 'lesbian' has been limited to clinical
associations, and that in setting apart female friendship from the
erotic, the erotic itself is limited. 'Woman-identification' can be
a source of energy that the ideological pressure on 'compulsory
heterosexuality' stultifies. Robyn Rowland (1996) acknowledges the
value of Rich's 'continuum' but suggests that it does not adequately
deal with women who are heterosexual. Instead she refers to the
usefulness of Janice Raymond's (1986) work on passionate friendships between women that are not necessarily genital or erotic.
Emotional bonding between women affirms their importance to
each other. Sarah Hoagland (1988) rejects traditional feminine
virtues of self-sacrifice but endorses 'attending' as the basis for
a lesbian ethics that is sensitive to women's needs and aware of
lesbians' moral agency under conditions of oppression.

Controversially, Sheila Jeffreys (1990) argues that heterosexual
desire is founded on the ideology of difference where otherness

and power differentials are eroticized. In same-sex relationships otherness emerges through age, race, class, sadomasochism or roles. Jeffreys's argument is that when lesbians and men eroticize differences in control, they experience heterosexual desire. Jeffreys contends that the demolition of this desire is necessary for women's liberation and she presents homosexual desire as the way forward – the eroticizing of sameness of power, equality and mutuality. In a society that was not founded on the subordination of women, homosexual desire as she has defined it can fit into an opposite-sex relationship, but she insists that it is the 'eroticized power difference' which 'provides the excitement of heterosexuality today' (1992: 487). Heterosexual feminists challenge any assumed inevitability of eroticized power differences.

During the mid-1980s, **sadomasochism** (sm) emerged strongly in the lesbian community. Those opposed to sm were defined as anti-sex. Lesbian pro-sex sm advocates accused the 'vanilla' section of the lesbian community of being 'lesbian police'. Discourse is revealing. Sm's presentation of itself as 'tops' and 'bottoms' rather than as 'sadists' and 'masochists', 'belies the actual violence inherent in sm discourse and practice' (Lewis and Adler 1994: 435). In sm, physical or emotional pain is encouraged as part of the sexual experience. Some claim 'that by enacting fantasies of what we most fear, the desired goal of self-knowledge could be attained' (1994: 435). Typical gadgets used in sm are chains, leather, belts, slavery imagery, harnesses and white flimsy frocks.

Two dominant themes of signification in lesbian erotic fiction are penetration and anonymity. The 'dramatic increase in fucking and violent sex, heretofore associated with heterosexual sexual practice, is accompanied by the displacement of sex from nurturing, sisterly relationships to isolated and casual sexual encounters' (Lewis and Adler 1994: 435). 'Good' sex is kinky, risqué, penetrative, 'bad' sex is gentle and clitoral-fixated. Reina Lewis and Karen Adler (1994: 435) comment that the thrill of the unknown, the separation of the sexual from the emotional and political lives of some lesbians, the disregard for a commitment beyond the sexual encounter were part of the criticisms by feminists of men in the early Women's Liberation Movement. As Jews, these authors find it disturbing that the playing out of Nazi and slave roles is considered as therapeutic. An understanding of domination and exploitation should not disregard place and history. Given the emphasis in feminist ethics on nurture and minimizing hurt, sm is difficult to justify.

Queer transgressions

Queer theory developed in response to 'the pathologization of same-sex desire' and gives gay activists and queer culture a voice (Davis 1997: 13). **Queer politics** celebrates diversity. It addresses the 'discursive limits of sex' (Butler 1993). Queer defines strategies, attitudes, references to other identities and new self-understandings. It radically questions cultural norms relating to gender, reproductive sexuality and the family. Some lesbians are particularly attracted to queer as a rebellion against a prescriptive feminism that leads them to feel disenfranchised from lesbian feminism. Identity politics promotes equal representation and access to resources, but some lesbians feel that the political identification of lesbianism obscures lesbianism as a sexual identity (Smyth 1993). For some, the threat of censorship of sado-masochist practices sits unwelcomed in 'a growing need to discuss desire, fantasies and sexual practices without being policed or labelled "post-feminist"' (1993: 38).

Queer politics sits uneasily within feminism. Feminist politics are rooted in humanism's liberatory project. Identity politics of race, class and sexual differences sometimes is divisive in solely concentrating on lived experiences of oppression without contextualizing the broader picture. An avoidance of the potential divisiveness is possible when feminists theorize the structural interrelationships between oppressions. In this context, Mary McIntosh (1993) explains the rooting of queer theory in the deconstructiveness of categories and subjectivities. Theorists of the body like Elspeth Probyn (1992) and Elizabeth Grosz (1996) embrace queer theory as a radical approach to rethinking feminist body theory and of developing alternative politics as creative subversion rather than identity politics. Politics become 'performative' (Butler 1997), and 'the body takes on a central role in the transgressive aesthetic of performance and display' (Davis 1997: 13). Queer resists, it refuses labels, pathologies and moralities. It messes normality.

Queer sexuality is deliberately transgressive. Transgressive acts encompass heterosexuality for bisexuals as well as certain lesbian and gay acts. Its transgressive nature is directed 'against the stifling norms of political correctness, radical feminist separatism and binary oppositions' (Wilson 1993: 107). However, experimental kinky sexual acts that feel transgressive are not politically subversive. Violating sexual norms may be personally liberating, but as Elizabeth Wilson argues (1993), it cannot deal with systematic or structural oppressions. Trespassing makes an existential statement and creates distance from the dominant culture. But unless there is a strategy, transgression ends in mere posturing rather than in transformation. Queer politics embraces a 'defiantly perverted and pluralistic alliance of lesbians and gays and bisexuals, which denounces prescriptive heterosexuality and orthodoxies of feminist, lesbian, and gay activism' (Lewis and Adler 1994: 434). This positioning seems 'to undermine the basis for an engagement with feminism, replacing as it does a collective gender-based politics with aestheticized individual assertions of identity politics' (Kemp and Squires 1997: 318). Hence the broad feminist project of collective liberation is lost, and an agency that is solely self-directed loses a feminist ethical concern with selves-in-relationships.

Redefining heterosexuality

During the 1970s and 1980s lesbian radical feminism offered powerful critiques of the restrictiveness of heterosexuality and motherhood. During this time, many feminists decided to stay childfree and/or to be 'politically correct woman-loving' (Rowland 1996: 79). Rowland maintains that at a positive level lesbian identity was affirmed. On the negative side, libertarian claims of normalcy of practices like sm are based on relations of dominance and submission. To replicate male-defined relations 'within purportedly woman-loving relationships cannot hope to create a sexuality empowering women with dignity' (1996: 80). Dignity, autonomy and agency are fundamental to a feminist ethics of sexuality.

Similarly, Eva Feder Kittay argues that partners of any sex engaging in sado-masochistic sex that is mutually desired and not merely consented to, 'may hurt one another by engaging in physically painful or psychologically humiliating behaviour, without causing harm to one another' (1984: 153). Nevertheless, she questions why persons might desire to be humiliated or pained in sexual role-playing. If they believe themselves unworthy of love and can only attain sexual release when they imagine they are being punished, 'this masochistic role may serve to reinforce their lack of self-respect and self-esteem through their sexually demeaning behaviour' (1984: 154). For others, their partner's humiliation whets sexual appetite. Sadism that intends to harm as well as hurt is morally objectionable.

Radical feminists like Andrea Dworkin (1981) argue that heterosexuality is at the root of male supremacy and women's subordination and violence is central to women's objectification. Dworkin (1997) explains the context in which she sees men as the enemy who want to conquer women by force. Growing up as a Jewish child in the wake of the Holocaust, she was raped at nine, worked as a prostitute and married a man who beat her severely. Shame dominated her. Male philosopher Harry Brod (in Levin and Brod 1998) criticizes heterosexual privilege and argues that discrimination or hierarchical power relationships based on sexual orientation are unjustified. Alison Assiter responds amusingly that 'real penises, most of the time, are rather soft, tender and squashy. Why should these appendages attached to real men who can often be loving, caring and tender, symbolize violence' (1989: 65)? While many women suffer traumatic heterosexual abuse, 'viewing heterosexuality as simply a manifestation of male power' is problematic 'in that it encouraged all women to identify themselves as the victim of all men, and risked making speech about sexual pleasure taboo' (Kemp and Squires 1997: 317).

Heterosexual feminists redefine their sexuality so that for women who enjoy sex with a man, intercourse is not degrading and penetration is not intrusive. Feminists who have sons are challenged in their views of living in patriarchal society, knowing that men also suffer because of the constraints traditional masculinity imposes on them. Heterosexual feminists have changed practices of mothering as well as expectations of fathering. Likewise, they have altered the institution of marriage, legal and de facto, rejecting cultural role expectations of 'wife' and maintaining a strong independent separate identity that allows for growth and interest outside of that particular relationship. Feminists aim for an equitable power distribution in domestic labour and childcare if there are children, emotional support, economic independence and contribution. Within healthy feminist heterosexual relationships, sexuality sits alongside of emotional support and friendship. Partners respect other networks of intimacy and closeness. Both heterosexual and lesbian feminists can view 'the politics of intimacy' as a site of resistance and change that enriches our understanding of the personal as political (Rowland 1996: 86). Feminism is about critique and the articulation of anticipatory visions of new kinds of society with feminist ethics and politics as its base. 'Part of that vision must include healthy loving relationships with men, or there is no point in being part of a social movement for change' (1996: 81).

Pleasure and danger

Sexuality often contradicts. Carole Vance points to tensions where sexuality can be a site 'of restriction, repression, and danger', but also 'a domain of exploration, pleasure, and agency' (1992: 1). A sole focus on pleasure and gratification ignores the patriarchal structures in which women act, yet to speak only of sexual violence and oppression ignores women's positive experiences of agency and enjoyment. Some theorists concentrate on the dangers of sexuality, the violence, brutality and coercion of rape, incest, sexual harassment and exploitation, others see 'the positive possibilities of sexuality – explorations of the body, curiosity, intimacy, sensuality, adventure, excitement, human connection' as sustaining energy (1992: 1). Most people have sexual experiences that are pleasurable and immensely satisfying, and others that are less satisfying, some have humiliating or oppressive experiences. Pleasure and displeasure sit alongside desire, fantasy and reality. Vance maintains that feminists have exposed the violence of many sexual practices, but the anti-pornography ideology introduces new forms of shaming. If sexual desire is coded as male, women wonder about their desire and sexual agency. Women who are ignorant about their bodies, or have been socialized into repression and fear about sensuality, are particularly vulnerable to feeling shame when they experience strong desire. Feminists support sexual 'pleasure as life-affirming, empowering, desirous of human connection' (1992: 24) and vital to women as sexual subjects.

The liberal model of marriage contract presents a stumbling block. It instils the notion that a husband provides protection and access to property and, in exchange, the wife provides sexual, emotional and domestic services. This entails 'her complicity in denying her sexuality' (Coltheart 1986: 121). Hence, the urgent need to reinstate the integrity of pleasure. Lenore Coltheart draws on the motif of French theorists (Marks and de Courtivron 1981), *jouissance*, as 'a desire which is the counterpoint of desire to acquire', curious and delightful play, the learning with our lives as the way 'to burst the bonds of liberal desire' (1986: 121) and express full agency as a free, equal citizen. Free sexual agency requires consent.

Robin West questions the assumption 'that whatever is non-coercive is morally non-problematic' (1995: 55). Consensual sex is harmful when it shares in the attributes of non-consensual sex. Her example is those women who trade sex for something they value like keeping the peace, preventing violence, economic dependency, male protection. Unpleasurable sex sustains injury to selfhood, self-assertiveness, self-possession, bodily integrity and autonomy. When these harms are multiplied over years or an entire adulthood, the harm is profound, even though not fully grasped. Women are expected to provide sexual services, so these harms go unnoticed because the sex appears consensual. West's claim is that rape, domestic violence and violent sex have been theorized, but 'the harms that might be caused by consensual sexuality' (1995: 54) have not been articulated.

Objectification of women

Sexualized violence

Objectification is a prerequisite for violence. Much of the indoctrination in military training centres around depersonalizing the 'enemy' as an object of war, thus a 'legitimate target'. What is different about this 'objectification and the objectification of women is that the latter is sexualized' (Jeffreys 1992: 465). An example is throat rape where men believe they can deep-thrust to the bottom of a woman's throat. The woman suffers pain yet pornography portrays her as loving it. 'He could kill me with his cock. . . . He didn't need a gun in his hand' (Dworkin 1988: 238). The tragedy is that 'pornography makes sexism sexy' (MacKinnon 1987b: 171) and it is primarily women who are objectified as sexual symbols.

What constitutes the major site of women's oppression is a key disagreement. Radical feminists like Catherine MacKinnon see sexuality as occupying this position, because a male-dominated sexuality is central to matters of vital importance to women like abortion, contraception, domestic battery, sexual abuse of children, genital mutilation, rape, incest, sexual harassment, sterilization abuse, unnecessary caesareans or hysterectomies and pornography. Liz Kelly suggests that male control of women's sexuality is a key factor in women's oppression and that sexuality is based on men's experiences of legitimated use of coercion within heterosexual encounters (1988: 20).

Many black feminists and feminists of colour dispute this view of oppression, arguing that while sexuality is important, other forms of inequality may be primary for certain groups of women. Tracey Gardner (1994) suggests that the connections between pornography and racism capitalize on the history and myths that oppress people of colour. American slavery relied on the denial of the humanity of black persons, undermining their sense of family and nationhood. 'Much of this was achieved through the sexual exploitation, brutalization, and degradation of the enslaved people' (1994: 172). Sexual and racial oppression are inseparable. White men exploited black women while protecting white women from black men. Patricia Hill Collins suggests that in pornography, the image of black women is almost consistently one featuring them enslaved, breaking from chains, whereas Asian women are depicted being tortured (1993: 99).

Most feminists agree that female genital mutilation (FGM) is a form of sexual violence. The idea that it is culturally specific and should be accepted is troublesome. It is widely practised in Africa and the Middle East and in areas as diverse as Brazil, El Salvador, Malaysia, Pakistan and in the Australian and United Kingdom communities of Muslims. Official World Health Organisation figures for FGM is more than 75 million (Viney 1996: 193), but unofficial figures put it higher at 130 million (Neustatter 1998: 14). There are different degrees. Circumcision, or incision, removes the hood and tip of the clitoris; clitoridectomy, or excision, removes the clitoris and all or part of the labia minora and part of the labia majora; infibulation removes the clitoris, the labia minora and majora and pulls the scraped side of the vulva together across the vagina, securing it with thorns or sewing it, leaving a small gap for urine and menstrual flow. Women must be cut open for intercourse and childbirth, then may be sewn up again. An aim is to guarantee virginity and fidelity. About 80 per cent of cases involve infibulation (Neustatter 1998: 14).

Westernized women who are not virgins (or women who have been sexually abused) have a hymen reconstructed so that they appear as virgins if they marry in their community. The fear is that if there is not a bloody show on the sheets on their wedding night, their families will be ashamed and they risk violence or banishment. Some medical practitioners consider this practice unethical in colluding with deceit and confirming sexual inequality. Others justify it on the grounds that it minimizes women's suffering or even the 'cleansing' murders that happen in some cultures if the woman is not a virgin.

Case study. Responding to female circumcision

A Kenyan National Women's Group committed to ending FGM has begun a programme called 'Circumcision Through Word'. This brings young women together in seclusion to learn traditional teachings like roles of young women and mothers, as well as personal health, reproduction, hygiene, communication, self-esteem, peer pressure. Instead of the isolated hut with pain and tears, the emphasis is on community, song, dancing and feasting.

Somalian-born Waris Dirie is one of the world's top models. She is also a United Nations 'goodwill ambassador' with a mission to end FGM. As a five-year-old she was circumcised, cutting 'everything that God gave me to enjoy being a woman . . . done to give men enjoyment at our expense' (in Neustatter 1998: 14–15). Despite her enormous success, photographed for *Allure, Elle* and *Vogue* magazines and cosmetic company Revlon, she writes, 'I still feel helpless and desperate about my body' (1998: 15). Dirie is attempting to make sense of her experience by actively campaigning to end FGM.

Box 5.1 Violence against women

Violence permeates sexual politics. Women in pornography are often victims of child sexual abuse. 'Some studies show that 65–75 per cent of the current population in prostitution and pornography have been abused as children, usually in the home' (Dworkin and MacKinnon 1993: 80). These children run away from the abuse to cities where their vulnerability means they are picked up by pimps, raped, beaten, drugged and forced into prostitution or pornography to survive. Consider the different case of a woman in an Orthodox Jewish community in 1998. An Israeli married woman with children was raped by three men after she left a Jewish ritual bath. She told her husband who is a descendant of the Jewish Temple priests. He sought advice from other rabbis. Despite the couple's desire to stay together, they were ordered to divorce, as she was now 'unclean'. If the husband had said to his wife, 'I don't believe you', the command may have been overruled. The couple sought a rabbi to find a loophole. Women's groups are outraged at the lack of support for the woman, a victim, and that the entire tragedy was dependent on the husband's assessment of belief of his spouse.

What is at stake in all forms of sexualized violence is the violation of women's will and autonomy. Kelly defines sexual violence to include '*any physical, visual, verbal or sexual act that is experienced by the woman or girl, at the time or later, as a threat, invasion or assault, that has the effect of hurting her or degrading her and/or takes away her ability to control intimate contact*' (1988: 42). At the core of gender domination lies a subjugation of woman by man, a logic of domination, indifferent to personal desire. Domination 'is a twisting of the bonds of love' (Benjamin 1990: 219), subjugating the other. Gay men who eroticize sexual domination and submission 'constitute a serious obstacle to women's liberation' (Jeffreys 1992: 484). Campaigns of zero tolerance expose and condemn men's use of violence against women.

Pornography

The only professions where women earn more money than men are modelling and prostitution where 'women's economic value is determined largely by sexual value: how much the woman's body is worth in the marketplace as a commodity' (Dworkin and MacKinnon 1993: 81). Pornography is a massive industry. Pornography derives from the Greek roots *porne*, meaning 'sexual slave' or 'harlot', and *graphos*, meaning 'description of'. Thus, 'pornography means a description of sexual slavery or the purchase of sex from women' (Carse 1995: 159). The 'sexual revolution' of the 1960s 'derepressed' pornography (Jeffreys 1990). The pornographic industry exploded in the late 1960s and early 1970s, becoming increasingly explicit, concerned with sm and brutal in its portrayal of women. While some define pornography as 'explicit sexual materials intended to arouse the reader or viewer sexually' (Garry 1984: 313), others add 'the exposure of genitals with abuse or degradation in a manner that appears to endorse, condone, or encourage such behaviour' (Russell 1993: 2–3).

Pornography is the explicit representation of sexual behaviour that degrades, humiliates or harms persons (usually women) for the sexual gratification of other persons (usually men). It is intentionally injurious, hurtful, coercive or violent and disregards another's desires by treating them as a sex object. Much pornography depicts the imbalanced power of the master–slave paradigm. Typically it involves images of women as commodities, enjoying pain, humiliation or rape, being tied up, cut, mutilated, bruised, in postures of servility, presented in scenarios of degradation, injury, torture, filth, inferiority, bleeding, reduced to body parts, penetrated by objects or animals and sexually objectified (MacKinnon 1987b: 176; 1993: 300).

Pornography differs from the erotic where the expression of sexual interest is an appropriate response. The erotic is sensuous rather than crude and does 'not sexualize coercion, violence, or denigration' (Carse 1995: 159). While sexually explicit, **erotica** presumes equality. It is 'sexually suggestive or arousing material that is free of sexism, racism, and homophobia, and respectful of all human beings and animals portrayed' (Russell 1993: 3). Every society 'makes some distinction between a legitimate and an illegitimate sexuality' (Kittay 1984: 149) and the erotic as opposed to the pornographic reflects this distinction. Feminists dispute the view that, while tasteless and debased, the vicarious enjoyment of pornographic representations of eroticized domination is harmless (Carse 1995: 163; Kittay 1984: 171).

The ethically objectionable nature of pornography 'is its abusive and degrading portrayal of females and female sexuality, *not* its sexual content or explicitness' (Russell 1993: 4). What makes a work pornographic is not simply a representation of degrading or abusive sex, but its approval of sexual behaviour that is immoral, by which Helen Longino means it 'physically or psychologically violates the personhood of one of the participants' (1994: 155). Pornography endorses degradation by devaluing or ignoring the desires of a participant. 'Abusive' sexual acts are derogatory, demeaning, contemptuous, damaging, brutal, cruel, exploitative, painful, or violent, and 'degrading' acts are humiliating, insulting and disrespectful (Russell 1993: 3). Pornography undermines ethical agency.

Eroticized subordination of women

Feminists who gained liberation from the 1960s were outraged that what constituted sex under male supremacy was, as Sheila Jeffreys expresses it, 'the eroticized subordination of women' (1992: 462). It made inequality appear sexy 'and the sexiness of this inequality was the grease that oiled the machinery of male supremacy' (1992: 462). Jeffreys points particularly to the depiction of male violence against women as pleasurable to men. Women raped, gagged, bound, tortured are shown to love it. Pornography is a lie. Most women do not ecstatically relinquish sexual self-determination. Pornography implies the inferiority of women. Dworkin describes the ideology of pornography as implied male superiority, of the natural right of the male to physically possess women, that sex is 'conquest and possession of the female', that the use of the female body is men's prerogative, that 'the sexual will of men properly and naturally defines the parameters of women's sexual being' (1981: 203).

Likewise, MacKinnon explains the systematic abuse women suffer in pornography which 'sexualizes rape, battery, sexual harassment, prostitution, and child sexual abuse; it thereby celebrates, promotes, authorizes, and legitimizes them. More generally, it eroticizes the dominance and submission that is the dynamic common to them all' (1993: 297). Male aggression is equated with sexual pleasure and sexualized subordination with feminine pleasure. Dominance and submission are the ruling codes. MacKinnon argues that 'in pornography, the violence *is* the sex. . . . If there is no inequality, no violation, no dominance, no force, there is no sexual arousal' (1984: 343). Male dominance, she explains, is so pervasive that the harm of pornography as an act of supremacy is hard to discern because we 'live in the world pornography creates' (1984: 335). Pornography institutionalizes male sexual supremacy which creates an eroticized gendered inequality (MacKinnon 1987b: 172) as if women's desire is solely to be violated and possessed, men to violate and possess. Pornography plays a large part in constituting the meaning of sexuality (MacKinnon 1993: 298).

Pornography as sex discrimination

Pornography focuses on mechanistic, coercive, anonymous sex emphasizing breasts and genitals at the expense of intimate, affectionate consensual sensuality. However, self-proclaimed 'pro-sex feminists' refer to compassionate contact as 'vanilla sex' and suggest it idealizes femininity as another form of objectification (Vance 1992). They suggest that anti-pornography campaigns invite reactionary alliances. By seeking state authority to bar pornography, censorship could extend to sex education, erotica, lesbian and gay literature. Other feminists suggest that anti-pornography movements represent the embodiment of caring, that 'the moral message is that the unit of responsibility and care – that group with whom one has sexual or sensual relations – must be based on tenderness, not violence; equality, not hierarchy' (Katzenstein and Laitin

1987: 271). Wendy Brown (1995) criticizes MacKinnon's ideas for being relentlessly dualistic as subject/object, person/thing, dominant/subordinate; understating other differentials like race; sexualizing and totalizing subjectivities; and ignoring lesbian sexuality.

The anti-pornography lobby see pornography to be the root cause of women's oppression, as objects of aggressive male sexuality. Others see it 'as being simultaneously symptom and cause' (Kittay 1984: 145). As symptom it reflects sexual politics, as cause direct correlations have been documented between exposure to violent images and aggressive actions toward women. The anti-pornography cause gathered momentum when feminists amassed evidence of the ways in which pornography encouraged men to abuse women. Women gave accounts of how pornography was implicated in their torture or was their husbands' textbook for sexual abuse. Some men would act out a scene they had read in a magazine. One woman was forcibly stripped and gagged and her husband helped a German Shepherd dog to rape her. Others took their wives to watch porn with a prostitute then insisted their wives act out the scenes with the prostitute. Numerous women are filmed by husbands, pimps, clients, stepbrothers, not knowing how the film is used.

In 1983, on the invitation of the City of Minneapolis, Andrea Dworkin and Catherine MacKinnon proposed a civic human rights ordinance that made pornography a justifiable act of sex discrimination. They define pornography 'as a practice of sex discrimination, a violation of women's civil rights, the opposite of sexual equality' (1993: 300). The ordinance declares that pornography fosters contempt for women, harming opportunities for equality in employment, education and public service. The aim of the ordinance is to classify pornographic speech as a civil rights violation, hence the production, sale, display or distribution of pornographic materials would be civilly actionable. Defamation 'captures the relation between pornographer, consumer, and women' (Davies 1988: 134). Pornography lies about women's sexuality, desire, dignity and personhood. Women fear rape and assault, few are masochistic by nature or are singularly driven by carnal lust.

The harm of pornography is 'the harm of the civil inequality of the sexes made invisible as harm because it has become accepted as the sex difference' (MacKinnon 1987b: 178). The ordinance facilitates individual women harmed by pornography to take action and collect damages. This includes those who are coerced into being part of a pornographic production, anyone made to watch it, assaulted as a result of pornography or defamed. The point was to make those who profit accountable to those who are injured. Sex equality is meaningless if women's damage, pain and enforced inferiority outweighs the pleasure and profits of pornographic producers and consumers. The law was passed by the council but vetoed by the mayor, a sequence repeated in other cities like Indianapolis and Cambridge, Massachusetts. Legal actions against violent images of women are based in civil rights claims to equality, not in claims of obscenity.

Pornographic harms

Feminists object to pornography when it degrades people. Pornography is morally objectionable when it 'exemplifies and recommends behaviour that violates the moral principle to respect persons' (Garry 1984: 314). Pornographic materials affront the dignity of women who 'are viewed as objects, dehumanized and depersonalized instruments for the satisfaction of men's sexual desires and whims' (Carse 1995: 166). Individual women are signifiers of sexual desire, dehumanizing the particular woman and by implication, objectifying all women (Davies 1988: 138). Subjectivity is lost and all women become sexual objects. When the depiction of violent sexuality causes harm, pornography is unacceptable. Pornography legitimizes the eroticization of violence, yet if 'it constitutes even a remote cause of violent, nonconsensual, nondesired sex, the "rights" of such adherents to acquire pornographic products deemed important for their sexual gratification must take second place' (Katzenstein and Laitin 1987: 274). Racist cartoons may give pleasure to some, 'but such rights to pleasure must surely be subordinated to the more fundamental right to be free from serious harm' (1987: 275).

Feminists shift the emphasis from pornography's offence to its harm. MacKinnon talks of the direct causality of exposure to pornography to produce harm through increasing an inability to distinguish sex from violence; the willingness of men to aggress against women; their hostility; propensity to condone rape or to predict they would force sex on a woman if they could get away with it (1993: 302). It is implicated in crimes against women, desensitizing men to rape. Tolerance to pornographic representations fosters a climate for the actual abuse of women. Jacqueline Davies evaluates pornography in terms of 'the harm principle, which states that the liberty of the individual may legitimately be limited only when it causes direct harm to other individuals' (1988: 127). A liberal privileging of free expression is wrong when pornography causes sexual assault. 'The nuisance argument counts something like a right to privacy as vulnerable to harm and therefore to be accorded protection' (1988: 129). Nuisance arguments require caution. Pornography is not a private fantasy, it exists in a sexist media and influences popular conceptions of sexuality. A strong argument against pornography lies in the threat argument which considers the harm suffered to be considerably more than a nuisance.

Harm includes contempt. What is wrong with pornography is not just the harm to the individual women being used as objects, but the general view of women it reflects (Carse 1995: 165). Images of women bound, beaten, gagged, spreadeagled, raped and serving men sexually, objectify and subordinate women in the attainment of men's ends. The eroticization of male dominance affects all women. Sexual acts are illegitimate when they harm another person or obtain pleasure at someone's expense (Kittay 1984: 150). This reiterates the Kantian imperative not to treat persons as means only, but as ends. Not all depictions of sexuality are pornographic or illegitimate, such as news coverage, films exploring sexual abuse and incest, educational materials, or feminist analyses of media representations of sexy women. What is morally reprehensible is the immorality of using another person. Kittay (1984: 159) suggests that this moral objection covers the image as representative of a group like all women, all blacks, all whores, all black women. 'Pornography lies explicitly about women's sexuality, and through such lies fosters more lies about our humanity, our dignity, and our personhood' (Longino 1994: 156).

What's wrong with being a sex object?

Feminists are liberated women who are comfortable with their bodies and free about their sexuality. So, is there anything wrong with being a sex object, being treated as a sex object or treating someone as a sex object? Ann Garry (1984) says that even if she thinks that sex is healthy, she would object to being treated *only* as a sex object in the same way she would object to be treated only as a cookie-maker or a tennis partner. She explains the connection between losing respect for a woman and treating her as a sex object in terms of the double standard of sexual behaviour where all men are assumed to be sexually active but where some women are classified as pure, delicate, fragile, refined and deserving of respect and others have fallen off the moral pedestal and can be used. Garry writes, 'one's mother, grandmother, Sunday School teacher, and usually one's wife are "good" women' (1984: 316). Classifying women as 'good' and 'bad' is unhelpful. Feminists are concerned with respect for all. All women deserve dignity and respect. Although 'bad' women are treated as sex objects, and thus not as full-fledged people, 'good' women also are not considered fully autonomous persons (1984: 317).

Linda Lemoncheck maintains that it is only when women are regarded as bodies, 'where their status as the moral equals of persons has been demeaned or degraded, that the expression "sex objectification" is correctly used' (1994: 202). The context in which one is considered a sex object is relevant. While it is appropriate to be sexually desirable and an object of sexual desire in a relationship, it is inappropriate where one is a passer-by, or where one should be treated as a business associate, stranger or client. We often find other women and men sexually attractive without acting on this inclination. The context ascertains the moral offence. When spouses are treated as mere objects rather than sexual partners, 'the sex objectifier treats the sex object as less than a moral equal, as one less deserving, not equally so, of the rights to well-being and freedom that he enjoys' (1994: 205). Objectification degrades, it lessens the status from person to object, moral equal to subordinate, diminishing or negating individual desires and interests. The person treated as a sex object is dehumanized.

Case study. Proud to be sex objects

Debi Sundahl has a double major in Women's Studies and History, was active in Marxist and feminist politics, was an advocate at a shelter for battered women and worked with women against pornography. She came out as a lesbian through this work and the awakening helped her to explore sexual taboos. She worked full-time as an erotic performer, loving being a stripper. She staged erotic performances for masturbation fantasies. Her hardest task was dealing with her feminist principles of objectification. She 'liked being a sex object, because the context was appropriate' (1994: 118). Her job was to sexually arouse. She went into burlesque where her self-respect as an erotic dancer increased. She claims 'it is a rare stripper who is not a feminist' (1994: 119) and she took the show to women-only strip events.

Nina Hartley, a trained nurse, states she is a 'feminist porno star'. She claims that a tenet of feminism is 'the *right* to sexual free expression, without being told by society (or men) what was right, wrong, good, or bad' (1994: 176). She is an exhibitionist with a cause to make sexually graphic porn. She finds her work satisfying in providing her with a safe environment to live out her fantasies; supporting her sexual growth; giving her erotic material to watch; and allowing her to celebrate her sexuality. She lives with her husband and his lover in a *ménage-à-trois*. She has 'always refused to portray rape, coercive pain-as-pleasure, woman-as-victim, domination, humiliation and other forms of nonconsensual sex' (1994: 178).

Sunny Carter's newborn son was diagnosed with a disease that would cost her more than she earned. She decided to learn to 'hook' and went shopping for appropriate clothing. After her first client she felt 'no pangs of guilt, no remorse, no shame. What I felt was smug, joyous elation' (1994: 114). She only selected professional well-paying clients who 'became my friends. I refused to deal with men who held me in low regard, those who wanted my services, yet still looked down on hookers' (1994: 116). She claims that prostitution was her 'useful tool' in providing her the money she needed to give her boy as full a life as his nine years allowed.

Can pornography be nonsexist and nondegrading?

How do feminists respond to these examples? The right to free expression is not unqualified. There is no right to incite violence or to misrepresent. Control of pornography diminishes freedom, but even if we could support the right to do as we please as long as the rights of others are respected, while pornography violates the rights of women to respect and freedom from defamation, it cannot be defended (Longino 1994: 160). The fact that a person has 'consented to be harmed, abused, or subjected to coercion does not alter the degrading character of such behaviour' (1994: 155). Garry suggests that the key to making pornography morally acceptable 'is to break the connection between sex and harm' (1984: 321). By example she cites the depiction of sexual activity that treats men and women as equal sex partners. The man would not control the circumstances, positions or acts, the woman's preferences would be considered equally. There would be no conquest, power-play or emphasis on male ejaculation. Both partners would express enjoyment. Women's pornography for lesbians would depict nonexploitative, nonviolent consensual sexuality. Why such depictions would be pornographic rather than erotic is unclear.

Many feminists believe that, 'the acceptance of pornography means the decline of feminist ethics and an abandonment of feminist politics' (Dworkin 1994: 152). Employing the political language of feminism, like choice, freedom, power, repression, is insufficient justification when subordination is eroticized 'to the point that objectification/humiliation feels basic to our sexuality' (Carola 1988: 174). Where women are portrayed 'as "tits, cunt, and ass", not as multi-faceted human beings deserving equal rights' (Russell 1993: 6) then sexual objectification depersonalizes. Objectification extends to movies, advertisements, lyrics, magazines, art, cartoons, posters, music covers. To insist on the liberal right to pornography is to miss the wider implications of power, class, race and big business. A liberal defence of freedom of expression is often a negative freedom, an absence of constraint. Realistically, the freedom of the individual as the 'unit of moral regard and blame' (Assiter 1989: 44), is the producer, writer, camera-man, consumer, the woman is the 'means' of satisfying the desires rather than an autonomous moral agent (1989: 15–16). This liberal defence 'relies on moral individualism', a self-sufficiency that interacts only contingently with others. In focusing on the fantasy object, pornography encourages a self-absorption, 'an exclusively "individualist", as opposed to an "other-directed", view of the self' (1989: 45) that is crucial to feminist ethics.

Prostitution

The view of **prostitution** as 'the oldest profession' prevails. Historically, prostitution is viewed as inevitable, a necessary evil that protects young girls from rape and shields the family from men's insatiable appetites, or as the only option for a girl or woman who is destitute and in poverty. Some societies prohibit and criminalize prostitution, punishing the prostitute. Regulationist systems legalize prostitution but make it subject to licensing and official control. Abolitionist systems eliminate regulation provided there is no overt soliciting. Generally, the prostitute is harassed, arrested, fined, but the client is left alone.

Is there a right to prostitute?

Liberals subscribe to the view that a woman has the right to prostitute herself if she chooses. Some believe that prostitution expresses women's right to sexual self-determination and equality through working for themselves. Liberals' appeal to equality and rights stress the need for decriminalization and minimal government interference in the 'private' sphere. Prostitution is seen as a business transaction of a sexual service, a contract of exchange between a buyer and seller. A prostitute can be of either sex and liberals claim that women and men should have equal opportunity to purchase or sell sexual services, regardless of colour, disability, gender.

Marxist feminists view prostitution as the exchange of the services 'a married woman provides to her husband in return for economic support' (Jaggar 1994: 104). Sexuality is a commodity, alienating and dehumanizing human capacity. Western men purchase mail-order brides from places like the Philippines, giving men 'sexual access to women's bodies in the capitalist market' (Pateman 1989: 189). Radical feminists contend that 'prostitution is the archetypal relationship of women to men' (Jaggar 1994: 106). The social function of prostitution extends 'to all men the right of unconditional sexual access to women and girls in addition to those privileges enjoyed by husbands and fathers within the institution of marriage' (Giobhe 1994: 121). Prostitution commercializes 'the sexual abuse and inequality that women suffer in the traditional family' (1994: 125). All prostitution is viewed as an assertion of dominance resulting in slavery and a violation of human rights.

The International Committee for Prostitutes' Rights (1994) drew a charter demanding changes in laws to decriminalize adult prostitution; human rights guarantees; adequate working conditions; health screening; full social benefits; regular taxes; and educational programmes to change the stigma. These prostitutes 'object to being treated as symbols of oppression and demand recognition as workers' (1994: 135). They explain that because many feminists hesitate to accept prostitution as legitimate work, they do not identify as feminist, however, many 'identify with feminist values such as independence, financial autonomy, sexual self-determination, personal strength, and female bonding' (1994: 135). Their research controversially suggests 'that fifty per cent of prostitutes were not abused' as children (1994: 137). The Committee write of the demands of the World Whores' Congress for rights to life, liberty, justice, family life, free expression, join a union, own possessions, leave a country, protection from degrading treatment, discrimination or servitude. These groups assume the validity of prostitution as legitimate sex work.

Is prostitution a human rights violation?

The distinction between prostitution as a choice and enforced prostitution was formalized in international law from the start of this century when treaties banned international traffic in persons. Later, procurement and the exploitation of prostitution was equated with slavery and an international convention was drawn up under United Nations auspices. Prostitution is regarded 'as a human rights violation only if it involves overt coercion or exploitation' (Reanda 1991: 202). Yet 'the distinction between "voluntary" and "enforced" prostitution has been increasingly difficult to sustain' (1991: 204). The element of 'choice' is problematic given that the United Nations Educational, Scientific and Cultural Organization (UNESCO) 'found that the majority of female prostitutes had been victims of incest, violence, or rape' which destroyed women's identity, transforming the 'body into a sexual item of merchandise for commercial purposes' (1991: 204). Many prostitutes cope by disassociating from their bodies or using drugs or alcohol to numb the emotional pain.

Consequently, arguments considering prostitution a coercive alienated relationship based in a denial of fundamental rights are compelling. The coercion includes a range of aspects like no money, unemployment, escape from a family situation or the clutches of a pimp. Once entered, 'prostitution results in "a state of servitude"' which is often 'the result of emotional blackmail, economic deprivation, marginalization, and loss of identity' (Reanda 1991: 205). Even the escort girls or adult male prostitutes who are not subject to a pimp 'are "unfree" in the sense that they are expected to submit to their client's wishes, often for degrading or violent sex' (1991: 205). UNESCO concludes that prostitution violates the Universal Declaration of Human Rights, Article 1, 'All human beings are born free and equal in dignity and rights', Article 4, 'No one shall be held in slavery or servitude' and Article 5, 'No one shall be subjected to torture or to cruel, inhuman or degrading treatment or punishment' (in Reanda 1991: 205).

The international traffic of girls, boys and women is particularly strong in the Asian region and in Eastern Europe. Poverty drives families to sell their children in anticipation of them returning shortly. Some do, laden with gifts, most do not. The sex industry is incorporated into the economic system of many countries. Anecdotal evidence given to human rights researchers is disturbing. One young girl was told she could go home when she had 'served' one thousand men which she did in three months. She was then told she had to make payments for the clothing, food and medicine she had received. When the brothel was raided two years later, she was still there (Rowland 1996: 78). Sex tourism is a thriving industry in Thailand, South Korea and the Philippines with tours from industrialized countries for the specific purpose of buying the sexual services of women and children in the Third World. It is also growing in Europe where poverty and few possibilities of finding work lead young women from Eastern Europe to leave their countries to search for work. Many are deceived by **traffickers** who inform the girls they can become dancers or hostesses but, on leaving their country, find themselves in slave-like conditions under the control of a profiteer.

What's wrong with prostitution?

Carole Pateman claims that 'to argue that there is something wrong with prostitution does not necessarily imply any adverse judgement on the women who engage in the work' (1989: 193). She shifts the focus to 'why men demand that women's bodies are sold as commodities in the capitalist market' (1989: 194). She answers in terms of the sexual contract, that 'prostitution is part of the exercise of the law of male sex-right, one of the ways in which men are ensured access to women's bodies' (1989: 194). While prostitutes may cheat clients or take advantage of their vulnerability, ' "prostitutes" are subject to "clients", just as "wives" are subordinate to "husbands" within the structure of marriage' (1989: 194).

Pateman describes the argument that prostitution is merely 'sex without love' as nonsense. Whereas advocates of 'free love' assume a mutual pleasure, prostitution uses a woman's body for a man's satisfaction in exchange for money. While some prostitutes enjoy their work, and some enjoy sex with their regulars, many have to endure physically repulsive or degrading acts with men for whom they feel no desire. In buying the 'sex act' men assume a patriarchal right of access to women's bodies. Women are subordinated, the man who contracts to use the services 'gains command over the use of her person and body for the duration of the prostitute contract' (1989: 203). The subject of this contract is a woman's body and sexual access to that body. Market sale of bodies is a form of 'slavery' (1989: 203–4). Prostitution is wrong because it affirms the patriarchal right of men's sex right, and subordinates women. The relationship between the body, sexuality and identity is integral. The sale of a woman's body in prostitution differs to an athlete's contract to play sport and endorse products. A woman's self is fundamentally violated in the subjection and loss of freedom. 'She is thus selling *herself* in a very real sense' (1989: 207).

Mutual recognition

In contrast to the domination and submission of the master and slave, the husband using 'his' wife as property, the client using a prostitute, the pornographer using an objectified body, Jessica Benjamin paints a lovely picture of **mutual recognition**. She describes this as an attunement of different minds and bodies. In erotic union, 'receptivity and self-expression, the sense of losing the self in the other and the sense of being truly known for oneself all coalesce' (1990: 126). We engage in mutual recognition 'in getting pleasure *with* the other and taking pleasure *in* the other' (1990: 126). Desire thus is the desire for recognition, to be appreciated and desired simultaneously. The vision of recognition is paradoxical, because the need for recognition relies on the independence of free agents. Feminist perspectives on sexual politics have a critique of sexualized power, respect the complexities of lived sexualities and retain a commitment to freedom and justice.

Summary

- Sexual relations are influenced by gendered inequalities of power and privilege.

- Sexual difference is a positive affirmation of embodiment and a strategy for the social equality of the sexes.

- When dominance is eroticized, sexual violence hurts, degrades and undermines moral agency.

- The objectification in pornography harms the person being used as a mere sexual object and makes violent, hurtful, degrading acts appear sexy.

- Prostitution affirms the patriarchal right of men's sex right and subordinates women.

Further reading

Jaggar, A. (ed.) (1994) *Living with Contradictions. Controversies in Feminist Social Ethics*, Boulder and Oxford: Westview Press.

Pateman, C. (1989) *The Sexual Contract*, Cambridge: Polity Press.

Russell, D. E. H. (ed.) (1993) *Making Violence Sexy. Feminist Views on Pornography*, Buckingham: Open University Press.

Chapter 6

Abortion

Chapter outline

Debates surrounding abortion are always complex. The chapter begins by asking what is entailed in women's right to an abortion. Abortion rights:

- affirm women's autonomy
- are part of broader reproductive freedoms
- sit alongside social responsibilities.

However, a woman's right to choose an abortion threatens a foetus's right to life. A feminist perspective on abortion responds to this ethical dilemma by incorporating:

- women's autonomous decision-making
- the moral significance of pregnancy, a foetus and birth
- the pregnant woman's physical, psychological, spiritual, economic and family circumstances.

The chapter shows how restrictive legislation leads to unsafe practices or women travelling elsewhere to procure an abortion. The idea of an abortion spectrum with varying degrees of moral responsibility is tested. A central aim of the chapter is to demonstrate how abortion can be recast from a conflict of rights to a concern with responsible caring. Rights and responsibilities are interdependent.

Moral rights to choice

One of the most vexing issues in ethics is that of abortion. Arguments typically proposed are: principles, medical, pragmatic, legal, moral (Ketting and Van Praag 1986: 155). Principled arguments relate to women's rights, the importance of freedom and non-restrictive policies. Medical arguments react to the high risks of illegal abortion practices and assist the health of women. Pragmatic arguments support the need to reduce the incidence of abortion and facilitate contraception and education. Legal reasons clarify how illegal abortions undermine law's authority. Moral debates pivot around the sanctity of life. None of these explanations are necessarily feminist.

Feminist ethics takes seriously the moral experiences of women, sexuality and reproduction. As long as crisis pregnancies occur, for whatever reason, the dilemma of abortion will exist. Feminists claim that resolving this dilemma must be made primarily by women. Women are moral agents, the entire 'world of morality, decision-making, responsibility, social accountability' is entailed in being morally autonomous, choosing, responsible persons including making decisions on abortion (Riddicks 1990: 11). Indeed, 'the abortion decision brings to the core of feminist apprehension . . . the adult questions of responsibility and choice' (Gilligan 1983: 71). This chapter shows that with regard to abortion, the dilemma lies in women's moral right to act as their own protagonists. Debates surrounding whether there is a 'right to abortion' are more complex than those surrounding rights to freedom of speech or to vote because 'when a woman considers whether to continue or abort a pregnancy, she contemplates a decision that affects both self and others and engages directly the critical moral issue of hurting' (1983: 71). If there is a 'right to abortion' it is a right of a woman to decide about her body that conflicts with the right of another to life. Do women have a right to abortion? If so, is rights discourse the best way to claim this right?

Rights discourse

Western democracies are preoccupied with how individual rights can be justly balanced with other demands within the larger social and state framework. A major shortcoming with any emphasis on liberal rights is that with political liberty as envisaged by the founding fathers of liberal democracy, rights masquerade as gender-neutral and speak in general terms and thus 'silently assumes the male body as the individual with protected rights' (Eisenstein 1991: 108). In reality, rights were meant for free, rational, property-owning men who dominate public spaces. Rights for women, considered to be emotionally suited to the 'natural' realm of the family, were derivative from their father, husband or master. The proposition that women have the right to choose to control their bodies presupposes that women are heirs to the tradition of political liberty and thus are persons of moral autonomy (Riddicks 1990: 13).

Feminist proponents of rights arguments contend that rights are useful in staking legal claims in that using the language of rights symbolically empowers women to forge a collective identity (Fox and Murphy 1992: 460) that enables them to claim rights as women. **Specificity** is an essential corrective to the assumed gender-neutrality, distinguishing difference of rights (Eisenstein 1991: 108). One of these specifications is the right to choose an abortion. The impasse that occurs when we discuss the 'rights' of a woman to choose whether or not to terminate the pregnancy and the 'rights' of the foetus to life appear insurmountable. Both sides of the argument seem to offer plausible logic – women should have control over their bodies and a being that potentially is a baby should be able to live. Is the argument as simple as this? Does rights discourse offer the best rationale for feminist ethics? Before answering these questions we need to see how rights are often part of the protection of privacy.

Privacy rights

The right to privacy is the right of an individual to be free from unwarranted government intrusion on something that is considered essentially to be a 'private choice'. Its roots lie in the right to bodily self-determination. The notion of property in one's own person parallels the idea of a natural right to own property. In a positive sense **privacy rights** affirm the importance of autonomy and uncoerced decision-making in ethical decisions, thereby protecting personal choice from arbitrary interference or state intervention. 'Control over one's body is an essential part of being an individual with needs and rights, a concept which is, in turn, the most powerful legacy of the liberal political tradition' (Petchesky 1980: 96). Privacy rights also have negative connotations as being asocial and exclusionary. The right of privacy is bound with individual autonomy and non-interference that can be interpreted as isolationist, yet it is considered a fundamental right to some legal systems.

The Supreme Court in the United States of America decided in the landmark 1973 *Roe v. Wade* case that the right to choose an abortion is a woman's private decision, that rights of privacy belong to pregnant women. This case embodies a view of society as a cluster of separate autonomous individuals. It heightens feelings of being left alone to struggle with private choice. 'The notion that abortion is an individual and private decision is itself a moral notion' (Glendon 1987: 36) preferring not only freedom of choice, but the wish to make the decision by oneself, minimizing the way that social engagement contributes to moral judgement. Privacy rights reinforce the public/private dichotomy, inferring that abortion is a private consideration rather than a crucial part of women's collective freedom as equal citizens.

Rosalind Petchesky argues strongly 'that the struggle to achieve women's reproductive freedom cannot succeed in the long run if conducted as a civil liberties struggle for individual "privacy"' (1986: viii). The power of individual privacy, that one should be left alone in decisions that affect one 'personally', is enormous. However, privacy rights express a preferred relationship between the individual and the state that contains individual's privacy and curtails the responsibilities of the state in actualizing individual rights (Eisenstein 1991: 99). The individual legal right to privacy means an individual has the right to decide on an abortion, but the state does not necessarily provide adequate means to act on the decision.

What's wrong with rights?

The slogan, 'a woman's right to choose' was the platform for feminist pro-abortion campaigns in the 1960s and 1970s. The slogan was a powerful voice for women who had no choice. This right was considered an essential part of equality rights, to have the right to control one's body. These advocates became known as '**pro-choice**' and were positioned against '**pro-life**' groups who support the foetus's right to life. These terms are misleading, because 'pro-choice' advocates also affirm life, and pro-lifers also affirm choice. Contemporary feminist perspectives are critical of the slogan. Feminists see the need for the right to abortion, but criticize arguments from rights discourse alone because they are first individualistic, and second they rely on abstract ungendered assumptions.

First, the ideological underpinning of rights discourse is individualizing, it effaces the connectedness, mutuality and reciprocity that are crucial aspects of contemporary feminist ethics (De Gama 1993: 115). The ultimate flaw of liberal rights arguments resides in their inability to cope with interdependent relationships. A position which is based on the individual rights of the woman alone inevitably appears self-centred, yet the abortion decision 'is as much about the foetus's chance of a reasonable life as the mother's willingness to care for it' (Himmelweit 1988: 49). Free choice is central to liberal individualism. In asking 'what's wrong with rights?' Elizabeth Kingdom makes three points. First, abortion is one of a number of interrelated reproductive rights that are part of women's reproductive needs of contraception, sex education, antenatal care, childcare, and the economic requirements of diet, housing, health and daily maintenance (1991: 51). Second, the slogan of choice 'accentuates the notion of a right as inhering in an individual, as the moral entitlement of an individual human being which is possessed independently of prevailing social conditions' (1991: 54). Any inference that a pregnant woman is isolated understates the impact of social factors on moral choice made in contexts of family, religion, ethnicity, class, status and life experience. Third, 'appeals to a woman's right to choose are notoriously vague' (1991: 59) in skating over complex issues of specific proposals, strategies, laws.

Second, as well as being individualistic, the rhetoric of abstract rights fails to give voice to diverse women's experiences in sex, families, parenthood, gendered relationships and reproductive technologies. The reality of pregnancy affects the status and experience of women, just as the social expectations of mothering affect women who have not given birth. Liberal adherents of equality maintain that once differential treatment of women is removed, equality follows. This assumes that there are no significant differences between men and women. For example, in one legal case, a husband is seen to have an equal right to decide on a continuation or termination of his wife's pregnancy and this treats maternity and paternity as if they are the same when clearly they are not (Krieger 1987: 53). A simplistic 'right to choose' framework is inadequate on three grounds: it is premised on abstract notions of rights assumed to apply to all; it is individualistic; and it leaves the individual as the sole moral arbiter.

Beyond a woman's right to choose to reproductive freedoms

'The idea of "a woman's right to choose" as the main principle of reproductive freedom is insufficient and problematic' (Petchesky 1980: 99; 1986: 6). The principle itself does not address how reproductive decisions should be made. Determining that a woman should decide 'does not tell us anything about the moral and social values women ought to bring to this decision; *how* they should decide' (Petchesky 1980: 100). Having a critical stance toward the liberal formulation of individual rights does not necessitate abandoning rights discourse, but it pushes it to its logical conclusion (Petchesky 1986: xiv). Democratic traditions embedded in the idea of individual choice must understand the social context to such traditions. Part of this understanding is that **special rights** take into account actual differences as being morally relevant. Special rights restore meaning to people's ordinary experiences by allowing difference to be properly acknowledged in law and institution (Kingdom 1991: 123). Women's need of the special right of an abortion should avoid individualistic connotations of liberal rights.

Alison Jaggar's early important work (1976) maintains that moral philosophic questions of if or when an abortion can be justified often dominate the socio-political questions of applying such reflections to particular women. Her views involve two principles: first, that 'the right to life . . . means the right to a full human life' (1976: 351), by which she infers requirements for complete development as a human; and second, that the ultimate decision should rest with those most affected, that 'the potential mother . . . should have the ultimate responsibility for deciding whether or not an abortion should be performed' (1976: 353). Her point is that women's right to decide is not absolute but is contingent on women's prime nurture of children. Jaggar suggests moving the focus from individual rights to fulfilling human need within broader reproductive freedoms. Reproductive rights are part of **reproductive freedoms** that affirm ideals of equality and autonomy. Given women's reproductive potential, reproductive rights ensure bodily integrity and the self-determination that is part of being equal citizens. A defence of autonomy is important given women's social position and that they are not only responsible for pregnancy but usually for the care of children. Therefore, women's input into decisions on contraception, abortion and childbearing is imperative. This defence is certainly what Jaggar proposed in 1976, that equality is rooted in individual generalized rights and autonomy in socially determined particular needs.

Petchesky's similar argument is that reproductive freedom 'is irreducibly social and individual at the same time; that is, it operates "at the core of social life" as well as within and upon women's individual bodies' (1980: 94; 1986: 2). Platforms conducted solely on women's right to choose or on individual privacy cannot incorporate this dual emphasis. Working through specificity requires untangling dominant views and articulating what is involved in unspecified abstract rights. The rights of 'a pregnant woman of colour' urges rights 'to be inclusive, indicating possible differences race, ethnicity, and class make, not only to possessing rights but also to having access to them' (Porter 1994: 71). Some women may have the right to abort but not the finance to cover costs. Others might not legally possess the right and be forced to take desperate measures. Zillah Eisenstein argues that reproductive rights 'are located in this space *in between*: between our rights and our access to them, between our reproductive specificity and our universal claims' (1991: 12). Feminist ethics constantly reworks dualisms.

Competing rights

Do a pregnant woman and a foetus have rights? If the rights conflict, whose rights have ultimate sway? Such debates preoccupy women's groups, fathers, religious organizations, church beliefs, right-wing community groups, lawyers, politicians and sometimes state constitutions. Competing rights are opposed, causing an irresolvable moral-legal dilemma. There seems to be an impasse between those who believe a woman has an exclusive right to choose whether or not to terminate a pregnancy and those who believe the foetus has a right to life on the basis of a status as actual or potential person who should be protected by law. These rights are conflictual in that one can only be granted at the expense of the other. A woman's right to choice threatens the foetus's life. A foetus's right to life prevents the woman from acting as an autonomous chooser.

The agency implicit in choice is paramount to a feminist perspective on abortion. As competing rights, the conundrum appears unsolvable for both positions are 'logically defensible if one accepts certain premises' (Clarke 1991: 155) about the personhood or nonpersonhood of foetuses. The conundrum usually is resolved by disputing groups prioritizing one right over the other. A feminist morality of abortion cannot dismiss one debate as arbitrary, but must examine closely the premises on which debates are based. Taking a rights discourse alone leads to a win–lose situation that does not consider the relational dimension of pregnancy. A feminist perspective on abortion is responsive both to women's autonomy and to the moral significance of pregnancy and birth.

A woman's right to choice and a foetus's right to life conflict in that one cannot be granted without withholding the other. Granting women the right to choose means that the foetus's right to life is abridged and vice versa. Janet Farrell Smith argues that there is an incoherence in asserting that a foetus's right to life conflicts with a woman's right to choose 'when the "right to life" depends on and only makes sense in terms of that very woman's nurture and sustaining the pregnancy' (1984: 268). She argues that there are real problems in imposing a conflict of rights construction on the relationships between interdependent beings. Rights-conflicts only occur among social agents in decision-making contexts (1984: 269). Christine Overall also argues that 'the embryo/foetus has no right to occupancy of its mother's uterus, a specific instance of the more general principle that no one has the right to the use of anyone else's body' (1987: 77), part of the explanation as to what makes rape and slavery wrong. Maintaining autonomous bodily integrity is essential to moral identity.

The interdependent relationship between the pregnant woman and the foetus is not symmetrical, the foetus needs the woman to survive, the woman does not need the foetus. Smith argues that while talk of the 'foetus's right' requires the woman's care and nurture, it does not make sense to talk of foetal duties. 'A conflict of rights presumes independent beings capable of making countervailing claims upon one another' (Smith 1984: 268). Smith carefully explains that this argument does not mean that the foetus does not have a right to life, but it questions whether the right makes sense when asserted against the right to choose of the woman carrying the foetus. A woman's choice in reproductive matters is a *liberty-right* and the right to life for a foetus is a *welfare right*, that is, 'a right to well-being that imposes positive duties of care and nurture upon a particular person' (1984: 270). Petchesky makes a stronger claim that 'abortion is not simply an "individual right" (civil liberty) or even a "welfare right" (for those "in need") but a "social right"' (1986: 387). Abortion rights are part of in-clusive reproductive rights which are democratic rights of both reproductive specificity and universal human claims.

Reproductive rights encompass individual and common needs for reproductive freedom. Once the right is established, the specificity can be contested, that is, what are this or that woman's actual needs that require a resolution, given her lack of educa-tion; many earlier pregnancies; language barrier; religious beliefs; poverty; personal fears? This priority given to the interdependence between a woman's liberty rights and a foetus's welfare rights is significant. Without it, the politically powerful slogan, 'a woman's right to choose' places abortion in the adversarial territory of women's rights versus foetal rights, father's rights or surrogate rights. 'Rights arguments will always be of limited use in a situation which seems to admit of no compromise. Because rights "trump", "override", and "compete", they fail to fit the experience of being pregnant. Moreover, rights arguments seem to have an inevitable tendency to generate opposing claims' (Fox and Murphy 1992: 460). If rights arguments limit an appreciation of interdependence what moral status does a foetus have?

Foetal personhood

Foetal rights are couched in controversies of moral status, human potential and the relationship to a pregnant woman. When does personhood start? Is it with conception, brain life, quickening when the baby's movements are first felt, lung development, personality or rational choice? Varying responses seem plausible. Brain death usually marks the end of life, and brain life, occurring at about ten weeks, the start of personhood. In early common law, the kill-ing of a child in the womb was considered a misdemeanour until quickening at about eighteen weeks, and then it was treated more seriously, given the presumed ensoulment. Even Catholic doctrine disputes exactly when a foetus is animated with a soul. Petchesky argues that the concept of foetal personhood is offensive in ignor-ing the distinctiveness of human capacity for consciousness and sociability. She uses a stark example by suggesting that the assump-tion of foetal personhood places the death of Holocaust victims on the same level as aborted foetuses, demeaning the moral value of human sociability (1986: 341). Humans are rational and social, otherwise the concept of persons as moral beings makes no sense.

Even when the foetus is not regarded as a person in the fullest sense, 'it is not nothing, and important questions will still remain as to what sort of being it is and how it ought to be treated' (Overall 1987: 41).

What is the moral stature of the foetus? Some answer this in terms of what it might become, that is, its potential to be a full human being. Questions of **potentiality** help establish guidelines for research on embryos. The Warnock Report (1985) decided on a limit of fourteen days beyond fertilization. Some argue that if the potentiality argument makes sense, then any limit is arbitrary, hence no research can be justified. The foetus does not have legal rights, although some test cases challenge this in relation to radioactive exposure. Once the foetus is born and is a child then there are legal rights. As Mary Warren expresses it, 'there is room for only one person with full and equal rights inside a single human skin. That is why it is birth, rather than sentience, viability, or some other prenatal milestone that must mark the beginning of legal parenthood' (1989: 63) and of legal personhood.

The foetus is different from other body parts and has status worthy of protection. Having an abortion is not like having one's appendix out, or a tooth pulled, or even a leg amputated. While a genetic parent has no entitlement to destroy an embryo (Overall 1987) the embryo has no automatic right to occupy a woman's uterus. Compulsion to nourish a foetus is itself a moral issue (Petchesky 1986: 327) because maintaining bodily integrity is essential to moral dignity. The issue is not whether the mother should be prevented from destroying the embryo, but whether the law should compel her to sustain its life and growth for the nine months from fertilization to birth (Thompson 1997). Similarly, Sally Markowitz argues that in situations of structurally imbalanced power relations, the requirement of oppressed groups to make sacrifices that exacerbate oppression asserts the 'impossible sacrifice principle' (1990: 7) and is morally impermissible. To insist that pregnant women never assert their need for an abortion is to insist on an inconceivable sacrifice. Even if the foetus has no automatic right of occupancy, this does not mean it is never wrong to terminate.

Susan Sherwin (1997) maintains that the moral significance of foetuses lies in their relationality, in making emotional claims on pregnant women. The foetus is 'human life' but not a human person. The foetus's potentiality is significant, giving it a 'sanctity of life'. As a potentially human sentient being it is morally deserving of consideration. Lynn Morgan presents a complex critique of 'foetal relationality'. She argues that personhood and relationality are 'dynamic, negotiated qualities realized through social practice' (1996: 47). A pregnant woman's circumstances are embedded within a social context. Morgan is criticizing the view that persons 'are corporeally immutable and fixed, rather than susceptible to continuing social influences' (1996: 55). She explains how in many nonWestern cultures, nature–culture relations are permeable, the social world constructs the body/person. She argues that race, class, gender, religion, romance, family, medical coverage or constraints and national politics ensure that analyses of foetal personhood are filled with 'ambiguity, messiness, instability, and dynamism' (1996: 64). Personhood is a social category defined by interactions. Feminist ethics incorporates the well-being of the foetus and a respect for a woman's autonomy.

Legal provision

What legal provision is there for abortion? Women in many parts of Latin America, the Caribbean, Asia, Africa and the Pacific have no legal access to abortion. Many die through having illegal, unsafe abortions. These typically are women who have several children and cannot reasonably provide for more. Women who leave home to have backyard abortions often experience extreme guilt and subsequent health problems. Many of them have tried home remedies, jabbing themselves internally with knitting needles or sharp instruments, falling down stairs or having excessively hot baths. When frantic attempts fail, the backyard abortionist uses unsterilized instruments and dirty hands. As crisis pregnancies continue, total legal restriction appears naive and inhumane.

'Woman' in law

The legal equality women experience in democratic societies sits uncomfortably alongside of their subjection to notions that their bodies, sexuality, hormones and reproductive potential make them not proper moral agents capable of decision-making and accountability. Sally Sheldon examines comments made by Members of Parliament in English abortion laws about the 'type' of women who terminate a pregnancy. First, there is the woman as minor who in rejecting maternity 'is seen to reject the very essence of Woman-hood' (1993: 9) and must be both immature and unwomanly. Second, the mother so burdened down with her immediacy that she cannot fulfil her 'function as a mother, of holding together the family unit' (1993: 13) is seen as a victim. The third stereotype elevates the doctor as the epitome of common-sense professional-ism. To counter this undermining of women's agency, Sheldon proposes an image of 'Woman' as *rational, self-determining, respons-ible* and *mature*; as the person best placed to consider the needs of herself and the foetus, and to make the correct decisions with regard to whether or not to abort' (1993: 22). If women's moral agency was valued, crucial decisions affecting their bodies, womanhood and everyday lives would not be in others' hands.

Restrictive legislation

Ireland has the most restrictive abortion laws in the West. The ban includes rape, repeated caesarian sections, exposure to rubella or radioactive substances, incest, difficulties with previous pregnan-cies, allergies to contraception, severe psychological disturbances, multiple miscarriage or stillbirths and presence of one or more handicapped children in the family (Jackson 1986: 58). The 1937 Constitution of the Republic of Ireland reads, 'The State acknow-ledges the right to life of the unborn and . . . the equal right to life of the mother' (Article 40.3.3). In 1983 a referendum amended the wording to read 'the State acknowledges the right to life of the unborn and, with due regard to the equal right to life of the mother, guarantees to respect, and as far as practicable, by its laws to vindicate that right' (Barry 1988: 59). The Republic of Ireland became the first country to enshrine the 'right to life' of the foetus in law. 'Life' is interpreted as physical life, not quality of life. This interpretation ignores the fact that economic, familial and sexual conditions as well as those of physical health create genuine needs that justify abortion (Petchesky 1986: 289). The right to life of a pregnant woman was placed on equal terms with the foetus she carries.

Since 1986 it became unconstitutional in the Republic of Ire-land for women's health clinics to refer women to abortion clinics in Britain. Unable to express their fears openly, and deprived of non-directive counselling, women were driven to have an abortion as the only solution. In 1992 the European Court of Human Rights found Ireland's ban on information to contravene human rights.

A referendum in 1992 agreed that the equal right to life of the unborn with the equal right to life of the mother should not limit information of services lawfully available in another European state nor limit freedom to travel to procure an abortion. Legislation is only marginally relevant to what occurs. 'Restrictive legislation leads not to the reduction of the abortion incidence, but instead to bad practice' (Ketting and Van Praag 1986: 169). Censorious climates and prohibitive laws do not prevent women from having abortions, they ensure that the problem is exported and Irish women travel to England. An Irish woman in a crisis context has to face a peculiar mixture of a social consensus based on Catholic religion, law, the state, convention, strong family ties and personal beliefs. In most countries, there is 'little support for making all abortions illegal and little support for unrestricted freedom of choice' (Glendon 1987: 41).

Case study. Girls, rape and necessary abortions

In 1992 in the Republic of Ireland, a young girl was raped by a 'family friend'. The parents sought an abortion for her when she was about eight weeks pregnant. In this X case the 'due regard to the equal right to life of the mother' and the 'right to life of the unborn child' conflicted in interpretation. The case established that termination of the unborn was permissible in certain circumstances. A constitutional provision to protect the life of the mother meant a corollary right to relevant information. Since this case the 1995 Abortion Information Act entitles women seeking abortion to receive counselling and information. In 1997, a thirteen-year-old girl from the travelling community was raped by another traveller after she had minded his children. Miss C lived in squalor in a broken caravan. She was taken into care. The parents, who had twelve children to provide for, approved an abortion, then fought it when the anti-abortion lobby intervened, distributing pictures of aborted foetuses to her young siblings and promising financial support and a new caravan. In November 1997 the High Court accepted the advice of care professionals and supported an abortion against her parents' wishes. The girl had to travel to England for an abortion, as do the approximately 5,000 women from the Republic of Ireland and about 1,500 from Northern Ireland each year. Figures cannot be exact because many women give false addresses in fear of being discovered.

Box 6.1 Abortion law in Europe

Abortion law in Europe is categorized in four ways (Ketting 1993: 4).

1 The 'very strict' category permits abortion only if a pregnancy poses an immediate threat to a woman's life and includes the Republic of Ireland, Northern Ireland and Malta.
2 The 'rather strict' category views circumstances like a threat to the women's physical or mental health, foetal defects, rape or incest as justifiable and includes Poland, Portugal, Spain and Switzerland.
3 The 'rather broad' category permits abortion for socio-economic reasons like low income, poor housing, youth, old age, having many children and includes Finland, Iceland, Luxembourg, Hungary, Cyprus and the United Kingdom.
4 All other European countries offer abortion on request, although generally this applies in the first twelve weeks, and only on specific grounds in the second trimester.

Context and abortion

Cultural differences

Rights are never exercised in a vacuum. They exist within cultural communities where their meanings emerge. Wherever the abortion issue is politicized the church plays an important role in galvanizing opposition. The most Catholic countries are the least supportive of reproductive freedoms (Jelen, O'Donnell and Wilcox 1993: 379).

Mary Glendon compares the Nordic and Anglo-American-Australian worlds with the Romano-Germanic worlds. In the former, the legal emphasis is on the individual family members. In the name of neutral toleration about the good, modern family law relinquishes attempts to promote particular ideas about family life. In contrast, in Continental civil law, 'rights tend to be seen as naturally paired with responsibilities. The individual is more often envisioned in a social context' (Glendon 1989: 298). Such differences emerge starkly in assumptions influencing abortion law. While the right to privacy dominates in the West, German basic law protects the 'right to life', emphasizing 'the character of this right as a value of the community rather than as something that belongs to the foetus' (Glendon 1987: 38). The concern is with the state's obligation to promote public values rather than the rights these values give to individuals. Similarly, with the Spanish consti- tution the courts state that unborn life is a public good to be pro- tected. Glendon remarks that European laws do not only inform pregnant women that abortion is a serious moral consideration, but they communicate to fathers that having a child is a serious commitment 'and communicate to both that the welfare of each child is a matter in which the entire society is vitally interested' (1987: 58). Feminist ethics sees individual rights as part of social obligations.

Family

For most women, obligations revolve around families, yet their actual needs differ. Attention to particularity requires exploring why unintentional pregnancies occur. Impoverished abused girls are more likely to become pregnant than comfortable cared-for girls. Being a victim of childhood abuse, poverty and ill-health, and being pregnant with the prospect of becoming a mother, may be more traumatic than contemplating and undergoing an abor- tion. Specific variables to crisis pregnancies include the fact that many women do not consent to sexual relations, that even those who do may be subject to power imbalances or intimidating con- trol. Other women may be ignorant of contraceptive options, un- able to obtain them, or prevented by parents, health authorities, religious beliefs or a partner's control. Mistakes also happen even with consensual responsible sex. The responsibilities of sexual men to their contraceptive obligations often are ignored.

In most cultures women are defined by reference to their fam- ilies, partners and children. Matters of the womb frequently define women's status. Women who evade their 'reproductive destiny' are damned as selfish and sinful. In many cultures, abortion is viewed as abnormal, unnatural, contradicting nature, a defiance of fem- inine purpose and a sin against God. It is important to contextualize the representations of women, but 'locating the woman within the context of the family may allow her needs to be conflated with those of the family' (Fox and Murphy 1992: 459). This reinforces the idea that women's ethical domain is solely in the private, natural

realm of domestic life and nurturance. 'Nurturing responsibilities are both a traditional source of women's subordination and a
potential social strength, integral to feminine identity' (Porter
1996a: 290).

Faye Ginsburg (1991), in comparing American pro-life and pro-
choice activists, discovers that responsibilities of women in relationship to nurturance are the chief issue and contradiction for
women of all persuasions. Both sets of activists reject narrow cultural representations of nurturance that devalue the caring of
dependants. Rather, they reclaim nurturance as central to women's
moral authority in that it appreciates fundamentally, 'the pro-
life choice and the protection of nascent life, and the pro-choice
concern with the rights and obligations of women to whom the
care of that nascent life is culturally assigned' (1991: 669). Proponents of both pro-life and pro-choice have overlapping concerns
for nurturant societies, advocating responsive sex, decent parenting
and caring communities. Understanding the importance women
typically give to nurture grasps the social nature of the abortion
quandary in a way that rights discourse delineates individual
entitlements.

Sex-selective abortions

Rashmi Luthra (1993) challenges the limitations of 'choice' in the
abortion rights movement. She argues that in racist, classist societies, forced sterilization and high infant and maternal mortality
are reality for working-class women of colour. Where women do
not have 'access to abortion services, decent health care, decent
childcare, acceptable life options for their children, "choice" is a
hollow and abstract concept' (1993: 44). Also, for women of colour, 'the "choice to be a mother" is as important as the choice of
whether to abort or not' (1993: 45). Luthra is right to ask white
Western feminists to evaluate their opposition to the selective abortion of female foetuses where there is a preference for sons,
yet leave open the choice to abort disabled foetuses. Her agenda
redirects the focus to broad structural changes around racism,
poverty, illiteracy and universal health care.

Gail Weiss argues that **sex-selective abortion** is a 'moral mistake'
but the individual blame cannot be assessed because 'the decision
to undergo the procedure is directly tied to community beliefs and
practices' that construct different values for males and females
(1995: 203). This abortion occurs because the woman has discovered

through ultrasound and/or amniocentesis that she is carrying a foetus who is an unwanted sex. This practice (as well as female infanticide) occurs particularly in India and in China where there is social pressure to have a son to help in the fields, to care for the aged, to carry the family line and because sons are more prestigious. For poor women, the practice appears the only alternative to a life of misery, deprivation and degradation. Bombay feminists lobbied for a law to be passed in 1988 to ban prenatal testing for purposes of sex determination. Enforcing law is difficult. Across poor, middle- and upper-middle-class families, a primary motivation for the test 'is to increase the family's acceptability in its community' (1995: 209). Weiss sees the need to work with families to explore alternatives to altering the social acceptability of sex testing 'in a nonpatronizing manner that continues to "maintain the caring relation" between the community as a whole and the individuals and families who are members of it' (1995: 215).

Reverence for life

Few approach abortion lightly. Naomi Wolf (1995) argues for the need to incorporate moral, spiritual and legal issues. She views abortion as a 'necessary evil', something that should be treated with grief, respect, reverence and public mourning. She polemically claims that the pro-choice movement 'has ceded the language of right and wrong to abortion foes' (1995: 26). She criticizes the 'free-market rhetoric about abortion' (1995: 29) in that it introduces priorities of self-interested rational calculations into areas of life where considerations of empathy, mercy and the alleviation of distress are more appropriate. Given today's economic context, most women are compelled to consider qualifications, career, mortgage and costs of having children. Economic and employment issues impact enormously on families and must be addressed carefully. Wolf's point is that if the values of the market invade our notions of what is 'valuable' or 'worthless', instrumental values dehumanize subject matter so that an abortion is seen as mere 'uterine material' or 'foetal tissue' and the moral significance of conception and birth is diminished.

Wolf's idea that 'abortions occupy a spectrum, from full lack of alternatives to full accountability' (1995: 32) is useful. Her point is that there is a significant ethical difference between the desperate, accidental, medically necessary and violently conceived abortions and the 'I don't know what came over me, it was such good Chardonnay' ones (1995: 35). Actual experiences must be voiced rather than merely claiming absolute abstract rights. Wolf suggests that special considerations should be given to poor women who have many mouths to feed or who cannot afford contraception; ignorant youth; victims of coerced sex, incest and marital rape; and women whose male partners refuse to allow them to use contraception. Abortions undertaken for reasons of 'convenience' are wrong. Certainly they can be justified because women can offer reasons for them, but the reasons are morally weak, poor or inadequate. This moral **abortion spectrum** acknowledges that there are degrees of moral culpability. With educated, knowledgeable women who can afford contraception, abortion is less easy to justify. Carelessness, being caught in the passion of the moment or not liking the feel of a condom are not easily defended rationales for abortion. Wolf suggests that even the morally defensible 'desire to be a good mother' (1995: 32) explanation, given perhaps by a student who wants to continue her studies and wants a child when she can devote herself more fully to being a 'good mother', is often used for self-absorbed reasons. Yet, all abortions require an accountability for a decision that usually is combined with relief as well as grief. Abortion reflects an irresponsible morally weak choice or an ethically responsible choice (Porter 1999: 6).

Spirituality and conscience

Wolf talks of 'a paradigm abandoned by the left and misused by the right: the paradigm of sin and redemption' (1995: 33). Her prompt was a question from a conservative who said, 'You're four months pregnant. Are you going to tell me that's not a baby you're carrying?' (1995: 34). Wolf knew the typical pro-choice response was to evade, talk of 'privacy' and 'difficult personal decisions' and 'choice'. Instead, she snapped, 'Of course it's a baby. And if I found myself in circumstances in which I had to make the terrible decision to end this life, then that would be between myself and God' (1995: 34). In the relief of an honesty that includes conscience, grief, loss and guilt, she claims that the pro-life images of foetal graphics and little footprints are polemical but the pictures themselves are biological facts. The imagery cannot be accepted as mere propaganda, feminists must be honest to the facts and to conscience.

With a desire to instil spirituality into public debate, Wolf uses religious language to suggest that it is not inappropriate to be pro-choice yet to view abortion as a sin needing redemption. Her notion of 'sin' implies a falling short of moral potential and thus needing to ask for forgiveness. Grief accompanies the mourning of loss, but it places a heavy burden on women's conscience to permit an abortion then to ask women to endure the prolonged guilt of sin and shame. Some women experience enormous relief, not debasement, with an abortion. If abortion is a sin, then women who have an abortion knowingly commit a wrong, and given that accountability is crucial to ethical agency, it makes it difficult to accept that abortion can be justified, despite the possibility of redemption that frees one from the past, and the atonement that makes up for the loss and provides a reconciliation.

In countries where religious discourse remains vocal, the language of morality is part of abortion politics. Furthermore, within feminist ethics, there is a strong grounding in which to say that abortion is a matter of law, conscience, soul and moral agency. The fact that the majority of abortions are carried out in the first twelve weeks of gestation confirms a sense of developmental difference most people have that corresponds to differences in relationship and obligation to the foetus. Most people concede the value of unborn life and feel differently about early, mid- and late-term abortions. Later abortions tend to be teenagers who have procrastinated through fear and uncertainty of who to confide in. A stillborn birth and the death of a neonate may affect people differently. So too a miscarriage in the early months may assume a different meaning to that occurring in later months, and the state and medical profession distinguish between trimesters.

There is ambiguity in many ethical judgements. However, medical experiments often venture into the realm of the almost unbelievable. Discussion occurs on what 'use' the aborted foetus may be to medical research. Suggestions do not always consider responsibilities to the pregnant woman who had the abortion. Should her permission be given before research is done on the aborted foetus? Or, is the foetus no longer hers once it is removed from the body, given that she wanted it removed? Until these questions are debated more carefully, and ethical answers raised as contested options, some medical experimentation fails to respect bodily integrity and the sanctity of life. Glendon concludes, 'perhaps it is fitting that abortion law at present should mirror our wonder as well as our ignorance about the mystery of life, our compassion for women who may be frightened and lonely in the face of a major crisis, and our instinctive uneasiness at terminating a form of innocent human life, whether we call it foetus, an embryo, a baby, or an unborn child' (1987: 46).

Rights and responsibilities of moral selves

Responsibilities

In Carol Gilligan's abortion study, she discovered that women typically construct the moral problem 'as a problem of care and responsibility in relationships' (1983: 73). In discussing ethical conflicts, possible options and actual choice, she repeatedly heard the words 'selfish' and 'responsible'. She writes that pregnancy signifies a connection 'in which there is no way of acting without consequence to other and self. In understanding the reality of interdependence and the irrevocability of choice, the abortion dilemma magnifies the issues of responsibility and care' (1983: 108). Morality 'arises from the experience of connection and is conceived as a problem of inclusion rather than one of balancing claims' (1983: 160). The dilemma typically is worked out through considering all possibilities of potential hurt. How would this decision harm me? How would this decision affect my partner and my family? The ethic of responsibility that emerges is based on an identity defined through ties to others, and evaluated not by self-assertive individual rights claims, but through practices of care. Abortion is thus recast from a conflict of rights to a conflict of responsible caring.

Responsibilities push rights to articulate their terms. Men's right to sexual freedom is vacuous without a concomitant responsibility for contraception or the acceptance of active fatherhood. Do men have a right to consent to or dispute an abortion? It seems hard to justify a right simply on the grounds of their contribution of sperm. 'The only basis for such a claim to have moral weight is *through the social relationship established between the man and the pregnancy*' (Petchesky 1986: 350) or in actual demonstrations of care in prior co-parenting experiences. Many men mourn with spontaneous miscarriages or delight with feeling the foetus's movements or are actively responsible with other children. Most feminists encourage these men to voice their feelings and desires but accept that the ultimate choice lies with the woman. Responsibility-based arguments are not easier to solve, but 'they are inclusionary, they embrace questions women of all cultures, religions, and socio-political backgrounds ask of the self-other relationship, even though the answers vary' (Porter 1996a: 291).

Social reproduction

Abortion concerns the individual, family, state and society. To give substance to this idea theorists talk of the 'social relations of reproduction' (Himmelweit 1988: 53; Petchesky 1980: 104; Porter 1994: 77), to emphasize the impact of historical and social conflicts, access to power, agency, cultural interpretations of sexuality and material conditions under which choices are made. 'Abortion is the fulcrum of a much broader ideological struggle in which the very meanings of the family, the state, motherhood, and young women's sexuality are contested' (Petchesky 1986: vii). Meanings vary in contemplating or undergoing an abortion with a frightened teenager, a victim of rape or incest, a woman with more mouths to feed than she can afford and a wealthy single woman pregnant to a married man. It is disturbing to think that persons who have never been 'in the situation of a woman confronted with an unwanted pregnancy are telling women what she may or may not do about it' (Glendon 1987: 50).

A woman who suspects she is carrying a disabled child or who, through an amniocentesis or scan, knows she is may regret having to undergo an abortion, but her decision may also be 'an indictment of society and the help it offers for the care of the disabled' (Himmelweit 1988: 43). Moral societies provide adequately for vulnerable dependants, ensuring there is support for their care. Where the state restricts the availability of abortion and affirms the value of the unborn child, it has a responsibility to assist those who have children. Ethically responsible societies need to demonstrate a commitment to children's welfare. Abortion is a personal and social decision. Abortion debates, policies and law are part of a broad community concern for the rights and responsibilities of sexually active women and men. Abortion is not about single-issue politics, debates encompass related issues of family, sexuality, safe available contraception, sex education, negative connotations associated with being pregnant, representations of pregnancy, counselling, access to information for those unwillingly pregnant, prenatal care, maternity leave, childcare, father's involvement.

Ethical agency

The interdependence of rights and responsibilities is starkly obvious in pregnancy and abortion. This is a mutual dependency in a moral sense because 'there is no way of acting without consequence to other and self' (Gilligan 1983: 108). A woman's actions affect the unborn child. Heavy smoking, drinking or taking harmful drugs, listening to music, eating good foods, being relaxed or exhausted all have an influence. Unsurprisingly, quickening marked the limit of 'acceptable' abortions as the movement signalled a sign of life, a communication of dependence on another relationship. The interdependence is not reducible to one stage, rather, the moral significance of birth lies in ending one relationship and beginning another new existence as a rights-bearing socially responsive member, forming newly emergent relations (Warren 1989). Not all women experience abortion or birth as of moral significance. Feminist perspectives on abortion develop a morality that breaks down hostile dualisms of self/other, right/responsibilities and individuals/communities. 'This creative synthesis transforms the moral construct, self-identity, one's relationships and moral choice. With this synthesis, abortion ethics remains an emotionally intense issue, but it is transformed from a narrow rigid dilemma to a dynamic moral construct' (Porter 1994: 80–81).

Decisions about abortion are filled with questions, contingencies, multiple possibilities, and plausible or implausible options. Viable options must be available, along with a protagonist with the self-authority to make a choice. Access to reproductive rights includes both abortion needs and the conditions to raise healthy children. This access is fundamental to citizenship and moral agency. Its structural challenge 'moves beyond defending "privacy" as some abstract good to enunciate a discourse of *public* morality, one that acknowledges abortion access as a *social right* of women if they are to function as full persons in the public domain' (Petchesky 1986: xiv). The availability of abortion is a prerequisite to women's well-being and self-determination even if women never have to avail themselves of this right. Enabling conditions that actualize rights are needed for women, regardless of colour, race, occupation, status and wealth. The underlying foundation to a feminist ethic of abortion is an affirmation of the self-autonomy of social beings. This is not the liberal privacy rights of non-interference. Rather, the decisions that affect our bodies, personhood and citizenship affect our social participation as 'selves-in-relations' (Porter

1991). A decision to have an abortion made in the light of all available options, and one that a woman is fully accountable for, is a morally responsible choice.

An awareness of the complexity of abortion debates allows the adoption of a healthy caution about absolutist positions and a questioning of ongoing moral debates. All difficult decision-making involves multiple negotiations between social context and personal desires. For most women this involves an intricate consideration of religious beliefs, conscience, law, family views, partner's views, career and material situation. Women, accustomed to regular consideration of vulnerable others, are likely to be morally informed. The morality of abortion is connected to nurture and responsibility for others.

Summary

- Reproductive rights are part of reproductive freedoms that affirm equality and autonomy.

- A feminist perspective on abortion is responsive to both women's autonomy and to the moral significance of pregnancy and birth.

- Without legal provision for abortion, unsafe, life-threatening and illegal practices continue.

- Sometimes women must travel to other countries to have an abortion.

- An abortion spectrum acknowledges different degrees of moral culpability, ranging from irresponsible morally weak choices to ethically responsible choices.

- The rights and morality of abortion are connected to responsibilities to nurture others.

Further reading

Glendon, M. A. (1987) *Abortion and Divorce in Western Law*, Cambridge MA: Harvard University Press.

Petchesky, R. P. (1986) *Abortion and Woman's Choice: The State, Sexuality, and Reproductive Freedom*, London: Verso.

Riddicks, R. (1990) *The Right to Choose: Questions of Feminist Morality*, Dublin: Attic Press.

Smyth, A. (ed.) (1992) *The Abortion Papers, Ireland*, Dublin: Attic Press.

Chapter 7

Reproductive Choices

Chapter outline

This chapter shows how technological means to assist reproduction appear to increase women's choice but exert control over women's lives. Women are treated as mere body parts – wombs, cells, eggs and makers of embryos. Motherhood too is split into genetic, birth or social mothers. Much experimentation of women's fertility, contraception and sterilization occurs in developing countries and the nature of ethnic and racist exploitation is discussed. The chapter distinguishes between:

- involuntary childlessness
- voluntary childfreeness
- infertility.

The chapter critically examines:

- the importance *in vitro* fertilization (IVF) places on genetic ownership and biological birth
- the dehumanization and suffering of undergoing IVF treatment that does not lead to the birth of a healthy baby
- who is suitable for IVF treatment.

The chapter looks briefly at genetic engineering, sex selection and controversies surrounding who owns stored genetic material. The commodification of reproduction is criticized, particularly in commercial contract motherhood, because it reduces a woman to a uterus whose sole purpose is to produce a baby to relinquish. The pregnant woman's personhood is not given moral significance.

Feminist perspectives on reproductive choices

Reproductive choices abound. They concern preventing conception, stopping reproduction after conception, causing conception when it does not occur naturally, monitoring the progress of the conceptus and handling difficulties with newborns. Feminist perspectives highlight common experiences as well as distinct diversity. Our bodies differentiate us through effects of age, class, (dis)ability, ethnicity, (sub)cultures, health, sexual preference, fertility. Women's life experiences differ according to whether they have children or not. Feminism attends to the ways that women are oppressed or blessed by reproductive potential. It places questions of reproductive choice in wide parameters of sexuality, contraception, attitudes toward women's bodies and motherhood and autonomous agency. This chapter concentrates on those choices that are influenced by technology.

Technological 'progress' to limit and to assist reproduction is spectacular. Medical and scientific advances in reproductive technology offer a 'double-edged sword' (Stanworth 1987), the technical possibility to decide the conditions under which women have children appears to give women choice; and the domination of technology by the medical profession enables a greater capacity to exert control over women's lives. It is as if we should 'expect trouble' with reproductive technologies (Hartsock and Boling 1995). The power of women's reproductive potential is at the core of women's experiences, in oppressive or empowering ways. Some feminists suggest that men's sense of disconnection from the process of reproduction underpins a desire to master nature and to construct social and cultural institutions that convey a sense of procreative power (O'Brien 1983; Rowland 1985), or that reproductive and genetic engineering are logical extensions 'of the patriarchal quest to gain control over women's fertility' (Klein 1992: 15). Nancy Lublin (1998) contrasts 'technophiles' who advocate acceptance of technological intervention in the womb as liberating, 'technophobic feminists' who reject artificial invasions as anti-natural and anti-woman, and 'other' feminists who argue that 'technological intervention in the womb' should be legal and available.

With medical technology, 'the power to negate woman's indispensability to human reproduction' appears possible (Steinbacher 1984: 274). In reproductive technology, women are treated as disembodied parts – wombs, cells, eggs, makers of embryos, foetus's carriers. Motherhood itself is deconstructed – ovarian mothers supply eggs, uterine mothers give birth, social mothers rear children. Feminists are alarmed at this reductionism and view the whole of women's experiences as valid to reproductive ethics. Feminist reproductive health care is committed to serving women's needs holistically and queries whether what medical science considers 'progress' is best. For example, the World Health Organization concludes that 'the major hazard to the health of the woman and the newborn infant is poverty' (in Spallone 1989: 32), not the need for technology. Feminist health centres accept that women are the primary subject of their bodies, fertility and any pregnancies they have. Midwives assisting in comfortable hospitals or home births are best able to facilitate the birth experience. 'We need a different kind of science, one that respects women as full human beings and not just living incubators' (Klein 1992: 18). Australia is a world leader in new reproductive technologies where initial experimentation was used to enhance the genetic stock of animals and the vigour of plants (Brown, Fielden and Scutt 1990). The sorts of ethical questions feminists ask begins with an affirmation of individual respect. What do women want themselves? Which choices are best for the women concerned? Which options involve the least control from political, scientific and commercial interests? (Holmes 1981: 2).

Race, ethnicity and reproduction

The rhetoric of individual rights and choices to reproduce or not to reproduce is especially problematic in the Third World. Religious or cultural restrictions on taking contraception or the distortion of family planning programmes to serve population control rather than women's real needs means that women's reproductive fate often is beyond their control. Given that most cultures expect wives to defer to their husband's consent before limiting fertility, and many men refuse permission, family planning programmes geared exclusively to women ignore the basic reality of male dominance (Hartmann 1994: 332). Often the only form of contraception available are hormonal implants that cause enforced sterilization. Hormonal, immunological and surgical methods receive the majority of total public expenditure compared to safer barrier methods such as the diaphragm and condom. Multinational companies move their research to the expanding Third World market where drug regulations are less rigid. Research is carried out on women in India, China, Chile, Mexico and Brazil. The printed

---

Box 7.1 Reproduction in the Third World

In the Third World in particular, the physical hardship of repeated pregnancies takes its toll. Between the ages of fifteen and forty-five, women in rural Bangladesh can expect an average of eight pregnancies, and to spend seventeen years pregnant or breastfeeding, a burden to undernourished women (Hartmann 1994: 331). Childbirth kills many poor women. Maternal mortality rates in excess of 5 per 30 live births in Third World countries sit alongside of 5 per 1,000 in industrialized countries (Hartmann 1994: 331). Klein (1992) cites examples of ways in which poor Third World women are used as breeders. In Bangladesh, when poor women are in labour, they may be visited by a 'baby buyer' who pays ten USA dollars per child. The fate of these babies is not clear, it is possible they are killed and their organs flown to Western countries. In Sri Lanka, baby farms allow pregnant women to give their babies for inter-country adoption after birth. Janice Raymond (1989) reveals data from India showing how parents sell their female foetuses when they are still in the womb, and yield the baby girls at birth into prostitution in Arab countries. In some Asian countries an inability to give birth leads to the expulsion from home. Often another woman meets the same fate until the man reluctantly accepts that he is infertile. Adoption is not an option where cultures value genetic continuity. If a woman bears a female child, she may be outcast for not producing a desired male child. Embryo research in Western countries is increasingly difficult to pursue because of ethical concerns, hence reproductive biologists open clinics in Malaysia, Singapore, the Philippines, Indonesia and Hong Kong, where fewer restrictions operate on ethics committees, and where poor women accept a token payment in exchange for allowing the use of their bodies. Agency is undermined.

---

possible side-effects are often missing or not in the local language. Using strong words, Renate Klein describes choice as being 'structured by a technopatriarchal *unethics* of misogynist fragmentation, eugenic, racist selection, and, above all, (male) control of women' (1992: 18).

This control is imbued with racist overtones. In the West, pregnancy within the black community assumes a different meaning than in the white community. Within the black community, fecundity is valued, thus the stigma of teenage pregnancy is lessened by the positive status that motherhood brings. Children are accommodated into the extended community, sometimes being taken in by families they are not related to. Janet Gallagher draws on the African maxim 'it takes a whole village to raise a child' (1995: 361) to put in context considerations of pregnant women with substance abuse. These women are often poor, on welfare and the majority are from black or mixed-race communities. There have been cases in the USA where women with addiction problems have faced forced caesarians, prosecutions for newborns tested for positive toxicology, forced sterilization or use of Norplant, a contraception which may be effective for up to five years, removal of custody, or lawsuits brought against the mother for negligent infliction of prenatal injuries. Gallagher suggests we need to grapple with the complexity of the pregnant woman's addiction as well as the specificities of race, class and gender. What these women need is prenatal care, accessible and appropriate drug treatment, childcare, skills to overcome poverty and the provision of safe housing away from physical violence and being trapped in relationships with battering men who abuse drugs and alcohol.

Sterilization abuse

The first three decades of this century witnessed sterilization laws and restricted immigration in the USA and UK. In Germany, racist selection and eradication occurred. Much of our current knowledge of hormones and many of the procedures used in modern gene and reproductive technology 'were developed by Nazi scientists and doctors who performed cruel, often deadly, experiments on "unworthy" women in concentration camps' (Klein 1992: 8–9). The spurious aim was to improve fertility for 'worthy' women. Sterilization abuse involves coerced and unconsenting sterilization of women and men. Blatant abuse includes forced sterilization against people's will or without their consent, mainly of the mentally ill, physically disabled and immigrants, or subtle abuse where people's capacity to make genuine reproductive choice is hampered (Clarke 1994: 341). In the 1950s and 1960s many black and Native American women in the USA were sterilized without their knowledge. Subtle abuse includes lack of options, unnecessary hysterectomies, economic constraints causing reluctant agreement, ignorance of the operation's permanency, or 'package deals' where women in situations undergoing emotional stress are offered abortions or delivery of a child on the condition that they are sterilized.

Women in India, Bangladesh, the Philippines, Africa and South America are offered injectable contraception like Norplant or hormonal implants that effectively enforce sterilization. Indeed, Western governments often tie economic aid to population control targets. Research on contraceptive vaccines experiments on women who do not know what the contraception does to their bodies. Women in the Third World are the unknowing targets to test whether the vaccine is reversible as it promises or causes sterility. If the vaccine is administered on a large scale, new reproductive technologies are promised as methods 'of reversing this induced infertility for those few deemed fit to reproduce: the perfect solution for a world-wide control of population growth' (Klein 1992: 16).

Childfree women

A 1993 survey of 76,100 patients in Britain found that one in ten women choose not to have children and the figure is rising (Bartlett 1994: ix). Jane Bartlett interviewed women who chose not to have children. These women are distinctive in their courage to swim against the tide of expectations of the 'need to mother'. Yet given that children are often the passport to a 'normal' mainstream lifestyle, many interviewees experienced feelings of exclusion. Curiously one woman considered surrogate motherhood because she understood how deeply women who want children must feel because she so deeply did not want children. Instead, as a midwife, she assists women with their births. Many of the women interviewed were devoted aunts and godmothers, seeing these roles as fun without duties and pressures. Some of the women work with children as teachers, nurses, midwives. Others actively avoid contact. Those women who live with or marry a man with children from a previous relationship often miss their childfree lifestyle and this causes enormous tensions even if it is only weekend access to children.

'The idea that having a child actually involves making a decision is a modern one' (Bartlett 1994: 98). Prior to accessible contraception and changing attitudes to morality and the family, the natural progression was to marry and have children. Some women simply delay the decision to have a child, pursuing social and career possibilities, postponing it until it seems to be too late. The average age for first births is now over 27 and birth rates have increased most in the 35–39 and 40-plus groups (1994: 101). The decision against trying to conceive is influenced by the woman's

partner, her mother and feminist beliefs, as well as personal preferences. Finding a like-minded partner is often difficult because
'men can't believe that a woman doesn't want children' (1994:
163). Most of these women value their independence, economic
self-sufficiency and freedom of lifestyle, including moving between
sexual partners. The financial and emotional costs of juggling
family and work life are a major consideration. The freedom to
choose to be childfree is important but differs from the situation
of women who are involuntarily childless.

Reproductive technologies

Women who want a child but cannot conceive naturally may be
offered artificial reproduction which takes place without sexual
intercourse. It includes *in vitro* fertilization (IVF), a costly process,
and artificial insemination by donor (AID) that often is associated
with IVF. Its justification is its response to the needs of those
otherwise unable to become biological parents. Feminist critiques
of reproductive technologies do not lie in technology as an '*artificial* invasion of the human body' but whether the political and
cultural conditions can be created so that technologies can be
employed by women in ways that reflect their self-definitions
(Stanworth 1987: 35).

Infertility

The pressures on women to be mothers make it difficult for women
with fertility problems or women whose partners have fertility problems to forego technology that might deliver the wanted child. The
stigma of infertility contributes to internalized guilt that one is not
a 'proper' woman. A woman's worth and status usually is meas-
ured by her children. Women without children experience isolation within their own families, particularly at times like Christmas,
Easter, school holidays, Mother's Day. 'The concept of infertility is
both normative and prescriptive' (Overall 1987: 139). It describes
the physical inability to reproduce and it assumes appropriate
behaviour for medical personnel, women and men. These meanings have implicit ethical dimensions. Infertility is an impairment
in the sense that it is a loss of function of procreative capacities.

Infertility is stereotyped as a woman's problem, but is due to a female factor in approximately 40 per cent of cases, a male factor in 40 per cent of cases (Michie and Cahn 1997: 148), the other cases being indeterminate. To view the impairment as a handicap is to view it as a negative perception. Such a perception is consistent with the ideology of femininity that defines motherhood as an essential part of womanhood. Yet, 'how infertility is evaluated depends upon the total context of the person's life' (Overall 1987: 141).

Involuntary childlessness, voluntary childfreeness and infertility differ. A fertile woman may be involuntarily childless due to reasons like early widowhood, not having a male partner, or being in a lesbian relationship, or an infertile woman may regard herself as fortunate in not needing contraception or in giving her free time. For most women, indeed for most couples who try to have a child and find they cannot, anguish and heartbreak prevail. Many infertile individuals and their partners experience crises of personal esteem, sexuality and normality. The relationship itself may be jeopardized. Learning of one's infertility can cause deep grief which means going through the stages of 'disbelief, guilt, anger, rage, distress, deep sorrow and ultimately resolution' (Koval and Scutt 1990: 48). In referring to women who are involuntarily childless, Naomi Pfeffer and Anne Woollett refer to women's loss in the emotionally powerful experience of pregnancy and childbirth that shape life, contribute to self-identity and create bonds within the community, particularly with other women (1983: 127). Embarrassment and exclusion results, exacerbating feelings of vulnerability to which those with children may be awkward in responding.

Feminists are critical of a compulsion to motherhood, but not of mothering itself. Infertile women with the desire to mother experience intense feelings, given the obstacles they face (Berg 1995: 85). Infertility occurs for many reasons like environmental hazards of pesticides and weapons testing, infections, sexually transmitted diseases, some contraceptive devices, surgery, certain drugs, excessive weight loss, blocked fallopian tubes, stress and other unknown factors. Infertile people need the support of friends, self-help groups for counsel, therapy and space to come to terms with the fact that they will not be biological parents. Many provide new role models of childless wo/men who are happy, fulfilled and nurturant.

Rather than correcting the reason for infertility, new reproductive technology aims to enable a couple to have a child through artificial means. Part of the rationale for promising infertile couples the use of IVF or AID is a notion of ownership, interpreted as genetic ties. Before IVF, infertile couples were offered adoption but now most single mothers keep their child. In early IVF procedures that used AID, the husband's sperm was mixed with fertile sperm so the man would think that it might be his sperm that fertilized the ovum. In the case of Louise Brown, the first *in vitro* baby, born in 1978, the fertility researcher remarked that Mrs Brown, who had blocked fallopian tubes, would be childless without IVF despite the fact that Mr Brown had a fourteen-year-old daughter by a previous marriage.

The genetic connection dominates the ownership rationale. For men who are infertile, AID is problematic as it means they cannot achieve a genetic immortality. IVF enables a man and woman to have their 'own' child, AID enables a woman to have her 'own' child, contract motherhood enables a man to have his 'own' child. This emphasis on one's 'own' leads to bizarre examples like the elderly man with no children who hires a woman to have 'his' child so he can leave his estate to his 'own' child rather than to his nieces and nephews. The assumption is that genetic parenthood surpasses the value of social parenthood, the actual rearing of children. This emphasis probably is stronger in men. The double standard in sexuality that justifies men having extra-marital affairs while insisting on monogamy for women is motivated by the need for a man to ensure that his wife's child is also his child. Some men raise children they assume are their own, sometimes to find out that the child has a different biological father.

How does feminist ethics respond to genetic ties? Part of the context of becoming pregnant is the emerging identity of the foetus with the identity of the parents. Genetics is significant but should not be made the exclusive consideration. It must be considered in context. Within a loving relationship the genetic component is one factor of importance. Within a contract pregnancy, genetics and instrumentality is paramount. In other contexts, a desire for a child can be fulfilled through care of a child to whom one is not biologically related. Step-children, foster children, refugee or abused children taken in by a family, children parented in a community or by lesbian and gays can be lovingly nurtured as 'one's own'. Adopted children are rarely treated as substitutes for the real thing. Adoption raises important ethical questions on the relinquishing mother's rights, and of selecting adoptive parents for a child, particularly with rearing mixed-race children.

In vitro *fertilization*

For those women who are desperate to bear a child, *in vitro* fertilization (IVF) involves fertilization outside of the woman's body. Before a woman is accepted into an IVF programme, she is evaluated socially, psychologically and medically. Mostly, only heterosexual couples in stable relationships are eligible. Some private clinics consider lesbians and single women. Once accepted, a woman is subject to extreme physical intrusion and emotional trauma. Typically, a 'hormonal cocktail' is given to stimulate the production of more than one ripe egg. Many drugs have adverse affects on women. Monitoring of ovulation is the next stage. The woman must be available for minimally twice daily monitoring. Ripe eggs are removed from the ovaries, usually using a laparoscopy requiring anaesthesia. Initially, reports were that four, six, eight eggs were removed, then came reports of fourteen and seventeen eggs (Spallone 1989: 58). Meanwhile, semen is collected after masturbation. Eggs are put in a petri dish with sperm. If fertilized and embryo development commences, 2–4 are transferred to the womb at the 8–12 cell stage via a catheter pushed through the cervix.

Box 7.2 Success and failure of IVF

Spontaneous abortion or ectopic pregnancy is frequent at this stage. Success rates of live births are low. Statistics vary from 8.5 per cent in Britain (Spallone 1989: 63), between 10 and 15 per cent in the USA (Mahoney 1995: 48) and in Australia (Brown, Fielden and Scutt 1990: 95). The impact of 'failure' on women who do not get pregnant is ignored by the medical profession. One 'failed' woman who wanted to talk to her gynaecologist was told by the IVF scientist, 'You're history, we are on to the next one, we haven't time for you now, we want to get on with it' (in Murdoch 1990: 69). Few women take a baby home. The majority, 'ninety to ninety-five women out of one hundred, will have to give up, often after as many as ten or more IVF attempts' (Klein 1992: 5). These women, classified as non-responders, often feel devastated, as inadequate women. 'The message they have been given is that not even with the help of technology can they produce their own child' (Klein 1992: 5). In the IVF doctors' purposes, 'the unsuccessful woman with her bad eggs, diseased tubes, hostile womb is a "fertilization" failure' (1992: 5). She is an embarrassment, lowering their statistics.

With gamete intrafallopian transfer (GIFT) a maximum of three eggs are removed to mature and then are transferred with sperm to the fallopian tubes, replicating the site of natural fertilization. With donor insemination (DI) women are inseminated artificially with donor sperm (anonymous or known), sometimes assisted by a partner with everyday kitchen items or a syringe. With DI the father is deemed by law to be the husband, married or not, of the woman undergoing such treatment. Yet DI is used increasingly by lesbians. With the mother it is the gestational function that defines legal motherhood, not the genetic relationship. The Human Fertilization and Embryology Act 1990 provides for the maternal transfer of parental responsibility in the case of surrogacy to the commissioning couple, as long as the baby is genetically related to at least one (Frith 1996: 174). During the Gulf War, some departing servicemen banked their sperm so that their wives could be inseminated if necessary, 'letting them "father" children posthumously if they were lost in battle' (Callahan 1995: 20). Attempts are also made to inseminate HIV-negative women with 'cleaned' sperm from HIV-positive partners. Fertilized ova can also be flushed out of one woman's uterus and placed in another. In 1987 a test-tube sister of an English IVF child was born. The second child was, as a frozen embryo, thawed, implanted and born as a twin, two years apart. Debate on such 'experiments' must be ongoing.

Consent is crucial. Those women who participated in early successful IVF pregnancies in Britain and Australia were unaware how experimental their cases were. 'The appearance of voluntarism is deceptive, for the control over women begins long before they can voice a "free choice"' (Corea 1994: 352). Social pressures on women to reproduce and the association of womanhood with childbearing is deeply ingrained. A fear of barrenness signifies a nothingness, a void, an emptiness of identity and personhood. Lesley Brown, the first successful IVF mother in 1978, felt she was failing her husband by not giving him a baby. 'Given patriarchy's proscription that women must produce children for their mates, free choice is conditioned' (Corea 1994: 355). Certainly the anguish an infertile woman suffers is vivid and painful, but why she suffers and how society deals with the pain is revealing. Feminist ethics criticizes any definitions of women as nonentities if they are not biological mothers. Gena Corea argues that in view of infertile women's deep suffering, feminists do not believe that encouraging her 'to hand over her body to the pharmacracy for manipulation and experimentation is a truly sensitive response to her plight' (1994: 355).

The term 'pharmacracy' draws on medicine, theocratic rule by God, and rule by the people. The suffering that women endure while on IVF is rarely documented as an ethical issue. Corea summarizes the suffering: 'The cycle of hopes raised (she's accepted into the programme) and dashed (doctor could not get an egg), raised (got an egg) and dashed (egg was abnormal), raised (got a normal egg) and dashed (embryo did not implant), raised (embryo implanted) and dashed (miscarried) harms women in ways pharmacrats have not acknowledged' (1994: 358). In the case of Lesley Brown, her baby Louise was lifted triumphantly to the cameras by the medical staff, while the mother lay unconscious on the table.

Who needs fertility treatment?

What ethical guidelines can feminists draw on in deciding who should be eligible for fertility treatment? Who is an appropriate or an inappropriate mother? The general guideline for declining treatment is when the welfare of a child appears in jeopardy. The right to have a child sits alongside the responsibility to maximize the child's well-being. The least controversial case is that of loving heterosexual couples who can adequately provide for a child's many needs. With lesbians, assuming this is a loving couple committed to co-parenting, most feminist ethicists approve this situation. However, ethicists continue to debate the status of the man who donates sperm, the problem of the child's likely confused identity with an anonymous donor and the complications if he is known to the woman and wants to participate somehow. The question of a single woman's right to fertility treatment is controversial if we argue that having more than one parent is desirable. However, the increasing numbers of successful women-headed households strengthens single women's case.

The question of post-menopausal women raises media attention, and while undoubtedly older women can be good mothers, just as they are valued grandmothers, the question of whether it maximizes the infant's best interests is dubious. An Italian woman made history at sixty-four by becoming the oldest mother in the world. A sixty-year-old British woman lied about her age and received donor egg and sperm. The child is not her biological son, nor her adopted son, yet he is certainly hers. Elizabeth Buttle lives in a dilapidated remote farm with no running water. She sold her story for £100,000 and the treatment cost her £10,000. Benefits to older women must be weighed with the effects on the children. Further controversy is raised by a geneticist and bioethicist who seriously suggest that young women who want to pursue their career without interruption, or HIV-positive women 'should have the option to have some ova collected during their optimal years of child-bearing, fertilized, and stored, frozen as embryos for future transfer' (in Klein 1992: 9).

Many women who have children by DI are lesbians, but some single heterosexual women who want a child but have not found an appropriate partner find insemination suitable for them. Insemination can easily be done with someone's help. The most controversial aspect is the role of the donor. Ethically, the anonymous donor is problematic in terms of the child's search for identity and roots which is why more countries are enabling access to information once the child turns eighteen. This has resulted in a significant drop of donor contribution, because men do not want to have to face a young adult who is their biological child. A donor who is a friend, or known, sometimes chooses to become more involved than was originally planned. Given his contribution, it is difficult to dispute his right to do so, particularly where it is motivated by a genuine concern for the well-being of the child, or a bond with the child. Sometimes this desired involvement is welcome, mostly it raises conflicts. With lesbians and gays, the role of the non-biological parent who has no legal guardianship but is a prime parent is important.

Status of the embryo

Ethical discussions amongst IVF advocates revolve around embryos. 'Ignoring women and talking in terms of embryos is morally less problematic than admitting that women are the subjects of "human IVF" and "human embryo" experimentation' (Spallone 1989: 22). As Patricia Spallone explains, by talking of the scientific knowledge about embryos what is kept in the forefront is the need to help infertile couples, prevent congenital 'defects' and create ideal contraception, ensuring that the actual experience of women's bodies trying to get pregnant or experiencing pregnancy is ignored. As she says, 'ignoring women as the subject of pregnancy, the "experts" are left with embryos' (1989: 22). The embryo is a fertilized egg, and granting it moral status enables medical scientists to continue their research on reproductive technologies without necessarily incorporating considerations of women. The requirement of samples for reproductive research requires a pool of available or unknowing women. Women having abdominal surgery or sterilization are potential egg donors, birthing women are potential placenta donors, women seeking contraception are volunteers for fertility control products and women having an abortion are potential foetus donors. The danger is that women's bodies and intentions are subordinated in the pursuit of scientific knowledge about reproductive processes.

'The claims of "foetal rights" became imaginable only when it became possible to see and think of the foetus as separate from the woman within whose body it is carried' (Gallagher 1995: 347). Ultrasound coloured photographs portray the foetus as a fascinating free-floating entity. 'A pregnant woman is herself whole. Being woman-centred rather than embryo-centred, feminists reject the identification of a disembodied embryo' (Spallone 1989: 39). The embryo is not unconnected to the woman who carries it or who will carry it. Separate interests of anti-abortionists, doctors, ethicists, lawyers, politicians, scientists and theologians are harmful to an integrated understanding of the embryo in relation to the woman. New reproductive technologies literally split the woman from her embryo/s, but any conceptual division between women's bodies and medical science needs to be resisted as perpetuating harmful dualisms between subject and object, passive observer and scientific control.

Dualism splits the status of motherhood into genetic mother, carrying mother, social mother. Research on artificial wombs is the next logical extension, offered in the guise of allowing career women to continue work without a disruption or allowing fashion models to have a child without stretch marks. Dualistic splits make it hard to ascertain the status of a woman who carries an embryo created with another woman's egg. 'Is the mother the woman who contributes *genetically* to the child, or the woman who bears the child and gives birth?' (Spallone 1989: 174). Or is it the woman who rears and nurtures the child, or are they different sorts of mothers? Who does the child consider to be mother if s/he is reared solely by a man? What about the woman who has lovingly co-parented and economically supported a child in a lesbian or de facto relationship? What are her rights if the relationship splits? Is the biological aspect of reproduction reduced to egg donor? These are substantial questions to continue debating. Spallone argues that it is the woman who labours and gives birth who is the mother (1989: 174) but women who have not given birth and who adopt, co-partner in lesbian parenthood, step-mother or foster a child are no less mothers.

Barbara Katz Rothman argues (1989) that we should reject the genetic model's patriarchal concern with possession and domination. Feminist understandings of parenthood shift the emphasis from ownership to nurturance, from genetics to bonding. 'Valuing nurturing over genetics means that the way our children become members of our families is less important than the relationship that develops once they are here, and adoption becomes not only a viable alternative but a morally preferable alternative' (Mahoney 1995: 48) to technological options. For example, an anonymous sperm donor would not be classified as a parent, but a known donor who nurtures would, as well as a gay man or a lesbian if they are actively engaged in parenting responsibilities.

Neonates

Ethical issues in the neonatal intensive care field are poignantly complex. These issues are pertinent in all pregnancies, but because many IVF pregnancies are multiple births, it warrants some attention. No one wants a baby to die, but difficult decisions need to be made when the infant is so tiny to be hardly viable, currently at 23 or 24 weeks. Pam Miller (1996: 124) suggests four main approaches to decision-making:

1 *Value of life* approaches view every life as sacred, although some admit the relevance of quality of life arguments.

2 *Parental authority* approaches try to involve the parents as much as possible but appreciate that given it is such an emotionally fraught time, it is unfair to invoke the possibility of guilt with parents having to make a life or death decision.

3 *Best interests* approaches grant that aggressive intervention to save a baby's life or prolong it, are not always in the child's perceived interests.

4 *Personhood* approaches view the possession of capabilities, self-consciousness, ability to reason and suffer as the basis to the right to life. Some grant the potential of such capabilities as a consideration, otherwise a much-loved five-year-old might not be viewed as a 'proper person'.

Treatment of low birth weight pre-term infants born less than 600 grams is often not given, but the small baby is handed to the parents to cuddle usually until s/he dies in their arms (Miller 1996: 126–7). Sometimes hints are given that the neonate should be allowed to die. At such moments, 'quality of life' arguments are morally relevant. Where the prolonging of life clearly is not in the best interests of the child, or indeed the parent/s, particularly where there is a probable degree of brain damage, the decision is best made by all who are caring for the baby so that the significance of the decision is not solely on one person. This way, there may be a dignified death, cuddles, photographs and some final closing of the infant's last minutes with the family (1996: 128).

Genetic engineering

Is prenatal diagnosis a welcome safeguard to prospective parents that their offspring will be healthy, or is it a covert and dangerous form of eugenics (Overall 1987: 1)? **Eugenics** is the scientific improvement of the human species by genetic means. Does genetic engineering overcome the inadequacies of 'mother nature' or is such technology an instrument of control, what Klein calls, 'the ultimate colonization of life?' (1992: 3). Medically important genes are being patented, many 'looted' from the Third World, a fact which violates the sacredness of the human body.

Women who conceive naturally can have a fertilized egg 'flushed out' to enable genetic screening and replaced if 'acceptable' or discarded if otherwise. Methods used are those gained through IVF, not merely targeted at infertility but at reproduction. Klein cites the British embryologist Anne McLaren who suggests that 'only about one per cent of all babies born are affected by a severe genetic or chromosomal disability' (in Klein 1992: 11). Having a severely disabled baby puts enormous stress on families, particularly on mothers. Yet those who are crippled or disabled view genetic counselling as a commentary on them, as if they are 'non-desirable', their infirmity a possible rationale for abortions on eugenic grounds. As authors argue in Arditti, Klein and Minden (1984) disabled women who support pro-choice on abortion often do not contemplate pre-natal screening while pregnant themselves because it assumes that the life of a disabled foetus should be ended. Such assumptions question the sexuality of disabled women and their reproductive rights. Determining who deserves to be born is a tremendous decision. Laura Purdy sensitively addresses this issue, disputing the view that attempts to avoid the birth of individuals with serious impairments signals crude instrumental messages to the living. Rather, 'wanting a world where fewer suffer implies doing what we can to alleviate the difficulties of those who now exist as well as doing what we can to relieve future people of them' (1995: 313–14). Her point is 'that there is no good reason to conceive a child at special risk for disability when you could with little effort conceive one at only the usual odds' and further, there are 'good reasons for not doing so' (1995: 316).

Sex selection

'Foetal sex preselection' refers to techniques enabling prospective parents to predetermine the sex of their child in the process of conception. Those factors that women can influence like diet, timing of intercourse in relation to ovulation, coital position, douching to alter acidity are controversial in effectiveness. Technological interventions involve separating the gynosperm which carries the X chromosome which produces daughters, from the androsperm bearing the Y chromosome which produces sons. The primary ethical question is whether **sex preselection** can be morally justified. With sex-linked inherited diseases, sex preference can be defended.

Christine Overall argues that where people specifically want a boy or girl baby, they are anticipating parenting pleasures with a younger human who is fundamentally 'either like oneself or different from oneself in . . . respect of sexual identity' (1987: 27) and this is not sexist. This desire may be confounded by experience where a daughter may be more different in personality to her mother than a son. However, Overall questions whether the preference for a sex 'is also *sufficient* to justify the practice of sex preselection' (1987: 28) and she concludes that in a culture oppressive to women, it is not. Post-conception sex determination clinics are common in India and China, where separation of male- and female-bearing sperm, amniocentesis or ultrasound are used for determining the sex of the foetus. Many foetuses are aborted for no other reason than that they are female.

Who owns genetic material?

Ownership, consent and liberty to experiment are all complex ethical areas. It is hard to view a discarded foetus as mere 'medical waste'. Yet, does the aborted foetus have moral status? Further, given the woman has consented to her abortion, should she be involved in approving any use of foetal material? Similar questions about moral status apply to embryos. Embryo freezing (**cryopreservation**), once considered a complex ethical issue, is now routine in IVF. Consider a bizarre experiment conducted in Bologna, Italy. 'A spare IVF embryo was injected into a womb removed from a woman by hysterectomy and kept alive on a perfusion machine in the laboratory for fifty-two hours – before the womb collapsed. The embryo was said to develop normally' (Klein 1992: 17). The researchers were excited at the idea of a gestation that did not require a woman.

Reflect on a potential 'test-tube baby', a one to sixteen cell embryo that exists in a culture medium. Do the donors of the egg and sperm have the right to refuse to permit excess embryos to be implanted in the woman, in a surrogate or be frozen for later use? Do they have the right to discard 'excess' ones? Overall (1987: 74) maintains that the couple do not have a right because they do not own the embryo. An individual owns his or her genetic material, be it egg or sperm. An embryo may become a person, hence it is not something that can be owned. While the genetic parents are generally authorized to make decisions about the fate of embryos, they have no automatic entitlement to destroy it, just as the embryo has no automatic entitlement to the occupancy of a woman's body. No one has the right to use anybody's body. This principle is part of what makes rape and slavery wrong (1987: 77). Who makes decisions about frozen embryos if the couple die before the expiry date? In Australia 'the responsibility for two embryos "orphaned" after the death of the contracting couple was held to lie with the clinic' (Bonnicksen 1994: 228).

Consider the example of Mary Sue Davis who had nine ova removed in 1988 and fertilized by her husband. Two embryos were implanted but no pregnancy resulted. The remaining seven were cryopreserved for possible future attempts. The couple divorced and Mary Davis sought entitlement to have the embryos implanted to which her ex-spouse objected. Custody of the embryos was given to the woman for implantation (Overall 1995: 179). Junior Davis objected that this meant he was to be 'raped of reproductive rights', that making him become a parent against his will was to deny his right to control reproduction (1995: 181). This objection confuses genetic contribution with parental care. Overall maintains that men are entitled to reproductive choice when sperm leaves their body but 'there are no grounds for extending male reproductive freedom beyond this point' (1995: 182). Mary Davis remarried and changed her mind about wanting the embryos implanted. Where there is a disagreement, the argument for assigning decisional authority for embryos to the woman is future-oriented, to reduce the likelihood of having to endure future burdens of IVF (1995: 192).

The advantages in freezing eggs are presented to women before they have chemotherapy for cancer treatment, which seems sympathetic and justifiable, but the offer to younger women who want to delay their family for career purposes is purely instrumental and harder to defend. Klein fears the freezing of eggs will mean that 'embryo research can be conducted at much greater distance from a woman's body' (1990: 240), further undermining women's bodily integrity and autonomous choice. Cryopreservation is a stage in the process of the search for an artificial womb, undervaluing women, increasing technocratic masculinist control and separating reproduction from its interdependent processes. Helen Bequaert Holmes believes that success in freezing eggs is disastrous because it is 'another tooth in the saw that dismembers women into body parts' (1994: 197). Her allied deep uneasiness over donating eggs 'arises from the fact that an egg carries half one's genes. Any successful use of that egg means that one has a(nother) child on this planet' (1994: 198). Elsewhere, we discussed the issue of genetic contribution as not being sufficient to talk of parenting. Nevertheless, biology is significant. It means a child one cannot love or ever know lives with a false genealogy, a child who may inadvertently be attracted to, or marry her/his genetic relative.

Contract motherhood

Commodification of reproduction

Reproduction is commodified when it becomes an economic relationship. The embryo or foetus becomes a consumer good made to order and purchased in the market. Parents become consumers of services intended to enhance the quality of the product. People in the West 'have the freedom to choose whether to reproduce, when to reproduce, what to reproduce, and the number of offspring to reproduce – a godlike responsibility' (Overall 1987: 49).

Legal experts claim that people 'should have the freedom to pick egg, sperm, or gestational donors to maximize desirable physical features' (in Overall 1987: 50). The embryo or foetus, as if a new consumer product, becomes a costly type of property to be obtained from others who are willing to sell. A couple, as 'joint owners' might dispute the destiny of an embryo. Surgical separation may result in each partner 'owning' one of a pair of identical twin embryos that can be sold or frozen for later use.

Commercial transactions themselves are not morally objectionable, it is the introduction of economic considerations into reproduction as the sale of eggs, sperm, embryos and use of a uterus that is morally troubling. The manipulation of women's fertility in a womb or laboratory, 'can alter the "products" of reproduction' (Spallone 1989: 15–16), creating the potential for exploitation and misuse of power. When we ask who benefits from reproductive technology, it is often the scientists and physicians (who make the decisions as to who has abortions, which women are eligible for IVF, who will donate eggs and embryos and which embryos are transferred to which women) who profit in a financially lucrative or careerist way from these decisions.

Within feminist ethics, the most important consideration is that, 'a person is not the kind of thing that may be bought or sold' (Overall 1987: 52). Buying and selling a human corpse is highly disrespectful. Similarly, the buying and selling of an embryo or foetus is wrong because it violates 'the prima facie obligation not to buy or sell what is, was, or will be a person' (1987: 53). Overall advocates stringent restrictions on all research, institutions and contracts that promote the commodification of reproduction. Legally, this prohibits any commercial agreement where sperm, ova, embryos or bodily parts are bought or sold. Contracts for babies by contracting mothers are also invalid. It is difficult to limit profit-making and there is enormous potential for exploitation, but a serious problem is the moral obligation to the embryo or foetus. Whatever one's views of its status, it is not merely a piece of art, a scientific experiment, a product to be improved through medical ingenuity, a bit of property or a consumer good with a monetary value. All these attitudes depersonalize the value of life and undermine women's bodies, separating reproduction from the rest of women's lives and from nurturance. The principle of nonmaleficence, refraining from hurting a living being and the environment in which they live is a minimum requirement of responsible moral behaviour.

Who is a surrogate mother?

The term 'surrogate mother' is a distortion in that 'the surrogate mother *is* the mother, and she is giving up her child for adoption just as is the birth mother who gives up her child for adoption by an unrelated person' (Ketchum 1993, 102). The language buries the physical connection between the mother and child, suggesting she is a mere receptacle. For this reason, feminist ethics talk of **commercial contract motherhood**. Is this a valuable service to men whose female partners are infertile 'or is it a type of reproductive prostitution of women?' (Overall 1987: 1). A commissioning couple who are unable to bear a child pays a fee to a woman who generally is inseminated with the male's sperm, bears the child and surrenders it at birth. While the man's name can go on the birth certificate, the infertile woman who rears the child must formally adopt the child to become the legal mother. Some women gestate an embryo that is not genetically theirs but has been created through IVF using another woman's egg; occasionally this is from their sister or daughter. The debates on this topic are enormous (Holmes 1994).

When IVF is used, a woman who has 'good' eggs but no womb or fallopian tubes has these eggs fertilized by her partner then implanted into a commercially hired woman. Klein is sceptical of the argument 'by IVF doctors that by not using her own egg the risk of the surrogate mother bonding to the child after that pregnancy is less' (1992: 8). In the 1987 'Baby M' case Mary Beth Whitehead changed her mind about being a 'surrogate mother'. She felt she was a mother in the fullest sense. Initially she gave William and Elizabeth Stern the baby, then decided she could not keep the fee and asked for the baby back. Judge Sorkow emphasized the class differences, arguing that the Whiteheads could provide more materially, socially and morally. Significantly, he also claimed that because the child was genetically related to William Stern, 'he cannot purchase what is already his' (in Spallone 1989: 175). This reinforces patriarchal logic of male ownership (as one might own an expensive car), for the child was also genetically Whitehead's. A later decision restored Whitehead as the legal mother but custody remains with the Sterns.

Genetic ties are also important to women. In the USA, Christa Uchytils was born with ovaries but no uterus. In 1991, eggs taken from her ovaries were fertilized by her husband's sperm and implanted into her forty-three-year-old mother who bore twins. A similar case occurred in South Africa where a forty-eight-year-old woman gave birth to triplets, her grandchildren conceived by her daughter (Callahan 1995: 29). These examples are not subject to the concerns involved in fees for gestational mothers. The desire for biological motherhood may extend beyond a seeking of genetic ties to include 'the relational experiences of pregnancy, birth, and nursing' (Berg 1995: 81). Yet these experiences were not options in these two cases. Their controversial nature means that some think it is a lovely gesture of a mother to her daughter, others feel it does not seem quite right, others are adamant it is wrong. Part of the radical ethical unease surrounding the nature of 'choice' of a surrogate 'consists in agreeing (for love or money) to see herself as a mere incubator . . . unconnected to the embryo/foetus that grows in her body for nine months' (Klein 1992: 12). Even the distinction between commercial contracts and altruistic agreements reinforces gender norms that love rather than self-determination should underlie women's desire to have children (Anleu 1990).

Free market contracts

The free market model maintains that surrogacy is a service that uncoerced women can offer for payment to fertile men and their infertile women partners and it requires careful legal regulations of contract and public scrutiny of its operation (Birke, Himmelweit and Vines 1990). 'The couple freely decides to invest their money in their preferred form of consumer good: a child' (Overall 1987: 114). The contracting woman exercises free choice in selling her reproductive capacities. Given the choice between poverty and exploitation many women readily select the latter. However, this model maintains that contracting mothers freely choose to sell their services at an agreed price, hence it is not unjust. Regulation is needed 'to protect the interests of the women who participate' (Purdy 1994: 319). Those supporting commercialized contract mothering maintain that any restriction violates fundamental rights of autonomy, in reinforcing 'the negative stereotype of women as incapable of full rational agency' (Boone 1994: 350).

This is contentious. Women's competency as moral agents is not in question, but the desirability of the choice is. However, some maintain that a moral issue is women's freedom to determine their use of reproductive capacities and that renting one's capacities improves the opportunities presently available to women (Sistare

1988) 'by expanding their economic control over their reproductive powers' (Boone 1994: 350). Freedom is the central normative
consideration. This defence seems oblivious to how women experience contract motherhood, what the practice of buying and selling
reflects about women's social position, and it pays scant attention
to the possibilities of injustice and exploitation. A woman's choice
between poverty and exploitation is not a free choice in the sense
of a moral agency that permits women to flourish as full human
beings. ·

Sarah Boone casts reasonable doubt on the defence of autonomy.
From the vantage point of women of colour she argues that 'commercialized contract motherhood is morally objectionable because
it reinforces the multi-tiered oppression of all women' (1994: 351).
She maintains that contract motherhood and African-American
enslavement are different expressions of the same underlying ideological forms. It is mainly poor women who are likely to be contract mothers. New reproductive technologies make it possible
to implant fertilized ova so that women of colour can bear white
babies. This option assumes that a woman has less emotional ties
to a baby with whom she has a gestational but not genetic relationship. This assumption represents a state of alienation, separating the woman from the experience of pregnancy. Racial and
gender oppression is reinforced. Andrea Dworkin argues that the
scientific separation of sex from reproduction and of reproduction from sex 'enable women to sell their wombs within the terms
of the brothel model' (1983: 181). Reproduction is commodified
as sex is with prostitution. The womb is extracted from the woman
as a whole person. Dworkin calls the surrogate mother a 'reproductive prostitute' (1983: 188). Lawyers and doctors who recruit
the surrogate and match her with the commissioning couple act
as pimps.

Carole Pateman (1989) argues that surrogacy is another part of
the sexual contract, 'a new form of access to and use of women's
bodies by men' (1989: 210). The surrogate mother agrees to be
inseminated, bear a child and relinquish it to the genetic father.
While IVF permits an embryo to be inserted into a surrogate, the
former example is more typical. The baby produced becomes the
property of the man. Pateman suggests that to see surrogacy as a
gift relation ignores who the service is for. Prostitution is defended
as a therapy for men not getting enough sex and surrogacy is defended on compassionate grounds for infertile women. Pateman's
point is that just as a prostitute sells sexual services, a contracting

mother does not sell a baby but a service. Her payment is for entering a contract which allows a man to use her services. 'The contract is for use of the property a woman owns in her uterus' (1989: 212). From the view of contract, 'the fact that provision of a service involves motherhood is purely incidental. The womb has no special status as property' (Pateman 1989: 212–13).

Even the qualifier 'surrogate' signifies a denial of the relevancy of 'motherhood' to the contract. The woman has to stultify the unique creative, physiological and emotional changes in her body, and perhaps most crucially, she has to separate herself from the possibility of a bond forming. Pateman argues that the separation of motherhood from womanhood expands patriarchal rights. The contractual exchange is between sperm and a uterus. If the woman 'performs her service faithfully, he can claim the property thereby produced as his own' (1989: 214). The sexual contract takes a peculiar twist, in that 'the surrogacy contract enables a man to present his wife with the ultimate gift – a child' (1989: 214).

Some writers toy with the idea of contract motherhood as a career option. Christine Sistare (1988) argues that surrogacy reveals a meaningful respect for maternity in the capitalist mode of paying well for what is deemed rare and precious. Mary Gibson also argues that it is not surprising that working-class women welcome the opportunity for contract mothering to 'get paid for engaging in one of the most meaningful activities available to them' (1994: 403). However Gibson does not welcome the perpetuation of exploitative practices implicit in 'the commodification of the child that . . . includes the alienation of the child from the birth mother' (1994: 405). Most writers view commercial contract motherhood as alienated labour where the woman gives her body for a product she is to relinquish. She surrenders her individuality in that her fee is not for the expression of her personality but for her reproductive capacities. It is not that personal dimensions are insignificant to her pregnancy, but that her personhood is permitted no moral significance. She is reduced to a womb for rent, producing a product for sale. All commodification of persons is morally inappropriate because it fragments human capacity. It is morally repugnant that some women are faced with the option of selling a baby to provide for basic needs.

Most people find the practice of contract motherhood morally unacceptable. The Committee of Inquiry into Human Fertilization and Embryology headed by Mary Warnock recommended that surrogacy contracts be rendered legally unenforceable because treating others as means, however desirable the consequences, is morally objectionable, becoming exploitative when financial interests are involved (1985: 46). It recommends that agencies and professionals who recruit surrogates are criminally liable although private persons who participate in such arrangements are not. Rosemarie Tong (1995) supports the assimilation of surrogacy arrangements into adoption laws. She advocates gestational mothers being assured they have a 'change of heart' period. This acknowledges that a parental relationship has moral significance and challenges the notion that a contract is more important than people. She believes that adoption is preferable to contract, for the latter focuses on the paternal genetic relationship, the former on allowing contracting mothers to gain access to children. 'The adoption approach with its change of heart clause, replaces . . . the *heartless* contract approach' (1995: 75).

Case study. Fees for a baby

In 1985, Mrs Kim Cotton was the first British woman to give birth to a baby by commercial arrangement with a surrogate agency with the plan to give the baby to the father for the agreed fee of £6,500. She was artificially inseminated using the prospective father's sperm. The news of her pregnancy broke in the media shortly before the Warnock Committee's report was released. This woman had two children and was, to a large extent, motivated by money and altruism. A considerable sum was also received from tabloid newspapers. When she was asked her intentions, she replied, 'How could I even have considered keeping the baby, when it wasn't Geoff's (husband) child?' (Cotton and Winn 1985: 36). When pressed to explain this she responded, 'I think we do love children more if they are our own' (1985: 61). Closer to the time of birth she said, 'to give away a baby that looked like my own two meant I might have to face that I really was the mother, despite all my ways of distancing myself' (1985: 143). When the baby girl was born, she had no flood of maternal love, 'just joy that she was so lovely; happiness that her gift to the parents-to-be was such a perfect one; and pride in a job completed' (1985: 153). Her prime feelings was of a duty to get the baby to her father. The baby was placed in the couple's care but made a ward of court with a birth certificate sealed by court order. She never met the couple but pondered on whether the baby made them happy.

Affect on the child

Adopted children often experience a strong longing to search for their genetic parents or relinquishing mothers for their adopted child. Children born through AID may experience difficulty in grasping their origins. Increasing numbers of sperm donors consent to detailed information made available and in Australia donors can be contacted through a registry when the child reaches eighteen years (Berg 1995: 89). One adult born through AID says, 'no one considers how the child feels when she finds that her natural father was a $25 cup of sperm' (Rowland 1991: 38–41). There is a concern for how a child might be affected by knowing that a gestating mother conceived and carried with the deliberate intention of giving the child up. Should a child have access to a surrogate mother? Laura Purdy defends a utilitarian viewpoint, arguing that the consequences for babies are no worse from being born through IVF or surrogacy, that if technology can prevent harm to women at the cost of some emotional upset to children, women 'have a right to have their interests prevail' (1996: 174). Yet a child who is born as a result of donor egg and sperm, and who grows up with a sense of being dispossessed, not having a distinct parentage, may resent feeling alienated from the parent/s who raised her/him or from the unknown genetic parents. Considerations of the self and others are intrinsic to feminist ethics. The costs of commercial contract motherhood outweigh the benefits, because the security and integrity of identities is threatened.

Summary

• In reproductive technology, women are treated as disembodied beings with wombs, cells, eggs, embryos.

• Distinctions must be made between involuntary childlessness, voluntary childfreeness and infertility.

• Ethical discussions amongst IVF advocates revolve around embryos, ignoring the experimentation of women as subjects.

• Debating the ethical justification for genetic engineering, embryo freezing and sex preselection must be ongoing.

- Commercial contract motherhood expands patriarchal rights, allowing payment for a contract to allow a man to use a woman's reproductive services.

Further reading

Callahan, J. (ed.) (1995) *Reproduction, Ethics, and the Law. Feminist Perspectives*, Bloomington and Indianapolis: Indiana University Press.

Holmes, H. Bequaert (ed.) (1994) *Issues in Reproductive Technology*, New York and London: New York University Press.

Overall, C. (1987) *Ethics and Human Reproduction: A Feminist Analysis*, Boston: Allen & Unwin.

Scutt, J. A. (ed.) (1990) *The Baby Machine. Reproductive Technology and the Commercialisation of Motherhood*, London: Green Print.

Glossary

Abortion spectrums acknowledge there are degrees of moral culpability from full lack of alternatives through to full accountability.

Agape is an other-regarding love that demonstrates an unselfish concern for the well being of others.

Anger is a morally legitimate emotion which helps to identify wrongs.

Autonomy involves self-determination.

Beneficence is a responsibility to help someone who is in need.

Benevolence is the inclination to be generous, kind and sympathetic.

Commercial contract motherhood, often called **surrogacy**, involves a woman agreeing to being inseminated, bear a child and relinquish the child, usually to the genetic father in return for a fee. Some women gestate an embryo that is not genetically theirs, but most are genetically related to the child.

Communicative ethics are open, free, unconstrained and accessible forms of dialogue.

Compassion is the capacity to feel for others and, to some extent, share their emotions and enter into their predicaments.

Consent requires voluntariness, information, competence and a conscious decision.

Cryopreservation is embryo freezing.

Deliberative morality is morality open to criticism, self-criticism and debate.

Deliberative universalism accepts core universal principles and the need to debate publicly how conflicts on social justice can best be addressed.

Dialogic communitarianism assumes democratic institutions that provide access to political processes of dialogue in deliberating on collective ideas of how to achieve public goals.

Discourse ethics aims at communication and mutual understanding with those with whom an agreement must be reached.

Dualism involves hierarchically valued binary divisions that are perceived to be oppositional and antagonistic.

Embodiment as positionality refers to communities of knowing subjects who are empowered in their entitlement to speak and be heard.

Emotions are crucial for responding sensitively to people's situations.

Epistemology is a framework for understanding knowledge.

Essentialism is the view that human life has certain central defining features.

Ethics is the systematic and critical reflection on the goodness and rightness of human action.

Erotica is sexually suggestive and respectful of humans portrayed.

Eugenics is the scientific improvement of the human species by genetic means.

Feminist ethics is a moral reasoning about goodness, rightness and desirable practices that is directed toward the personal, social and political changes that feminism requires to end women's subordination.

Friendship is a practical and emotional relationship marked by mutual and equal goodwill, liking and pleasure.

Impartiality assumes that moral agents are emotionally distanced and objectively neutral.

Intimate relationships are particular, partial, specific and familiar relationships.

***In vitro* fertilization** involves fertilization outside of the woman's body.

Lesbian continuum refers to the range of woman-identified experiences from intense bonding through to sensual and sexual relationships.

Loyalty expects faithfulness, dependability and devotion.

Justice includes fairness, equity, reasonable treatment, rejecting injury, due regard, toleration and respect for others.

Moral agents have the capacity to make ethical judgements, to engage in decent practices and be accountable for themselves.

Moral boundaries are the lines between what is right and wrong, good and evil, permissible and impermissible, worthy and unworthy.

Moral deliberation is the process by which conflicting moral claims are constructed.

Mutuality is a reciprocal exchange that bolsters well-being.

Mutual recognition simultaneously appreciates, desires and gains pleasure from another as well as giving pleasure.

Nonmaleficence means to do no harm.

Normative ethics are concerned with guiding right and good action.

Objectification views people as objects and is dehumanizing, demeaning the moral equality of persons.

Obligations are the bases of duties.

Palliative care alleviates suffering.

Partiality responds to specific distinctiveness.

Particularity pays attention to particular others in actual contexts.

Paternalism is where someone's capacity to make their own judgement is ignored.

Political ethics critically reflects on good and bad decisions and right and wrong actions in the polity.

Politics of need interpretation involves a struggle over contesting legitimate needs; the rights required to satisfy human needs; and how to translate the rights effectively.

Pornography is the explicit representation of sexual behaviour that degrades, humiliates and harms persons for the sexual gratification of others.

Potentiality of personhood establishes guidelines for research on an embryo up to a limit of fourteen days beyond fertilization.

Practical reasoning is reasoning intended to identify morally desirable or permissible actions and practices.

Privacy rights are the rights to be free from unwarranted intrusion on something considered to be a personal matter.

Pro-choice advocates support a woman's right to choose an abortion.

Pro-life supports the foetus's right to life over a woman's right to choose an abortion.

Prostitution is the use of someone's body for sexual satisfaction in exchange for money.

Queer politics radically challenges social and cultural norms of gender, reproductive sexuality and the family.

Queer sexuality deliberately transgresses norms of sexuality.

Reproductive freedoms affirm ideals of equality and autonomy, ensuring bodily integrity and the reproductive self-determination that is part of equal citizenship.

Respect for autonomy allows people to make choices as self-determining, responsible and capable persons.

Rights are fundamental entitlements that enable people to participate in social life with dignity as equal citizens.

Sadomasochism is where physical or emotional pain is encouraged as part of sexual experience.

Self-respect is the due regard for one's dignity and worth.

Selves-in-relations is an understanding that the interconnections between oneself and those with whom we are attached are integral to moral judgements.

Self-sacrifice is when the interests and needs of others are prioritized over the desires of one's self.

Sex preselection refers to techniques which enable prospective parents to predetermine the sex of their child.

Sex-selective abortions abort female foetuses where there is a cultural preference for sons (or a practice of female infanticide occurs).

Sexual difference is about embodied subjectivity and the desire to speak as a woman or as a man.

Sexual politics is about unequal power relations.

Special rights take into account actual differences as being morally relevant factors that should be incorporated into law, policy and institution.

Specificity articulates differences that are ethically relevant.

Traffickers are those responsible for luring women and young girls and boys from their homes into sexual slavery.

Trust is a reliance on others not to harm, but to care for our well-being.

Universalism is the belief that there are rules, norms and principles that are equally applicable to everyone.

References

Afshar, H. and Maynard, M. (eds) (1994) *The Dynamics of 'Race' and Gender: Some Feminist Interpretations*, London: Taylor & Francis.

Almond, B. (1988) 'Women's right: reflections on ethics and gender', in M. Griffiths and M. Whitford (eds) *Feminist Perspectives in Philosophy*, Bloomington: Indiana University Press, pp. 42–57.

Almond, B. (1995) *Introducing Applied Ethics*, Oxford: Blackwell.

Andolsen, B. Hilkert (1994) 'Agape in feminist ethics', in L. K. Daly (ed.) *Feminist Theological Ethics. A Reader*, Louisville, Kentucky: Westminster John Knox Press, pp. 146–59.

Anleu, S. Roach (1990) 'Reinforcing gender norms: commercial and altruistic surrogacy', *Acta Sociologica* 33 (1): 63–74.

Annis, D. (1987) 'The meaning, values and duties of friendship', *American Philosophical Quarterly* 24 (4): 349–55.

Anthias, F. and Yuval-Davis, N. (1992) *Racialized Boundaries. Race, Nation, Gender, Colour and Class and the Anti-Racist Struggle*, London and New York: Routledge.

Arditti, R., Klein, R. D. and Minden, S. (eds) (1984) *Test Tube Women: What Future for Motherhood*, London: Pandora.

Aristotle (1977) *The Nicomachean Ethics*, Middlesex: Penguin Books.

Assiter, A. (1989) *Pornography, Feminism and the Individual*, London: Pluto Press.

Aziz, R. (1992) 'Feminism and the challenge of racism: deviance or difference?', in H. Crowley and S. Himmelweit (eds) *Knowing Women, Feminism and Knowledge*, Cambridge: Polity Press, pp. 291–305.

Bacchi, C. (1996) *The Politics of Affirmative Action*, London: Sage.

Badhwar, N. Kapur (1987) 'Friends as ends in themselves', *Philosophy and Phenomenological Research* 48 (1): 1–23.

Baier, A. C. (1985) 'What do women want in a moral theory?', *Noûs* 19 (1): 53–63.

Baier, A. C. (1986) 'Trust and antitrust', *Ethics* 96 (2): 231–60.

Baier, A. C. (1987) 'Hume, the woman's moral theorist?', in E. Feder Kittay and D. T. Meyers (eds) *Women and Moral Theory*, Totowa, NJ: Rowman & Littlefield, pp. 37–55.

Baier, A. C. (1993) 'What do women want in a moral theory?', in M. J. Larrabee (ed.) *An Ethic of Care*, London: Routledge, pp. 19–32.

Baier, A. C. (1994) *Moral Prejudices: Essays on Ethics*, Cambridge MA: Harvard University Press.

Balbus, I. D. (1998) *Emotional Rescue. The Theory and Practice of a Feminist Father*, London and New York: Routledge.

Banks, S. (1995) *Ethics and Values in Social Work*, London: Macmillan.

Bar, B.-A. and Ferguson, A. (eds) (1998) *Daring to be Good. Essays in Feminist Ethico-Politics*, London and New York: Routledge.

Baron, M. (1991) 'Impartiality and friendship', *Ethics* 101 (4): 836–57.

Barry, U. (1988) 'Abortion in the Republic of Ireland', *Feminist Review* 29: 57–63.

Bartky, S. (1990) *Femininity and Domination. Studies in the Phenomenology of Oppression*, New York: Routledge.

Bartlett, E. A. (1992) 'Beyond either/or: justice and care in the ethics of Albert Camus', in E. Browning Cole and S. Coultrap-McQuin (eds) *Explorations in Feminist Ethics*, Bloomington: Indiana University Press, pp. 82–8.

Bartlett, J. (1994) *Will You Be Mother? Women Who Choose to Say No*, London: Virago Press.

Basu, A. (ed.) (1995) *The Challenge of Local Feminisms*, Boulder, Colorado and Oxford: Westview Press.

Benhabib, S. (1992) *Situating the Self. Gender, Community and Postmodernism in Contemporary Ethics*, Cambridge: Polity Press.

Benjamin, J. (1990) *The Bonds of Love. Psychoanalysis, Feminism, and the Problem of Domination*, London: Virago.

Benner, P. (1994) 'The role of articulation in understanding practice and experience as sources of knowledge in clinical nursing', in J. Tully (ed.) *Philosophy in an Age of Pluralism: The Philosophy of Charles Taylor in Question*, Cambridge: Cambridge University Press, pp. 136–55.

Berenson, F. (1991) 'What is this thing called "love"?', *Philosophy* 66 (255): 65–79.

Berg, B. J. (1995) 'Listening to the voices of the infertile', in J. Callahan (ed.) *Reproduction, Ethics, and the Law. Feminist Perspectives*, Bloomington and Indianapolis: Indiana University Press, pp. 80–108.

Bhavnani, K.-K. and Phoenix, A. (eds) (1994) *Shifting Identities, Shifting Racisms. A Feminism and Psychology Reader*, London: Sage.

Bickford, S. (1996) *The Dissonance of Democracy: Listening, Conflict and Citizenship*, Ithaca, New York and London: Cornell University Press.

Birke, L., Himmelweit S. and Vines G. (1990) *Tomorrow's Child: Reproductive Technologies in the 90s*, London: Virago.

Bishop, S. (1987) 'Connections and guilt', *Hypatia* 2 (1): 7–23.

Bishop, A. H. and Scudder J. R. (1996) *Nursing Ethics. Therapeutic Caring Presence*, Boston: Jones and Bartlett Publishers.

Blum, L. (1980) *Friendship, Altruism and Morality*, London: Routledge & Kegan Paul.

Blum, L. (1986) 'Iris Murdoch and the domain of the moral', *Philosophical Studies* 50 (3): 343–67.

Blum, L. (1988) 'Gilligan and Kohlberg: implications for moral theory', *Ethics* 98 (3): 472–91.

Blum, L. (1991) 'Moral perception and particularity', *Ethics* 101 (2): 701–25.

Blum, L. (1993) 'Gilligan and Kohlberg: implications for moral theory', in M. J. Larrabee (ed.) *An Ethic of Care. Feminist and Interdisciplinary Perspectives*, London and New York: Routledge, pp. 49–68.

Bock, G. and James, S. (eds) (1992) *Beyond Equality and Difference. Citizenship, Feminist Politics and Female Subjectivity*, London: Routledge.

Bonnicksen, A. L. (1994) 'Ethical issues in the clinical application of embryo freezing', in H. Bequaert Holmes (ed.) *Issues in Reproductive Technology*, New York and London: New York University Press, pp. 217–30.

Boone, S. S. (1994) 'Slavery and contract motherhood: a "racialized" objection to the autonomy arguments', in H. Bequaert Holmes (ed.) *Issues in Reproductive Technology*, New York and London: New York University Press, pp. 349–66.

Bordo, S. (1993) *Unbearable Weight. Feminism, Western Culture and the Body*, Berkeley: University of California Press.

Bowden, P. (1996) *Caring. Gender-Sensitive Ethics*, London and New York: Routledge.

Brabeck, M. (1993) 'Moral judgement: theory and research on differences between males and females', in M. J. Larrabee (ed.) *An Ethic of Care. Feminism and Interdisciplinary Perspectives*, London and New York: Routledge, pp. 33–48.

Braidotti, R. (1992) 'On the female feminist subject, or: from "she-self" to "she-other"', in G. Bock and S. James (eds) *Beyond Equality and Difference. Citizenship, Feminist Politics and Female Subjectivity*, London: Routledge, pp. 177–92.

Braidotti, R. (1993) 'Embodiment, sexual difference, and the nomadic subject', *Hypatia* 8 (1): 1–13.

Brown, M., Fielden, K. and Scutt, J. A. (1990) 'New frontiers or old recycled? New reproductive technologies as primary industry', in J. A. Scutt (ed.) *The Baby Machine. Reproductive Technology and the Commercialisation of Motherhood*, London: Green Print, pp. 77–107.

Brown, W. (1995) *States of Injury: Power and Freedom in Late Modernity*, Princeton: Princeton University Press.

Brownmiller, S. (1976) *Against Our Will: Men, Women and Rape*, New York: Simon & Schuster.

Bubeck, D. E. (1995) *Care, Gender and Justice*, Oxford: Clarendon Press.

Bubeck, D. E. (1998) 'Ethic of care and feminist ethics', *Women's Philosophy Review* 18: 22–50.

Burman, E. (1994) 'Experience, identities and alliances: Jewish feminism and feminist psychology', in K.-K. Bhavnani and A. Phoenix (eds) *Shifting Identities, Shifting Racisms. A Feminism and Psychology Reader*, London: Sage, pp. 155–78.

Butler, J. (1990) *Gender Trouble: Feminism and the Subversion of Identity*, London and New York: Routledge.

Butler, J. (1993) *Bodies That Matter: On the Discursive Limits of 'Sex'*, New York: Routledge.

Butler, J. (1997) *Excitable Speech. A Politics of the Performative*, London: Routledge.

Callahan, J. C. (ed.) (1995) *Reproduction, Ethics, and the Law. Feminist Perspectives*, Bloomington and Indianapolis: Indiana University Press.

Card, C. (1988) 'Gratitude and obligation', *American Philosophy Quarterly* 25 (2): 115–27.

Card, C. (1990) 'Caring and evil', *Hypatia* 5 (1): 101–8.

Card, C. (1991) *Feminist Ethics*, Kansas: University of Kansas Press.

Carola, E. (1988) 'Women, erotica, pornography – learning to play the game?', in G. Chester and J. Dickey (eds) *Feminism and Censorship. The Current Debate*, Dorset: Prism Press, pp. 168–77.

Carse, A. L. (1995) 'Pornography: an uncivil liberty?', *Hypatia* 10 (1): 155–82.

Carter, S. (1994) 'A most useful tool', in A. Jaggar (ed.) *Living with Contradictions. Controversies in Feminist Social Ethics*, Boulder, Colorado and Oxford: Westview Press, pp. 112–16.

Chen, M. (1983) *A Quiet Revolution: Women in Transition in Rural Bangladesh*, Cambridge, MA: Schenkman.

Chryssides, G. D. and Kaler, J. H. (1993) *An Introduction to Business Ethics*, London: Chapman & Hall.

Clarke, A. (1994) 'Subtle forms of sterilization abuse: a reproductive rights analysis', in A. Jaggar (ed.) *Living with Contradictions. Controversies in Feminist Social Ethics*, Boulder, Colorado and Oxford: Westview Press, pp. 341–52.

Clarke, J. (ed.) (1993) *A Crisis in Care? Challenges to Social Work*, London: Sage.

Clarke, L. (1991) 'Abortion: a rights issue?', in R. Lee and D. Morgan (eds), *Birthrights: Law and Ethics at the Beginning of Life*, London: Routledge, pp. 155–71.

Clement, G. (1996) *Care, Autonomy and Justice. Feminism and the Ethic of Care*, Boulder, Colorado and Oxford: Westview Press.

Cockburn, C. (1996) 'Strategies for gender democracy', *European Journal of Women's Studies* 3 (1): 7–26.

Code, L. (1987) *Epistemic Responsibility*, Hanover: University Press of New England.

Code, L. (1991) *What Can She Know? Feminist Theory and the Construction of Knowledge*, Ithaca: Cornell University Press.

Code, L. (1995) *Rhetorical Spaces: Essays on Gendered Locations*, London and New York: Routledge.

Code, L., Mullett, S. and Overall, C. (eds) (1988) *Feminist Perspectives. Philosophical Essays on Method and Morals*, Toronto: University of Toronto Press.

Cole, E. Browning and Coultrap-McQuin, S. (eds) (1992) *Explorations in Feminist Ethics*, Bloomington: Indiana University Press.

Collins, P. Hill (1990) *Black Feminist Thought: Knowledge, Consciousness, and the Politics of Empowerment*, Boston: Unwin Hyman.

Collins, P. Hill (1993) 'Pornography and Black women's bodies', in D. E. H. Russell (ed.) *Making Violence Sexy. Feminist Views on Pornography*, Buckingham: Open University Press, pp. 97–103.

Coltheart, L. (1986) 'Desire, consent and liberal theory', in C. Pateman and E. Gross (eds) *Feminist Challenges. Social and Political Theory*, Sydney: Allen & Unwin, pp. 112–22.

Connell, R. (1995) *Masculinities*, Cambridge: Polity.

Corea, G. (1985) *The Mother Machine – Reproductive Technologies from Artificial Insemination to Artificial Wombs*, New York: Harper & Row.

Corea, G. (1994) '"Informed consent": the myth of voluntarism', in A. Jaggar (ed.) *Living with Contradictions. Controversies in Feminist Social Ethics*, Boulder, Colorado and Oxford: Westview Press, pp. 352–61.

Corey, G., Schneider Corey, M. and Callanan, P. (1988) *Issues and Ethics in the Helping Professions*, Pacific Grove, California: Brooks/Cole Publishing Company.

Cornell, D. (1991) *Beyond Accommodation*, London and New York: Routledge.

Cornell, D. (1992) *The Philosophy of the Limit*, London and New York: Routledge.

Cornell, D. (1995) 'What is Ethical Feminism?', in S. Benhabib, J. Butler, D. Cornell and N. Fraser, *Feminist Contentions. A Philosophical Exchange*, London and New York: Routledge, pp. 75–106.

Cotton, K. and Winn, D. (1985) *Baby Cotton. For Love and Money*, London: Dorling Kindersley.

Crenshaw, K. (1997) 'Intersectionality and identity politics: learning from violence against women of color', in M. L. Shanley and U. Narayan (eds) *Reconstructing Political Theory. Feminist Perspectives*, Cambridge: Polity Press, pp. 178–93.

Crowley, H. and Himmelweit, S. (eds) (1992) *Knowing Women. Feminism and Knowledge*, Cambridge: Polity Press.

Cuomo, C. J. (1997) *Feminism and Ecological Communities. An Ethic of Flourishing*, London and New York: Routledge.

Davies, C. (1995) 'Competence versus care? Gender and caring work revisited', *Acta Sociologica* 38 (1): 17–31.

Davies, J. MacGregor (1988) 'Pornographic harms', in L. Code, S. Mullett and C. Overall (eds) *Feminist Perspectives. Philosophical Essays on Method and Morals*, Toronto: University of Toronto Press, pp. 127–45.

Davis, K. (1995) *Reshaping the Female Body. The Dilemma of Cosmetic Surgery*, New York: Routledge.

Davis, K. (1997) 'Embody-ing theory. Beyond modernist and postmodernist readings', in K. Davis (ed.) *Embodied Practices. Feminist Perspectives on the Body*, London: Sage, pp. 1–23.

de Beauvoir, S. (1975) *The Second Sex*, trans. H. M. Parshley, Middlesex: Penguin Books.

de Beauvoir, S. (1980) *The Ethics of Ambiguity*, trans. B. Frechtman, Secaucus, New Jersey: Citadel Press.

De Gama, K. (1993) 'A brave new world? Rights discourse and the politics of reproductive autonomy', *Journal of Law and Society* 20 (1): 114–30.

De Lauretis, T. (1990) *Sexual Difference: A Theory of Socio-Symbolic Practice*, Bloomington: Indiana University Press.

Dietz, M. (1985) 'Citizenship with a feminist face: the problem with maternal thinking', *Political Theory* 13 (1): 19–37.

Dietz, M. (1992) 'Context is all: feminism and theories of citizenship', in C. Mouffe (ed.) *Dimensions of Radical Democracy. Pluralism, Citizenship, Community*, London: Verso, pp. 63–85.

Dillon, R. (1992a) 'Toward a feminist conception of self-respect', *Hypatia* 7 (1): 52–69.

Dillon, R. (1992b) 'Care and respect', in E. Browning Cole and S. Coultrap McQuin (eds) *Explorations in Feminist Ethics*, Bloomington: Indiana University Press, pp. 69–81.

Diprose, R. (1994) *The Bodies of Women. Ethics, Embodiment and Sexual Differences*, London: Routledge.

DiQuinzio, P. and Young, I. M. (1995) 'Introduction: special issue on feminist ethics and social policy', *Hypatia* 10 (1): 1–7.

Draper, H. (1996) 'Consent in childbirth', in L. Frith (ed.) *Ethics and Midwifery. Issues in Contemporary Practice*, Oxford: Butterworth-Heinemann, pp. 17–35.

Dreifus, C. (ed.) (1978) *Seizing Our Bodies. The Politics of Women's Health*, New York: Vintage Books.

Dworkin, A. (1981) *Pornography: Men Possessing Women*, New York: Perigee Books.

Dworkin, A. (1983) *Right-Wing Women*, New York: Perigee Books.

Dworkin, A. (1988) *Letters from a War Zone*, London: Secker & Warburg.

Dworkin, A. (1994) 'Why pornography matters to feminists', in A. Jaggar (ed.) *Living with Contradictions. Controversies in Feminist Social Ethics*, Boulder, Colorado and Oxford: Westview Press, pp. 152–3.

Dworkin, A. (1997) *Life and Death: Unapologetic Writings on the Continuing War against Women*, London: Virago.

Dworkin, A. and MacKinnon C. (1993) 'Questions and answers', in D. E. H. Russell (ed.) *Making Violence Sexy. Feminist Views on Pornography*, Buckingham: Open University Press, pp. 78–96.

Eisenstein, Z. (1991), 'Privatizing the state: reproductive rights, affirmative action, and the problem of democracy', *Frontiers* 12: 98–125.

Elshtain, J. Bethke (1981) *Public Man, Private Woman, Women in Social and Political Thought*, Oxford: Martin Robertson.

Elshtain, J. Bethke (1993) 'Sovereignty, identity, sacrifice', in M. Ringrose and A. J. Lerner (eds) *Reimagining the Nation*, Buckingham: Open University Press, pp. 159–75.

European Network of Experts (1994) *Women in Decision-Making*, Brussels: Network of the European Commission on 'Women in Decision-Making'.

Evans, D. (ed.) (1990) *Why Should We Care?*, London: Macmillan Press.

Firestone, S. (1970) *The Dialectic of Sex*, New York: Bantam Books.

Flanagan, O. and Jackson, K. (1993) 'Justice, care and gender: the Kohlberg-Gilligan debate revisited', in M. J. Larrabee (ed.) *An Ethic of Care. Feminist and Interdisciplinary Perspectives*, London and New York: Routledge, pp. 69–84.

Flax, J. (1993) *Disputed Subjects, Essays on Psychoanalysis, Politics and Philosophy*, New York: Routledge.

Fox, M. and Murphy, T. (1992) 'Irish abortion: seeking refuge in a jurisprudence of doubt and delegation', *Journal of Law and Society* 19: 454–66.

Fraser, N. (1989) *Unruly Practices. Power, Discourse and Gender in Contemporary Social Theory*, Cambridge: Polity Press.

Fraser, N. and Gordon, L. (1994) 'Civil citizenship against social citizenship? On the ideology of contract-versus-charity', in B. van Steenbergen (ed.) *The Condition of Citizenship*, London: Sage, pp. 90–107.

Frazer, E., Hornsby, J. and Lovibond, S. (eds) (1992) *Ethics: A Feminist Reader*, Oxford: Blackwell.

Frazer, E. and Lacey, N. (1993) *The Politics of Community. The Feminist Critique of the Liberal-Communitarian Debate*, Toronto: University of Toronto Press.

Friedman, M. (1988) 'Individuality without individualism: review of Janice Raymond's *A Passion for Friends*', *Hypatia* 3 (2): 131–7.

Friedman, M. (1991) 'The practice of partiality', *Ethics* 101 (4): 818–35.

Friedman, M. (1993) *What Are Friends For?: Feminist Perspectives on Personal Relationships and Moral Theory*, Ithaca and London: Cornell University Press.

Friedman, M. (1995) 'Beyond caring: the de-moralization of gender', in V. Held (ed.) *Justice and Care. Essential Readings in Feminist Ethics*, Boulder, Colorado and Oxford: Westview Press, pp. 61–77.

Frith, L. (ed.) (1996) *Ethics and Midwifery. Issues in Contemporary Practice*, Oxford: Butterworth-Heinemann.

Frug, M. (1992) *Postmodern Legal Feminism*, London and New York: Routledge.

Frye, M. (1983) *The Politics of Reality: Essays in Feminist Theory*, New York: The Crossing Press.

Galeotti, A. E. (1993) 'Citizenship and equality. The place for toleration', *Political Theory* 21 (4): 585–605.

Gallagher, J. (1995) 'Collective bad faith: "protecting" the foetus', in J. Callahan (ed.) *Reproduction, Ethics, and the Law. Feminist Perspectives*, Bloomington and Indianapolis: Indiana University Press, pp. 343–79.

Gardiner, F. (1993) 'Political interest and participation of Irish women 1922–1992: the unfinished revolution', in A. Smyth (ed.) *Irish Women's Studies Reader*, Dublin: Attic Press, pp. 45–78.

Gardner, T. A. (1994) 'Racism in pornography and the women's movement', in A. Jaggar (ed.) *Living with Contradictions. Controversies in Feminist Social Ethics*, Boulder, Colorado and Oxford: Westview Press, pp. 171–6.

Garry, A. (1984) 'Pornography and censorship', in R. Baker and F. Elliston (eds) *Philosophy and Sex*, New York: Prometheus Books, pp. 312–26.

Gatens, M. (1995) 'Between the sexes: care or justice?', in B. Almond (ed.) *Introducing Applied Ethics*, Oxford: Blackwell, pp. 43–57.

Gatens, M. (1996) *Imaginary Bodies: Ethics, Power and Corporeality*, London and New York: Routledge.

Gibson, M. (1994) 'Contract motherhood: social practice in social context', in A. Jaggar (ed.) *Living with Contradictions. Controversies in Feminist Social Ethics*, Boulder, Colorado and Oxford: Westview Press, pp. 402–19.

Gilligan, C. (1983) *In a Different Voice: Psychological Theory and Women's Development*, Cambridge, MA: Harvard University Press.

Gilligan, C. (1984) 'The Conquistador and the Dark Continent: reflections on the psychology of love', *Daedalus* Summer 1984: 74–95.

Gilligan, C. (1986) 'Reply', *Signs* 11 (2): 324–33.

Gilligan, C. (1987) 'Moral orientation and moral development', in E. Feder Kittay and D. T. Meyers (eds) *Women and Moral Theory*, Totowa, New Jersey: Rowman & Littlefield, pp. 19–33.

Gilligan, C. (1988) 'Remapping the moral domain: new images of self in relationships', in C. Gilligan, J. V. Ward, and J. McLean Taylor (eds) *Mapping the Moral Domain. A Contribution of Women's Thinking to Psychological Theory and Education*, Cambridge MA: Harvard University Press, pp. 3–19.

Ginsburg, F. (1991) 'Gender politics and the contradictions of nurturance: moral authority and constraints to action for female abortion activists', *Social Research* 58 (3): 653–76.

Giobhe, E. (1994) 'Confronting the liberal lies about prostitution', in A. Jaggar (ed.) *Living with Contradictions. Controversies in Feminist Social Ethics*, Boulder, Colorado and Oxford: Westview Press, pp. 120–6.

Glendon, M. A. (1987) *Abortion and Divorce in Western Law*, Cambridge MA: Harvard University Press.

Glendon, M. A. (1989) *The Transformation of Family Law: State, Law, and Family in the U.S. and Western Europe*, Chicago: University of Chicago Press.

Gould, C. (ed.) (1984) *Beyond Domination. New Perspectives on Women and Philosophy*, Totowa, New Jersey: Rowman & Allanheld.

Gould, C. (1988) *Rethinking Democracy*, Cambridge: Cambridge University Press.

Govier, T. (1992) 'Trust, distrust and feminist theory', *Hypatia* 7 (1): 16–33.

Govier, T. (1993) 'Self-trust, autonomy, and self-esteem', *Hypatia* 8 (1): 99–120.

Griffiths, M. (1995) *Feminisms and the Self. The Web of Identity*, London: Routledge.

Griffiths, M. and Whitford, M. (eds) (1988) *Feminist Perspectives in Philosophy*, Bloomington: Indiana University Press.

Grimshaw, J. (1986) *Feminist Philosophers*, Brighton: Wheatsheaf Books.

Grosz, E. (1994) 'Sexual difference and the problem of essentialism', in N. Schor and E. Weed (eds) *The Essential Difference*, Bloomington: Indiana University Press, pp. 82–97.

Grosz, E. (1996) *Space, Time and Perversion. Essays on the Politics of the Body*, New York: Routledge.

Gutmann, A. (1993) 'The challenge of multiculturalism in political ethics', *Philosophy and Public Affairs* 22 (3): 171–206.

Habermas, J. (1971) *Knowledge and Human Interests*, trans. J. J. Shapiro, Boston: Beacon Press.

Hanen, M. and Nielson, K. (eds) (1987) *Science, Morality and Feminist Theory*, Calgary: University of Calgary Press.

Haraway, D. (1997) *Modest_Witness@Second_Millenium.FemaleMan_Meets_ OncoMouse*, London: Routledge.

Harding, S. (1987) 'The curious coincidence of feminine and African moralities: challenges for feminist theory', in E. Feder Kittay and D. T. Meyers (eds) *Women and Moral Theory*, Totowa, New Jersey: Rowman & Littlefield, pp. 296–316.

Hartley, N. (1994) 'Confessions of a feminist porno star', in A. Jaggar (ed.) *Living with Contradictions. Controversies in Feminist Social Ethics*, Boulder, Colorado and Oxford: Westview Press, pp. 176–8.

Hartman, A. and Laird, J. (1998) 'Moral and ethical issues in working with lesbians and gay men', *Families in Society* 79 (3): 263–76.

Hartmann, B. (1994) 'Reproductive rights and wrongs', in A. Jaggar (ed.) *Living with Contradictions. Controversies in Feminist Social Ethics*, Boulder, Colorado and Oxford: Westview Press, pp. 330–40.

Hartsock, N. and Boling, P. (1995) *Expecting Trouble: Surrogacy, Fetal Abuse, and New Reproductive Technologies*, Boulder, Colorado and Oxford: Westview Press.

Hasse, L. (1987) 'Legalizing gender-specific values', in E. Feder Kittay and D. T. Meyers, (eds) *Women and Moral Theory*, Totowa, New Jersey: Rowman & Littlefield, pp. 282–95.

Hekman, S. J. (1995) *Moral Voices, Moral Selves. Carol Gilligan and Feminist Theory*, Cambridge: Polity Press.

Held, V. (1984) *Rights and Goods*, New York: Macmillan Free Press.

Held, V. (1987) 'Feminism and moral theory', in E. Feder Kittay and D. T. Meyers (eds) *Women and Moral Theory*, Totowa, New Jersey: Rowman & Littlefield, pp. 111–29.

Held, V. (1993) *Feminist Morality. Transforming Culture, Society, and Politics*, Chicago and London: The University of Chicago Press.

Held, V. (ed.) (1995) *Justice and Care. Essential Readings in Feminist Ethics*, Boulder, Colorado and Oxford: Westview Press.

Henry, C. (ed.) (1995) *Professional Ethics and Organisational Change in Education and Health*, London: Edward Arnold.

Herman, B. (1991) 'Agency, attachment, and difference', *Ethics* 101 (4): 775–97.

Hill, T. (1987) 'The importance of autonomy', in E. Feder Kittay and D. T. Meyers (eds) *Women and Moral Theory*, Totowa, New Jersey: Rowman & Littlefield, pp. 129–38.

Himmelweit, S. (1988) 'More than a "Woman's Right to Choose"?', *Feminist Review* 29: 38–55.

Hoagland, S. L. (1988) *Lesbian Ethics: Toward New Value*, Palo Alto: Institute of Lesbian Studies.

Hoagland, S. L. (1990) 'Some concerns about Nel Noddings' *Caring*', *Hypatia* 5 (1): 109–14.

Holmes, H. Bequaert (1981) 'Reproductive technologies. The birth of a women-centred analysis', in H. Bequaert Holmes, B. B. Hoskins and M. Gross (eds) *The Custom-Made Child? Women-Centred Perspectives*, Clifton, New Jersey: Humana Press, pp. 1–18.

Holmes, H. Bequaert (1994) 'To freeze or not to freeze: is that an option?', in H. Bequaert Holmes (ed.) *Issues in Reproductive Technology*, New York and London: New York University Press, pp. 193–200.

Houston, B. (1987) 'Rescuing womanly virtues', in M. Hanen and K. Nielson (eds) *Science, Morality and Feminist Theory*, Calgary: University of Calgary Press, pp. 237–62.

Houston, B. (1990) 'Caring and exploitation', *Hypatia* 5 (1): 115–19.

Hugman, R. and Smith, D. (eds) (1995) *Ethical Issues in Social Work*, London: Routledge.

International Committee for Prostitutes' Rights (1994) 'International Committee for Prostitutes' Rights. World Charter and World Whores' Congress Statements', in A. Jaggar (ed.) *Living with Contradictions. Controversies in Feminist Social Ethics*, Boulder, Colorado and Oxford: Westview Press, pp. 133–42.

Jack, R. and Jack, D. Crowley (1989) *Moral Vision and Professional Decisions: The Changing Values of Women and Men Lawyers*, New York: Cambridge University Press.

Jackson, D. (1990) *Unmasking Masculinity. A Critical Autobiography*, London: Unwin Hyman.

Jackson, P. Conroy (1986) 'Women's movement and abortion: the criminalization of Irish women', in D. Dahlerup (ed.) *The New Women's Movement. Feminism and Political Power in Europe and the USA*, London: Sage, pp. 48–63.

Jaggar, A. (1976) 'Abortion and a woman's right to decide', in C. C. Gould and M. W. Wartofsky (eds) *Women and Philosophy: Toward a Theory of Liberation*, New York: Putnam, pp. 347–60.

Jaggar, A. (1994) 'Prostitution', in A. Jaggar (ed.) *Living with Contradictions. Controversies in Feminist Social Ethics*, Boulder, Colorado and Oxford: Westview Press, pp. 102–12.

Jaggar, A. (1995) 'Caring as a feminist practice of moral reason', in V. Held (ed.) *Justice and Care. Essential Readings in Feminist Ethics*, Boulder, Colorado and Oxford: Westview Press, pp. 179–201.

Jaggar, A. and Bordo S. (eds) (1989) *Gender\Body\Knowledge*, New Brunswick, New Jersey: Rutgers University Press.

Jakobsen, J. J. (1998) *Working Alliances and the Politics of Difference: Diversity and Feminist Ethics*, Bloomington: Indiana University Press.

James, S. (1992) 'The good-enough citizen: female citizenship and independence', in G. Bock and S. James (eds) *Beyond Equality and Difference. Citizenship, Feminist Politics and Female Subjectivity*, London: Routledge, pp. 48–65.

Jeffreys, S. (1990) *Anticlimax*, London: The Women's Press.

Jeffreys, S. (1992) 'Pornography', in E. Frazer, J. Hornsby and S. Lovibond (eds) *Ethics: A Feminist Reader*, Oxford: Blackwell, pp. 458–88.

Jelen, T., O'Donnell, J. and Wilcox, C. (1993), 'A contextual analysis of Catholic and abortion attitudes in Western Europe', *Sociology of Religion* 54: 375–83.

Johnson, D. G. (1985) *Computer Ethics*, New Jersey: Prentice-Hall.

Jones, K. B. (1990) 'Citizenship in a woman-friendly polity', *Signs* 15 (4): 781–812.

Jones, K. B. (1993) *Compassionate Authority: Democracy and the Representation of Women*, New York: Routledge.

Kapur, N. Badhwar (1991) 'Why it is wrong to be always guided by the best: consequentialism and friendship', *Ethics* 101 (3): 483–504.

Karl, M. (1995) *Women and Empowerment. Participation and Decision Making*, London: Zed Books.

Katzenstein, M. Fainsod and Laitin, D. D. (1987) 'Politics, feminism, and the ethics of caring', in E. Feder Kittay and D. T. Meyers, (eds) *Women and Moral Theory*, Totowa, New Jersey: Rowman & Littlefield, pp. 261–81.

Keller, E. Fox (1985) *Reflections on Gender and Science*, New Haven, Conn: Yale University Press.

Keller, M. (1984) 'Resolving conflicts in friendship: the development of moral understanding in everyday life', in W. M. Kurtines and J. Gewirtz (eds) *Morality, Moral Behaviour, and Moral Development*, New York: John Wiley, pp. 140–58.

Kelly, L. (1988) *Surviving Sexual Violence*, Cambridge: Polity Press.

Kemp, S. and Squires, J. (eds) (1997) *Feminisms*, Oxford: Oxford University Press.

Ketchum, S. A. (1993) 'Selling babies and selling bodies', in J. Kourany, J. P. Sterba and R. Tong (eds) *Feminist Philosophies*, New York: Wheatsheaf, pp. 95–102.

Ketting, E. (1993) 'Abortion in Europe: current status and major issues', *Planned Parenthood in Europe* 22: 4–6.

Ketting, E. and van Praag, P. (1986), 'The marginal relevance of legislation relating to induced abortions', in J. Lovenduski (ed.) *The New Politics of Abortion*, London: Sage, pp. 154–69.

Kingdom, E. (1991) *What's Wrong with Rights? Problems for Feminist Politics of Law*, Edinburgh: Edinburgh University Press.

Kiss, E. (1997) 'Alchemy or fool's gold? Assessing feminist doubts about rights', in M. L. Shanley and U. Narayan (eds) *Reconstructing Political Theory. Feminist Perspectives*, Cambridge: Polity Press, pp. 1–24.

Kittay, E. Feder (1984) 'Pornography and the erotics of domination', in C. C. Gould (ed.) *Beyond Domination. New Perspectives on Women and Philosophy*, Totowa, New Jersey: Rowman & Allanheld, pp. 145–74.

Kittay, E. Feder and Meyers, D. T. (eds) (1987) *Women and Moral Theory*, Totowa, New Jersey: Rowman & Littlefield.

Klein, R. (1990) 'Genetic and reproductive engineering – the global view', in J. A. Scutt (ed.) *The Baby Machine. Reproductive Technology and the Commercialisation of Motherhood*, London: Green Print, pp. 235–73.

Klein, R. (1992) *The Ultimate Colonisation. Reproductive and Genetic Engineering*, Dublin: Attic Press.

Koehn, D. (1994) *The Ground of Professional Ethics*, London and New York: Routledge.

Koehn, D. (1998) *Rethinking Feminist Ethics. Care, Trust and Empathy*, London and New York: Routledge.

Koggel, C. M. (1997) *Perspectives on Equality. Constructing a Relational Theory*, New York and London: Rowman & Littlefield.

Kourany, J., Sterba, J. P. and Tong, R. (eds) (1993) *Feminist Philosophies. Problems, Theories, Applications*, New York: Wheatsheaf.

Koval R. and J. A. Scutt (1990) 'Genetic and reproductive engineering – all for the infertile?', in J. A. Scutt, (ed.) *The Baby Machine. Reproductive Technology and the Commercialisation of Motherhood*, London: Green Print, pp. 33–57.

Krieger, L. (1987) 'Through a glass darkly: paradigms of equality and the search for a woman's jurisprudence', *Hypatia* 2 (1): 45–61.

Kuhse, H. (1997) *Caring: Nurses, Women and Ethics*, Oxford: Blackwell Publishers.

Kurtines W. M. and Gewirtz J. (eds) (1984) *Morality, Moral Behaviour, and Moral Development*, New York: John Wiley, pp. 140–58.

Langan, M. and Day, L. (eds) (1992) *Women, Oppression and Social Work. Issues in Anti-discriminatory Practice*, London: Routledge.

Larrabee, M. J. (ed.) (1993) *An Ethic of Care. Feminism and Interdisciplinary Perspectives*, London and New York: Routledge.

Lemoncheck, L. (1994) 'What's wrong with being a sex object?', in A. Jaggar (ed.) *Living with Contradictions. Controversies in Feminist Social Ethics*, Boulder, Colorado and Oxford: Westview Press, pp. 199–206.

Levin, M. and Brod, H. (1998) *Sexual Preference and Human Rights*, New York and London: Rowman & Littlefield.

Lewis, R. and K. Adler (1994) 'Come to me baby, or What's wrong with Lesbian SM', *Women's Studies International Forum* 17 (4): 433–41.

Lewison, H. (1996) 'Choices in childbirth: Areas of conflict', in L. Frith (ed.) *Ethics and Midwifery. Issues in Contemporary Practice*, Oxford: Butterworth-Heinemann, pp. 36–50.

Lister, R. (1997) *Citizenship. Feminist Perspectives*, London: Macmillan Press.

Little, M. O. (1995) 'Seeing and caring: the role of affect in feminist moral epistemology', *Hypatia* 10 (3): 117–37.

Lloyd, G. (1984) *The Man of Reason. Male and Female in Western Philosophy*, London: Methuen.

Longino, H. E. (1994) 'Pornography, oppression, and freedom: a closer look', in A. Jaggar (ed.) *Living with Contradiction. Controversies in Feminist Social Ethics*, Boulder, Colorado and Oxford: Westview Press, pp. 154–61.

Lublin, N. (1998) *Pandora's Box. Feminism Confronts Reproductive Technology*, New York and London: Rowman & Littlefield.

Lucier, R. M., Childs, C. D., Parks S. M. and Yemba R. A. (1994) 'Heritage, surrogacy, and the ethics of community: choice and avoidance in African and African-American parenting traditions', in H. Bequaert Holmes (ed.) *Issues in Reproductive Technology*, New York and London: New York University Press, pp. 333–48.

Lugones, M. C. (1993) 'Sisterhood and friendship as feminist models', in C. Kremarae and D. Spender (eds) *The Knowledge Explosion. Generations of Feminist Scholarship*, London: Harvester Wheatsheaf, pp. 406–12.

Lugones, M. (1997) 'Playfulness, "world"-travelling, and loving perception', in D. Tietjens Meyers (eds) *Feminist Social Thought: A Reader*, New York and London: Routledge, pp. 148–59.

Luke, C. (ed.) (1996) *Feminisms and Pedagogies of Everyday Life*, New York: State University of New York Press.

Luthra, Rashmi (1993) 'Toward a reconceptualization of "choice": challenges by women at the margins', *Feminist Issues* 13 (1): 41–54.

Lutz, H., Phoenix, A. and Yuval-Davis, N. (1995) 'Introduction. Nationalism, racism and gender – European crossfires', in H. Lutz, A. Phoenix and N. Yuval-Davis (eds) *Crossfires. Nationalism, Racism and Gender in Europe*, London: Pluto Press, pp. 1–25.

McIntosh, M. (1993) 'Queer theory and the war of the sexes', in J. Bristow and A. Wilson (eds) *Activating Theory: Lesbian, Gay and Bisexual Politics*, London: Lawrence & Wishart, pp. 30–52.

MacIntyre, A. (1982) *After Virtue. A Study in Moral Theory*, London: Duckworth.

MacIntyre, A. (1988) *Whose Justice? Which Rationality?*, London: Duckworth.

MacKinnon, C. (1984) 'Not a moral issue', *Yale Law and Policy Review* 2 (2).

MacKinnon, C. (1987a) 'Feminism, Marxism, method, and the state. Toward feminist jurisprudence', in S. Harding (ed.) *Feminism and Methodology*, Bloomington and Indianapolis: Indiana University Press, pp. 135–56.

MacKinnon, C. (1987b) *Feminism Unmodified: Discourses on Life and Law*, Cambridge, MA: Harvard University Press.

MacKinnon, C. (1993) 'Pornography, civil rights, and speech', in J. Kourany, J. P. Sterba and R. Tong (eds) *Feminist Philosophies, Problems, Theories, Applications*, New York: Wheatsheaf, pp. 295–308.

McMillan, C. (1982) *Women, Reason, and Nature*, Oxford: Blackwell.

McWilliams, M. with Kelly, L. (1997) 'Taking on the dinosaurs', *Trouble and Strife* 35: 7–15.

Mahoney, J. (1995) 'Adoption as a feminist alternative to reproductive technology', in J. Callahan (ed.) *Reproduction, Ethics, and the Law. Feminist Perspectives*, Bloomington and Indianapolis: Indiana University Press, pp. 35–54.

Manning, R. (1992) *Speaking from the Heart: A Feminist Perspective on Ethics*, Lanham, MD: Rowman & Littlefield.

Markowitz, S. (1990) 'Abortion and feminism', *Social Theory and Practice* 16 (1): 1–17.

Marks, E. and de Courtivron I. (eds) (1981) *New French Feminisms*, New York: Schocken Books.

Meehan, E. (1993) *Citizenship and the European Community*, London: Sage.

Meyers, D. T. (1986) 'The politics of self-respect: a feminist perspective', *Hypatia* 1 (1): 83–100.

Meyers, D. T. (1987) 'The socialized individual and individual autonomy: an intersection between philosophy and psychology', in E. Feder Kittay and D. T. Meyers, (eds) *Women and Moral Theory*, Totowa, New Jersey: Rowman & Littlefield, pp. 139–53.

Meyers, D. T. (1989) *Self, Society and Personal Choice*, New York and Oxford: Columbia University Press.

Meyers, D. T. (1993) 'Social exclusion, moral reflection, and rights', *Law and Philosophy* 12 (2): 217–32.

Michie, H. and Cahn N. R. (1997) *Confinements. Fertility and Infertility in Contemporary Culture*, New Brunswick: Rutgers University Press.

Miller, J. L. (1990) 'Making change: women and ethics in the practice of law', *Yale Journal of Law and Feminism* 2 (2): 453–76.

Miller, P. (1996), 'Ethical issues in neonatal intensive care', in L. Frith (ed.) *Ethics and Midwifery. Issues in Contemporary Practice*, Oxford: Butterworth-Heinemann, pp. 123–39.

Millett, K. (1969) *Sexual Politics*, London: Virago Press.

Minow, M. and Shanley, M. Lyndon (1996) 'Relational rights and responsibilities: revisioning the family in liberal political theory and law', *Hypatia* 11 (1): 4–29.

Mitchell, J. (1971) *Women's Estate*, Middlesex: Penguin.

Mohanty, C. (1988) 'Under western eyes: feminist scholarship and colonial discourses', *Feminist Review* 30: 61–88.

Morgan, L. M. (1996) 'Fetal relationality in feminist philosophy: an anthropological critique', *Hypatia* 11 (3): 47–70.

Morris, J. (1991) *Pride against Prejudice*, London: Women's Press.

Mouffe, C. (1992) 'Democratic citizenship and the political community', in C. Mouffe (ed.) *Dimensions of Radical Democracy. Pluralism, Citizenship, Community*, London: Verso, pp. 225–39.

Mouffe, C. (1993) 'Liberal socialism and pluralism: which citizenship?', in J. Squires (ed.) *Principled Positions. Postmodernism and the Rediscovery of Value*, London: Lawrence & Wishart, pp. 69–84.

Murdoch, A. (1990) 'Off the treadmill – leaving an IVF programme behind', in J. A. Scutt (ed.) *The Baby Machine. Reproductive Technology and the Commercialisation of Motherhood*, London: Green Print, pp. 67–70.

Murdoch, I. (1970) *The Sovereignty of Good*, London: Routledge.

Narayan, U. (1988) 'Working together across difference: some considerations on emotions and political practice', *Hypatia* 3 (2): 31–47.

Narayan, U. (1995) 'Colonialism and its others: considerations on rights and care discourses', *Hypatia* 10 (2): 133–40.

Narayan, U. (1997) 'Towards a feminist vision of citizenship: rethinking the implications of dignity, political participation, and nationality', in M. Lyndon Shanley and U. Narayan (eds) *Reconstructing Political Theory. Feminist Perspectives*, Cambridge: Polity Press, pp. 48–67.

Nardi, P. M. (ed.) (1992) *Men's Friendships*, London: Sage.

Nedelsky, J. (1989) 'Reconceiving autonomy. Sources, thoughts and possibilities', in A. Hutchinson and J. Leslie (eds) *Law and the Community. The End of Individualism?*, Toronto: Carswell, pp. 219–52.

Neustatter, A. (1998) 'The cruellest cut', *Australian Magazine* 18–19 July: 12–15.

Nicholson, L. J. (1993) 'Women, morality and history', in M. J. Larrabee (ed.) *An Ethic of Care*, London and New York: Routledge, pp. 87–101.

Noddings, N. (1984) *Caring: A Feminine Approach to Ethics and Moral Education*, Berkeley and Los Angeles: University of California Press.

Noddings, N. (1989) *Women and Evil*, Berkeley and Los Angeles: University of California Press.

Nunner-Winkler, G. (1993) 'Two moralities? A critical discussion of an ethic of care and responsibility versus an ethic of rights and justice', in M. J. Larrabee (ed.) *An Ethic of Care*, London and New York: Routledge, pp. 143–56.

Nussbaum, M. (1992a) 'Virtue revived', *Times Literary Supplement* 3 July: 9–11.

Nussbaum, M. (1992b) 'Human functioning and social justice. In defense of Aristotelian essentialism', *Political Theory* 20 (2): 202–46.

O'Brien, M. (1983) *The Politics of Reproduction*, London and Boston: Routledge & Kegan Paul.

Okin, S. (1989) *Justice, Gender, and the Family*, Princeton NJ: Princeton University Press.

Okin, S. (1994) 'Political liberalism, justice, and gender', *Ethics* 105 (1): 23–43.

Okin, S. (1995) 'Politics and the complex inequalities of gender', in D. Miller and M. Walzer (eds) *Pluralism, Justice, and Equality*, Oxford: Oxford University Press, pp. 120–43.

O'Neill, O. (1989) 'Friends of difference', *London Review of Books* 11 (17): 20–2.

O'Neill, O. (1996) *Towards Justice and Virtue. A Constructive Account of Practical Reasoning*, Cambridge: Cambridge University Press.

Overall, C. (1987) *Ethics and Human Reproduction: A Feminist Analysis*, Boston: Allen & Unwin.

Overall, C. (1995) 'Frozen embryos and "fathers' rights": parenthood and decision-making in the cryopreservation of embryos', in J. Callahan (ed.) *Reproduction, Ethics, and the Law. Feminist Perspectives*, Bloomington and Indianapolis: Indiana University Press, pp. 178–98.

Pankhurst, D. and Pearce, J. (1996) 'Feminist perspectives on democratisation in the South. Engendering or adding women in?', in H. Afshar (ed.) *Women and Politics in the Third World*, London and New York: Routledge, pp. 40–7.

Pateman, C. (1989) *The Sexual Contract*, Cambridge: Polity Press.

Pateman, C. (1992) 'Equality, difference, subordination: the politics of motherhood and women's citizenship', in G. Bock and S. James (eds) *Beyond Equality and Difference. Citizenship, Feminist Politics and Female Subjectivity*, London: Routledge, pp. 17–31.

Petchesky, R. Pollack (1980) 'Reproductive freedom: beyond "A Woman's Right to Choose"', in C. R. Stimpson and E. Spector Person, (eds) *Women, Sex and Sexuality*, Chicago: University of Chicago Press, pp. 92–116.

Petchesky, R. Pollack (1986) *Abortion and Woman's Choice: The State, Sexuality, and Reproductive Freedom*, London: Verso.

Pfeffer, N. and Woollett, A. (1983) *The Experience of Infertility*, London: Virago.

Phillips, A. (1991) *Engendering Democracy*, Cambridge: Polity Press.

Phillips, A. (1992) 'Universal Pretensions in Political Thought', in
M. Barrett and A. Phillips (eds) *Destabilizing Theory. Contemporary
Feminist Debates*, Cambridge: Polity Press, pp. 10–30.

Phillips, A. (1993) *Democracy and Difference*, Cambridge: Polity Press.

Phillips, A. (1994) 'Why should the sex of the representatives matter?',
paper for *Women and Public Policy: The Shifting Boundaries between the
Public and Private Domains*, Rotterdam: Erasmus University.

Phillips, A. (1995) *The Politics of Presence*, Oxford: Clarendon Press.

Porter, E. (1991) *Women and Moral Identity*, Sydney: Allen & Unwin.

Porter, E. (1994) 'Abortion ethics; rights and responsibilities', *Hypatia*
9 (3): 66–87.

Porter, E. (1995) *Building Good Families in a Changing World*, Melbourne:
Melbourne University Press.

Porter, E. (1996a) 'Culture, community and responsibilities: abortion in
Ireland', *Sociology* 30 (2): 279–98.

Porter, E. (1996b) 'Women and friendships: pedagogies of care and
relationality', in C. Luke (ed.) *Feminisms and Pedagogies of Everyday
Life*, New York: State University of New York Press, pp. 56–79.

Porter, E. (1997a) 'Diversity and commonality. Women, politics and
Northern Ireland', *European Journal of Women's Studies* 4 (1): 83–100.

Porter, E. (1997b) 'Feminist analysis', in D. Woodward, A. Parkin and
J. Summers (eds) *Government, Politics, Power and Policy in Australia*,
6th edition, Melbourne: Longman, pp. 392–412.

Porter, E. (1998a) 'Political representation of women in Northern
Ireland', *Politics* 18 (1): 25–32.

Porter, E. (1998b) 'Identity, location, plurality: women, nationalism
and Northern Ireland', in R. Wilford and R. L. Miller (eds) *Women,
Ethnicity and Nationalism. The Politics of Transition*, London and New
York: Routledge, pp. 36–61.

Porter, E. (1999) 'Bodies, Selves, and Moral Responsibilities', *Women's
Studies International Forum* 22 (1): 1–8.

Praetorius, I. (1997) 'Thinking beyond the androcentric order', in
Cymbals and Silences: Echoes from the First European Women's Synod,
Austria, 21–28 July, 1996, London: Sophia Press, pp. 53–70.

Pringle, K. (1995) *Men, Masculinities and Social Welfare*, London:
University College London Press.

Probyn, E. (1992) *Sexing the Self. Gendered Positions in Cultural Studies*,
London and New York: Routledge.

Purdy, L. (1994) 'Another look at contract pregnancy', in H. Bequaert
Holmes (ed.) *Issues in Reproductive Technology*, New York and London:
New York University Press, pp. 303–20.

Purdy, L. (1995) 'Loving future people', in J. Callahan (ed.)
Reproduction, Ethics, and the Law. Feminist Perspectives, Bloomington and
Indianapolis: Indiana University Press, pp. 300–27.

Purdy, L. (1996) *Reproducing Persons: Issues in Feminist Bioethics*, Ithaca: Cornell University Press.

Radner, H. (1995) *Shopping Around. Feminine Culture and the Pursuit of Pleasure*, New York: Routledge.

Randall, F. and Downie, R. S. (1996) *Palliative Care Ethics. A Good Companion*, Oxford: Oxford University Press.

Randall, V. (1991) *Women and Politics. An International Perspective*, 2nd edition, Hampshire: Macmillan Education.

Rawls, J. (1973) *A Theory of Justice*, Oxford: Oxford University Press.

Rawls, J. (1975) 'Fairness to goodness', *Philosophic Review*, 84: 536–54.

Rawls, J. (1993) *Political Liberalism*, New York: Columbia University Press.

Raymond, J. (1986) *A Passion for Friends. Toward a Philosophy of Female Affection*, London: The Women's Press.

Raymond, J. (1989) 'The international traffic in women: Women used in systems of surrogacy and reproduction', *Reproductive and Genetic Engineering: Journal of International Feminist Analysis* 2 (1): 51–57.

Reanda, L. (1991) 'Prostitution as a human rights question: problems and prospects of United Nations action', *Human Rights Quarterly* 13 (1): 202–28.

Rice, F. P. (1993) *Intimate Relationships, Marriages, and Families*, 2nd edition, Mountain View, California: Mayfield Publishing Company.

Rich, A. (1979) *Of Woman Born. Motherhood as Experience and Institution*, London: Virago.

Rich, A. (1980) 'Compulsory heterosexuality and lesbian existence', *Signs* 5 (4): 631–60.

Richards, J. Radcliffe (1982) *The Sceptical Feminist. A Philosophical Enquiry*, Harmondsworth: Penguin.

Riddicks, R. (1990) *The Right to Choose: Questions of Feminist Morality*, Dublin: Attic Press.

Roberts, D. E. (1995) 'Race, gender, and the value of mother's work', *Social Politics* 2 (2): 195–207.

Rothenberg, P. (1984) 'The political nature of relations between the sexes', in C. Gould (ed.) *Beyond Domination. New Perspectives on Women and Philosophy*, Totowa, New Jersey: Rowman & Allanheld, pp. 204–20.

Rothman, B. Katz (1989) *Recreating Motherhood: Ideology and Technology in a Patriarchal Society*, New York: Norton.

Rowland, R. (1985) 'A child at any price?', *Women's Studies International Forum* 8 (6): 339–46.

Rowland, R. (1991) 'Decoding reprospeak', *Ms Magazine* 1: 38–41.

Rowland, R. (1996) 'Politics of intimacy: heterosexuality, love and power', in D. Bell and R. Klein (eds) *Radically Speaking. Feminism Reclaimed*, London: Zed Books, pp. 77–86.

Rubin, K. (1998) 'Get smart about being casual', *Association of University Teachers Bulletin*, January 1998, pp. 12–13.

Rubin, L. B. (1985) *Just Friends: The Role of Friendship in Our Lives*, New York: Harper & Row.

Ruddick, S. (1987) *Maternal Thinking: Toward a Politics of Peace*, New York: Ballantine Books.

Ruddick, S. (1992) 'From maternal thinking to peace politics', in E. Browning Cole and S. Coultrap-McQuin (eds) *Explorations in Feminist Ethics. Theory and Practice*, Bloomington: Indiana University Press, pp. 141–55.

Ruddick, S. (1995) 'Injustice in families: assault and domination', in V. Held (ed.) *Justice and Care. Essential Readings in Feminist Ethics*, Boulder, Colorado and Oxford: Westview Press, pp. 203–23.

Russell, D. E. H. (ed.) (1993) *Making Violence Sexy. Feminist Views on Pornography*, Buckingham: Open University Press.

Sandel, M. (1982) *Liberalism and the Limits of Justice*, New York: Cambridge University Press.

Scaltsas, P. Ward (1992) 'Do feminist ethics counter feminist aims?', in E. Browning Cole and S. Coultrap McQuin (eds) *Explorations in Feminist Ethics*, Bloomington: Indiana University Press, pp. 15–26.

Scutt, J. A. (ed.) (1990) *The Baby Machine. Reproductive Technology and the Commercialization of Motherhood*, London: Green Print.

Segal, L. (1994) *Straight Sex: The Politics of Pleasure*, London: Virago Press.

Sevenhuijsen, S. (1991) 'Justice, moral reasoning and the politics of child custody', in E. Meehan and S. L. Sevenhuijsen (eds) *Equality, Politics and Gender*, London: Sage, pp. 88–103.

Sevenhuijsen, S. (1998) *Citizenship and the Ethics of Care. Feminist Considerations on Justice, Morality and Politics*, trans. L. Savage, London and New York: Routledge.

Shanley, M. Lyndon and Narayan, U. (eds) (1997) *Reconstructing Political Theory. Feminist Perspectives*, Cambridge: Polity Press.

Shapiro, J. Poliner and Smith-Rosenberg, C. (1989) 'The "other voices" in contemporary ethical dilemmas: the value of the new scholarship on women in the teaching of ethics', *Women's Studies International Forum* 12 (2): 199–211.

Sheldon, S. (1993) ' "Who is the mother to make the judgement?": the construction of women in English abortion law', *Feminist Legal Studies* 1 (1): 3–22.

Sher, G. (1987) 'Other voices, other rooms? Women's psychological and moral theory', in E. Feder Kittay and D. T. Meyers (eds) *Women and Moral Theory*, Totowa, New Jersey: Rowman & Littlefield, pp. 178–89.

Sherwin, S. (1997) 'Abortion: a feminist perspective', in T. A. Mappes and J. S. Zembaty (eds) *Social Ethics. Morality and Social Policy*, 5th edition, New York: McGraw-Hill, pp. 108–14.

Shilling, C. (1993) *The Body and Social Theory*, London: Sage.

Silvers, A. (1995) 'Reconciling equality to difference: caring (f)or justice for people with disabilities', *Hypatia* 10 (1): 30–55.

Singer, P. (ed.) (1993) *A Companion to Ethics*, Oxford: Blackwell.

Sistare, C. T. (1988) 'Reproductive freedom and women's freedom: surrogacy and autonomy', *Philosophical Forum* 19 (4): 227–40.

Smart, C. (1995) *Law, Crime and Sexuality*, London: Sage.

Smith, J. F. (1984) 'Rights-conflict, pregnancy and abortion', in C. Gould (ed.) *Beyond Domination: New Perspectives on Women and Philosophy*, Totowa, New Jersey: Rowman & Allanheld, pp. 265–73.

Smyth, A. (ed.) (1992) *The Abortion Papers, Ireland*, Dublin: Attic Press.

Smyth, C. (1993), 'Queer theory and the war of the sexes', in J. Bristow and A. Wilson (eds) *Activating Theory: Lesbian, Gay and Bisexual Politics*, London: Lawrence & Wishart, pp. 30–52.

Soble, A. (ed.) (1997) *The Philosophy of Sex. Contemporary Readings*, 3rd edition, New York and London: Rowman & Littlefield.

Spallone, P. (1989) *Beyond Conception. The New Politics of Reproduction*, London: Macmillan Education.

Spelman, E. V. (1989) 'Anger and insubordination', in A. Garry and M. Pershall (eds) *Women, Knowledge, and Reality*, Boston: Unwin Hyman, pp. 263–73.

Spelman, E. V. (1990) *Inessential Woman. Problems of Exclusion in Feminist Thought*, London: The Women's Press.

Spelman, E. V. (1991) 'The virtue of feeling and the feeling of virtue', in C. Card (ed.) *Feminist Ethics*, Kansas: University Press of Kansas, pp. 213–32.

Squires, J. (ed.) (1993) *Principled Positions. Postmodernism and the Rediscovery of Value*, London: Lawrence & Wishart.

Stack, C. B. (1993) 'The culture of gender: women and men of color', in M. J. Larrabee (ed.) *An Ethic of Care*, London and New York: Routledge, pp. 108–11.

Stanley, L. (1992) 'Epistemological issues in researching lesbian history: the case of romantic friendship', in H. Hinds, A. Phoenix and J. Stacey (eds) *Working Out: New Directions for Women's Studies*, London: Falmer Press, pp. 161–72.

Stanworth, M. (1987) 'Reproductive technologies and the deconstruction of motherhood', in M. Stanworth (ed.) *Reproductive Technologies: Gender, Motherhood and Medicine*, Cambridge: Polity Press, pp. 10–35.

Steinbacher, R. (1984) 'Sex preselection: from here to fraternity', in C. C. Gould (ed.) *Beyond Domination. New Perspectives on Women and Philosophy*, Totowa, New Jersey: Rowman & Allanheld, pp. 274–82.

Stocker, M. (1987) 'Duty and friendship. Toward a synthesis of Gilligan's contrastive moral concepts', in E. Feder Kittay and

D. T. Meyers (eds) *Women and Moral Theory*, Totowa, New Jersey: Rowman & Littlefield, pp. 56–68.

Strikwerda, R. and May, L. (1992) 'Male friendship and intimacy', *Hypatia* 7 (3): 110–23.

Sundahl, D. (1994) 'Stripper', in A. Jaggar (ed.) *Living with Contradictions. Controversies in Feminist Social Ethics*, Boulder, Colorado and Oxford: Westview Press, pp. 117–20.

Sypnowich, C. (1993a) 'Some disquiet about "difference"', *Praxis International* 13 (2): 99–112.

Sypnowich, C. (1993b) 'Justice, Community, and the Antinomies of Feminist Theory', *Political Theory* 21 (3): 484–506.

Tanner, K. (1996) 'The care that does justice. Recent writings in feminist ethics and theology', *Journal of Religious Ethics* 24 (1): 171–91.

Taylor, C. (1989) *Sources of the Self, The Making of the Modern Identity*, Cambridge: Cambridge University Press.

Taylor, C. (1992) 'The politics of recognition', in A. Gutmann (ed.) *Multiculturalism and 'The Politics of Recognition'. An Essay by Charles Taylor*, Princeton, New Jersey: Princeton University Press, pp. 25–73.

Thompson, J. Jarvis (1997) 'A defence of abortion', in S. Dwyer and J. Feinberg (eds) *The Problem of Abortion*, Belmont, CA: Wadsworth, pp. 75–87.

Thompson, N. (1993) *Anti-discriminatory Practice*, London: Macmillan.

Tong, R. (1993) *Feminine and Feminist Ethics*, Belmont, CA: Wadsworth.

Tong, R. (1995) 'Feminist perspectives and gestational motherhood: the search for a unified legal focus', in J. Callahan (ed.) *Reproduction, Ethics, and the Law. Feminist Perspectives*, Bloomington and Indianapolis: Indiana University Press, pp. 55–79.

Treviño, L. Klebe and K. A. Nelson (1995) *Managing Business Ethics. Straight Talk About How To Do It Right*, New York: John Wiley.

Tronto, J. (1987) 'Beyond gender difference to a theory of care', *Signs* 12 (4): 644–63.

Tronto, J. (1989) 'Women and caring: what can feminists learn about morality from caring?', in A. Jaggar and S. Bordo (eds) *Gender\Body\Knowledge*, New Brunswick: Rutgers University Press, pp. 172–87.

Tronto, J. (1993) *Moral Boundaries. A Political Argument for an Ethic of Care*, London and New York: Routledge.

Tronto, J. (1995) 'Care as a basis for radical political judgments', *Hypatia* 10 (2): 141–9.

Tuana, N. (1992) *Woman and the History of Philosophy*, New York: Paragon House.

Udayagiri, M. (1995) 'Challenging modernization. Gender and development, postmodernism, feminism and activism', in M. H. Marchand and J. L. Parpart (eds) *Feminism/Postmodernism/ Development*, London and New York: Routledge, pp. 159–77.

United Nations (1991) *The World's Women 1970–1990: Trends and Statistics*, New York: United Nations.

United Nations Division for the Advancement of Women (1992) 'Public life: Women make a difference', *Women 2000*, 2.

Vance, C. (ed.) (1992) *Pleasure and Danger: Exploring Female Sexuality*, London: Pandora.

Viney, E. (1996) *Dancing to Different Tunes. Sexuality and Its Misconceptions*, Belfast: Blackstaff Press.

Waerness, K. (1987) 'On the rationality of caring', in A. Showstack Sassoon (ed.) *Women and the State*, London: Hutchinson, pp. 207–34.

Walker, M. Urban (1989) 'Moral understandings: alternative "epistemology" for a feminist ethics', *Hypatia* 4 (2): 15–28.

Walker, M. Urban (1991) 'Partial consideration', *Ethics* 101 (4): 758–74.

Walker, M. Urban (1997) *Moral Understandings. A Feminist Study in Ethics*, London and New York: Routledge.

Walker, V. (1998) 'Child abuse reports lag behind law', *Weekend Australian* August 15–16: 43.

Walzer, M. (1985) *Spheres of Justice, A Defence of Pluralism and Equality*, Oxford: Basil Blackwell.

Warnock, M. (1985) *A Question of Life: The Warnock Report on Human Fertilisation and Embryology*, Oxford: Basil Blackwell.

Warren, M. A. (1989) 'The moral significance of birth', *Hypatia* 4 (3): 46–65.

Weeks, J. (1993) 'Rediscovering values', in J. Squires (ed.) *Principled Positions. Postmodernism and the Rediscovery of Value*, London: Lawrence & Wishart, pp. 189–211.

Weiss, G. (1995) 'Sex-selective abortion: a relational approach', *Hypatia* 10 (1): 202–17.

Weiss, P. A. (1997) *Conversations with Feminism. Political Theory and Practice*, New York and London: Rowman & Littlefield.

West, R. (1995) 'The harms of consensual sex', *American Philosophical Association Newsletters* 94: 52–5.

Whitbeck, C. (1984) 'A different reality: feminist ontology', in C. C. Gould (ed.) *Beyond Domination. New Perspectives on Women and Philosophy*, Totowa, New Jersey: Rowman & Allanheld, pp. 64–88.

Willett, C. (1998) *Maternal Ethics and Other Slave Moralities*, London and New York: Routledge.

Wilson, E. (1993) 'Is transgression transgressive?', in J. Bristow and A. Wilson (eds) *Activating Theory: Lesbian, Gay and Bisexual Politics*, London: Lawrence & Wishart, pp. 107–16.

Wise, S. (1995) 'Feminist ethics in practice', in R. Hugman and D. Smith (eds) *Ethical Issues in Social Work*, London: Routledge, pp. 104–19.

Wolf, N. (1991) *The Beauty Myth. How Images of Beauty Are Used Against Women*, New York: William Morrow.

Wolf, N. (1995) 'Our bodies, our souls', *New Republic* October, 16: 26–35.

Wolgast, E. (1980) *Equality and the Rights of Women*, Ithaca: Cornell University.

Wolgast, E. (1987) 'Wrong rights', *Hypatia* 2 (1): 25–43.

Women Aid International (1998) *Helping Those in Need*, publicity material, London.

Young, I. M. (1990) *Justice and the Politics of Difference*, Princeton, New Jersey: Princeton University Press.

Young, I. M. (1993) 'Together in difference: transforming the logic of group political conflict', in J. Squires (ed.) *Principled Positions. Postmodernism and the Rediscovery of Value*, London: Lawrence & Wishart, pp. 121–50.

Young, I. M. (1995) 'Mothers, citizenship, and independence: a critique of pure family values', *Ethics* 105 (3): 535–56.

Yuval-Davis, N. (1994) 'Women, ethnicity and empowerment', in K.-K. Bhavnani and A. Phoenix (eds) *Shifting Identities, Shifting Racisms. A Feminism and Psychology Reader*, London: Sage, pp. 179–97.

Yuval-Davis, N. (1996) 'Women and the biological reproduction of "the nation"', *Women's Studies International Forum* 19 (1/2): 17–24.

Zohar, D. (1997) *ReWiring the Corporate Brain. Using the New Science to Rethink How We Structure and Lead Organizations*, San Fransisco: Berrett-Koehler Publishers, Inc.

Index